Nebraska
Symposium on
Motivation
1981

_____

Nebraska Symposium on Motivation, 1981, is Volume 29 in the series on CURRENT THEORY AND RESEARCH IN MOTIVATION

University of Nebraska Press
Lincoln/London 1982

Nebraska Symposium on Motivation 1981

Response Structure and Organization

Herbert E. Howe, Jr.   *Series Editor*

Daniel J. Bernstein   *Volume Editor*

Robert G. Wahler   *Professor of Psychology*
University of Tennessee

James J. Fox   *Assistant Professor of Psychology*
Vanderbilt University

John B. Reid   *Research Scientist*
Oregon Social Learning Center

G. R. Patterson   *Research Scientist*
Oregon Social Learning Center

Rolf Loeber   *Research Scientist*
Oregon Social Learning Center

George H. Collier   *Professor of Psychology*
Rutgers University

Howard Rachlin   *Professor of Psychology*
State University of New York at Stony Brook

Peter R. Killeen   *Professor of Psychology*
Arizona State University

Donald M. Baer   *Professor of Human Development and Family Life*
University of Kansas

Copyright 1982 by the University of Nebraska Press
International Standard Book Number 0–8032–1171–6 (Clothbound)
International Standard Book Number 0–8032–6064–4 (Paperbound)
Library of Congress Catalog Card Number 53–11655
Manufactured in the United States of America

The paper in this book meets the guidelines for permanence and durability of the Committee on Production Guidelines for Book Longevity of the Council on Library Resources.

"The Library of Congress has cataloged this serial publication as follows:"
Nebraska Symposium on Motivation.
   Nebraska Symposium on Motivation. [Papers] v. [1]—1953—
   Lincoln, University of Nebraska Press.
      v. illus, diagrs. 22 cm. annual.
   Vol. 1 issued by the symposium under its earlier name: Current Theory and Research in Motivation.
   Symposia sponsored by the Dept. of Psychology of the University of Nebraska.
   1. Motivation (Psychology)

BF683.N4   159.4082   53–11655

Library of Congress

Preface

*A*mong the many traditions that mark the Nebraska Symposium on Motivation, one that has continued for the last five years is the dedication of the Symposium to the memory of Harry K. Wolfe, one of America's early psychologists. A student of Wilhelm Wundt, Professor Wolfe established the first undergraduate laboratory in psychology in America at the University of Nebraska. As he was the pioneer psychologist in Nebraska, it is especially appropriate that funds donated to the University of Nebraska Foundation in his memory by his late student Dr. Coral L. Friedline are used to support the Nebraska Symposium. The editors thank the University of Nebraska Foundation for its support.

As has been true for the last several volumes, this edition of the Nebraska Symposium on Motivation focuses on one broad theme: Response Structure and Organization. Many thanks are due the volume editor, Professor Daniel Bernstein, for the energy and thought he devoted to organizing this symposium and bringing it to fruition. The care Dan showed in selecting the outstanding speakers and organizing their presentations made the symposium an especially thought-provoking one.

HERBERT E. HOWE, JR.
Series Editor

Contents

Introduction

---

*T*he topic of this year's symposium is response structure, and the term *structure* is meant to imply the opposite of independence. This particular structural view assumes that understanding any behavioral event requires consideration of the entire stream of behavior within which an individual action is embedded. Another way to state the same assumption is to say that behavior is organized and that there is an orderly relationship among the activities within any behavioral system. There are classes of responses or activities that have a special relationship with each other. It follows from such a view that changes in one response category will indirectly result in changes in other responses that are related to it. A list of examples of structural phenomena might include motivational similarity among activities, cycles of preference across time, biological systems activated by specific stimuli or consequences, sequential regularities or stereotype chains of occurrence in naturalistic observation, and families of demand curves. Specific topics might run from a global analysis such as symptom substitution to a microanalysis such as the distribution patterns of pauses between instances of a particular type of response.

If a relationship among responses is to be studied, then the observation of behavior must include all the responses that are thought to be related. A pattern across activities can be assessed only if the data include a sufficiently broad multiple-response observation scheme. The common element in all the papers in this volume is the inclusion of data from multiple-response research in which more than one activity is observed at the same time. Researchers in many areas of psychology are moving toward an ethological style of recording behavior without necessarily adopting the traditional biological perspective of ethology. Researchers who have included theories of organization in their work have helped to expand the breadth of data collected in many areas of psychological research.

Given a broad record of behavior, it is possible to assess a variety of patterns in behavior that may reflect a fundamental structural relationship among responses. Selective substitution of one response for another has often been used as an index of motivational similarity and as the basis for developing response classes that are related to a motivational system. This has been especially important given the broad records of behavior, for in any exhaustive system all changes in one response necessarily result in a change in some other category in the response system. In addition, particular sequential patterns among the responses also can occur repeatedly, suggesting a special relationship among certain instances or classes of behavior. In both of these cases, a change in one response category will indirectly result in a change in other response categories not directly affected by the intervention. For example, in human behavior analysis it has long been considered good practice to use complementary contingencies for most effective treatment; in addition to punishing the undesired behavior, it is also good to reinforce the desired response that is to fill the behavior void created by punishment. In a similar vein, applied behavior analysts will often identify a chain or sequence of responses that terminates in the target behavior. Once we have made this analysis, the intervention can be directed at a behavior earlier in the chain (either breaking it or activating it), making the effect on the terminal response an indirect one. In both these cases psychologists are taking advantage of a property of connectedness among members of a response repertoire. The literature on biological constraints on learning that has flourished in the past decade provides another whole set of examples in which a knowledge of special relationships between responses makes certain conditioning tasks easier.

The methodological aspect of this approach to the study of behavior has helped to produce a new perspective on the effects of reinforcement operations on a repertoire of responses. When all categories of behavior are recorded, it becomes clear that any increase or decrease in one response will by definition result in a complementary decrease or increase somewhere else in the repertoire. Research done in this format has led some theorists to view reinforcement as a process of redistributing time among response alternatives rather than a process of strengthening individual response tendencies. This change in thinking is an example of an important theoretical possibility that has emerged partially as a result of viewing the reinforcement question as a broad structural problem.

The papers in this volume represent a broad range of psychological work, and all include a multiple-response view of research. There are studies of basic behavior process and studies of applied research problems. There are data from human research and data from work with animals. The point of gathering all this research together is to see how several research areas share certain approaches to the study of behavior and also to examine how each area can profit from the others' findings and theories.

The first paper, by Robert Wahler, is organized around the topic of response substitution. Wahler first provides an excellent introduction to the literature on response substitution and behavior analysis, summarizing the general principles that can be derived from that research. He then generates his own model of family intervention based upon his thinking in the area of response substitution. This provides an interesting and very useful example of the interaction between a structural concept and an applied program of behavior analysis.

John Reid's paper is also an example of the use of a structural concept to understand a complex behavior analysis problem. In this case the pattern is one of sequential tendencies rather than response substitution, but it shares the important data base provided by a multiple-response (even multiple-person) observational system. Reid also suggested during the symposium that the problem of generalization of intervention is related to the assumption of response structure. It is not always possible for a therapist to deliver appropriate intervention directly to the target behavior, so therapy is directed either at a similar or at a structurally related response available in the therapeutic situation. Changes in the available responses will then have an indirect effect on the real target behavior as a result of the connection between those two classes of responses.

The paper by George Collier represents the finest in multiple-response methodology. Collier has long been known for his research conducted in a 24-hour-a-day environment, and his pioneering work on schedule performance under these conditions anticipated the current fascination with open/closed economies. He has repeatedly demonstrated that animals resolve the constraints of a complex environment differently when all their sustenance is obtained in the experimental setting than under conditions of occasional experimental performance. In this paper Collier presents an analysis of biological and nutritional determinants of the structure of the response repertoire in any given species.

The next two papers are very abstract representations of the choices made within a repertoire of responses. Howard Rachlin presents choice as a path through a multidimensional consumption space, in which each dimension represents the time devoted to one response class. By definition, a change in the time devoted to any one member of the repertoire must change the representation of the consumption choice on at least one other dimension within the space. This very elegant model represents the epitome of a multiresponse approach to the study of the effects of reinforcement operations on behavior. The incentive model by Peter Killeen is less directly derived from a multiple-response approach, but Killeen does apply his model to multiple-response problems. In this paper he discusses the application of his model to mutual effects among concurrent operants and to a position taken by one of his students, which predicts the distribution of time across an entire repertoire of responses. Killeen's model, like Rachlin's model, makes predictions about the direction that behavior will follow through a multidimensional consumption space.

The final paper in this volume is by Donald Baer, who takes a skeptical stance toward the entire issue of response structure. Baer has reviewed many examples of structural constructs in behavior analysis, and he argues that any structure that is modifiable is therefore not a fundamental property of the behavioral repertoire. He cites many examples of procedures that can be used to modify or create structural effects, and he argues that any nonfundamental structure does not pose a problem for straightforward behavior analysis. This retrospective on the utility of the concept of response structure provides an interesting comment on the constructs described in the preceding five papers.

One of the tasks of the volume editor is to explain how the topic being presented actually relates to the concept of motivation. This year that task is easy, for motivational models are among the classic examples of assumed structures in a set of responses. When responses substitute freely for each other it is readily assumed that they share at least a functional, if not a motivational, similarity. When models of choice are generated to describe the flow of behavior, the concept motivation cannot be left far behind. A theory of incentive and arousal is on the face of it a description of a motivational system. It is my hope that these papers will provide a sample of the ways the concept of response structure or organization can be meaningfully used in understanding the concept of motivation.

DANIEL J. BERNSTEIN

Response Structure in Deviant Child-Parent Relationships: Implications for Family Therapy[1]

Robert G. Wahler and James J. Fox

University of Tennessee and Vanderbilt University

Developmental portrayals of child behavior usually include ample reference to the child's interpersonal life. Theorists have presumed that social relationships with "significant others" eventually culminate in the child's developing some sort of interpersonal *characteristics* or *personality*. Both these terms depict a set of stable social behaviors that will mark that child's individuality. The eventual presence of social individuality is hardly contested by either theorists or empiricists. There is, however, a marked divergence of opinion and circumstances concerning the separation of that individuality and the environmental settings in which the individual behaves. While a child can be roughly characterized by his or her social actions within a particular setting, such as a school playground, there is no certainty that the same characterization will materialize in a second setting. For example, a preschool child who frequently seeks adult help during structured play may show little dependency in a free-play setting where the same adults are available. Since the early and "shocking" observations of elementary school children's *honesty* by Hartshorne and May (1928), the uniform, across-setting presence of any social behavior has been held as questionable (see Mischel, 1968).

Despite the obviously powerful influence of environment on social behavior, many developmental theorists continue to argue

1. Preparation of this paper was funded by research grant MH 18516 from the National Institute of Mental Health, Crime and Delinquency Section.

1

for the existence of character style or personality. These arguments appear to be based on the things people *say* about themselves and on *some* observational evidence of interpersonal consistency across settings. In reference to the former, it is clear that members of the lay public believe they possess stable and generally evident social characteristics. For instance, when Kelly (1955) obtained adults' self-reports about their interpersonal behaviors, the test-retest reliabilities of such statements were remarkably high—even over spans of up to twenty years (Pearson rs from .45 to .60). In addition, observers of human behavior have recently discovered limited evidence of across-setting consistencies. Even the setting-specific results of Hartshorne and May (1928) revealed small but significant across-setting correlations when subjected to new analyses (Burton, 1963). More impressive in this light are the playground versus classroom observations of normal children's aggressive behavior reported by Harris (1979). If one is willing to regard consistency in terms of rank ordering within groups of individuals, these fifth- and sixth-grade boys were fairly predictable in their production of aggression ($r = .85$). But this stable rank ordering of children did not appear across settings for another same-age sample of boys that teachers regarded as presenting problems in aggression ($r = .12$). Thus Harris (1979) found some rather strange characteristics separating the two groups of children. The normal children's production of aggressive responses reflected consistency across situations, but the deviant, highly aggressive children's responses did not—quite the opposite of previous findings on the differential stability of deviant versus normal individuals (Raush, Farbman, & Llewellyn, 1960). More unusual yet in this light were the separate analyses conducted by Harris (1979) on the aggressive responses of one boy who was considered extremely aggressive. When his nine categories of aggressive behavior were subjected to rank-order correlation between playground and classroom, a remarkably stable pattern emerged ($r = .93$). Such across-setting consistency in deviant aggressive children had already been reported between home and school by Patterson and Maerov (Note 1). Their similar rank-order correlations conducted separately for two clinic-referred children were .73 and .85. Likewise, on the deviance dimension, Lichstein and Wahler (1976) found a lesser but still impressive across-setting consistency in the various social and nonsocial behaviors of an autistic child. When the child's responses were subjected to rank-order correlations between his home and two different school settings, a stable pattern emerged (.51, .63, and .85 for the three home versus school comparisons).

These correlational studies suggest an ordering of response likelihood within the behavior repertoires of some children—an ordering that appears independent of environmental settings. Although the evidence thus far is restricted to a few studies and though some peculiar differences did appear between normal and deviant children, there seems little doubt that the phenomenon *can* occur. That is, within social relationships some children may adopt roughly stylized manners of interchange; if a manner is observed in one social context (e.g., playground), one can be reasonably certain that it will emerge in a second social setting (e.g., home). However, in drawing conclusions about the nature of such a stylized manner, one must be equally aware of its currently documented molarity. In all three studies surveyed, the investigators conducted their correlational analyses on all response categories they thought to be relevant to the children in question (aggression categories for Harris, Patterson, & Maerov; social and nonsocial categories for Lichstein & Wahler). The investigators did not begin their searches for across-setting consistencies by first extracting those categories displaying the highest intercorrelations in one setting and then seeing if the same pattern emerged in the second setting. This distinction in method appears to be important in the following sense. When Lichstein and Wahler (1976) followed this latter strategy with the same autistic child, they extracted a smaller number of more highly intercorrelated responses in each of the three settings. But *none* of these more tightly covarying response patterns appeared in any two settings. Likewise, Wahler (1975) extracted covarying response clusters in two clinic-referred boys who were considered oppositional in their homes and classrooms. In both settings the two children's behavior repertoires were shown to contain dependably covarying sets of responses, but none of the covarying sets were similar between settings. Recently, however, Voeltz and Evans (Note 2) presented factor-analytic findings that did portray some consistencies. Their observational coverage of an austistic child extended across three different settings in the child's school. Despite the drastically different actions of teachers in the various settings, some consistent response covariations could be extracted. The clearest of these, called an activity factor, reflected a correlated cluster of simple motor responses (walking, running, sitting, and lying). Two other factors (negative social and play) also appeared in all three settings but did not consistently include the same covary-ing responses. Thus, while Voeltz and Evans provided some of the first evidence of inductively derived response consistencies, only the child's nonsocial response categories appeared as clear-cut clusters across settings.

All in all, evidence that response interdependencies will trans-cend environmental boundaries must be considered equivocal. Early observational findings (see Mischel, 1968 review) were nota-ble for the absence of across-setting behavioral consistencies. The recent studies, perhaps more sophisticated in observation technol-ogy, have indeed provided evidence that the phenomenon can occur. However, these data must be tempered with a methodologi-cal caveat. While it seems evident that researchers can pick re-sponse categories that will covary dependably across settings, an inductive selection of covarying categories may not produce the same consistency. Just why this difference should occur is not at all clear.

Regardless of the above interpretive constraints, the fact that across-setting consistencies *can* materialize in children is of enor-mous clinical importance. All therapeutic strategies must depend on generalization, at least in some degree. Therapeutic contingen-cies cannot be established for all the possible environmental set-tings that compose a child's day-to-day life. Typically, clinicians presume that covering some of these settings (e.g., mother-child interchanges in the evening; teacher-child interchanges during free time in the classroom) will yield outcomes extending into other stimulus conditions that make up the child's environment. The same presumption governs nonbehavioral treatment strategies in which the principal focus of change is on discussions between child and clinician. Once again, the therapeutic strategy counts heavily on generalization—in this case between the clinic and the child's natural environment. In essence, all therapeutic strategies are based on the notion that *indirect* modification of behavior is feasi-ble. That is, if change is produced in some aspects of a child's behavior under certain environmental conditions, predictable shifts will occur in other aspects. Obviously the importance of this assumption varies with the treatment strategy of choice. It is less important (but still relevant) for those social learning theory strategies (e.g., Tharp & Wetzel, 1969) implemented in the child's natural environment. The assumption is absolutely *critical* for the psychodynamic strategies usually implemented in clinic settings (Levitt, 1967). Thus, if the child's behavior repertoire is indeed organized with some degree of environmental independence, that organizational pattern must be understood. Perhaps the most striking new evidence behind this contention is seen in the *adverse* treatment side effects reported by Forehand, Breiner, McMahon, and Davies (1981). These investigators monitored the home and school behaviors of sixteen children referred for help because of their oppositional behaviors in the home. When a parent training program was shown to produce therapeutic effects in the home, an opposite trend occurred with these children in their school settings. The desirable shifts in home behavior correlated $-.72$ with changes in oppositional behaviors at school. In fact, the multiple-regression model using home therapeutic change scores and pretreatment levels of school oppositional behavior accounted for 70% of the variance in the oppositional changes at school! It seems evident that some process apart from direct environmental control was operating with these children.

Response Structure

These searches for consistencies in child behavior have generated little speculation about process factors. There have been allusions to the clinical importance of such research (i.e., producing indirect therapeutic change) but very few conclusions on why one would expect to find classes of behavior that transcend environmental settings. And, in those cases where consistencies actually were documented, the authors were reluctant to offer guesses on why they materialized.

As far as we are concerned, this reluctance to speculate is at least partly due to theoretical associations—both past and present. Early work on across-situation consistencies (e.g., Allport, 1966; White, 1964) was fostered by theories in which mediational constructs provided explanatory notions. According to these notions (e.g., psychodynamic), organized patterns of behavior *should* characterize individuals regardless of the settings in which they behave. Of course much of that early observational work could not document these consistencies. The more recent observational studies cited in this paper have had more of an ethological bent, in which the investigators typically did not entertain mediational explanations. If anything, most of these researchers have inclined toward social learning theory explanations that favor an environmental view of behavioral causality. We share this kind of theoretical strategy—admittedly a difficult position in which to conceptualize some of the data sets we have just reviewed. Nevertheless, we do believe one can adopt such a strategy in the useful search for organizational patterns in social behavior. We employ the term *response structure* in describing interdependencies among two or more responses within an individual's repertoire of behaviors. A response such as whining can be said to have structural properties if it either covaries with another of the child's responses or holds a predictable rank order of occurrence likelihood within the reper- toire. As the next section of this paper will document, structural properties of response repertoires have been demonstrated primarily within environmental settings. Few instances have been shown to occur across settings.

Social learning theory views of response structure seem easier to live with for within-setting cases of the phenomenon than for the across-setting covariations. But whereas stimulus control can be demonstrated in some instances of the former case, it is by no means "easier" to account for these cases than for the more sparsely reported across-setting variety. Either way, of course, the non- mediational social learning proponent would hope to demonstrate functional relationships between the response pattern and some observable events within the environment. As we see it, there are several possibilities for such relationships to materialize within the framework of reinforcement principles.

1. *Response chaining.* In response chaining an individual produces a sequence of responses that are interspersed with a sequence of stimuli provided by the behavior of other people. Presumably the stimuli function as reinforcers or discriminative stimuli for each response in the chain. Some ultimate stimulus in the chain may serve as the end point reinforcer for the entire response sequence. Thus a child's nagging, whining, yelling, and hitting may produce a covarying pattern because they occur in a predictable sequence. The functional control of that sequence may lie in mother-produced stimuli offered predictably after each child response.

2. *Response class.* Though more ambiguous, response class is also a demonstrable phenomenon governed by reinforcement principles. The ambiguity arises because a predictable time-line sequence is not necessary in producing stimulus control over the response pattern. Rather, one must conceptualize a situation or setting in which two or more of the individual's responses have roughly equivalent probabilities of generating the same reinforcer. For example, when a child's father enters the house smiling and

laughing, this stimulus event could predict the likelihood that the child's yelling, jumping, asking questions, and making demands will each be followed by the father's approval. The child would thus be reinforced for any one or all of these responses regardless of their order of occurrence. One could not predict which of the responses will occur given the discriminative setting, but the total *class* could be predicted.

3. *Stimulus class.* Like the response-class concept, the notion of stimulus class specifies a functional equivalence among two or more components—in this case, stimulus events. In other words, each of the stimuli, although they differ in physical similarity, becomes discriminative for the same response-reinforcer relationship. When a stimulus in the class is presented, it signals the likelihood that some particular response or response pattern will generate a dependable reinforcer. Using the earlier response-class example, it is possible that the child's mother, by simply sitting down in her favorite chair, may serve exactly the same discriminative function as the father does by smiling and laughing. As long as the same child behaviors are dependably reinforced under both stimulus conditions, the two stimuli will become members of one discriminative class. In essence, an across-setting consistency in this child's behavior would be understandable if such historical conditions prevailed.

4. *Response topography.* The concept of response topography does not share the reinforcement conceptions described in the three previous means of developing response structure. Rather, response topography refers to those physical characteristics of responses that affect their simultaneous occurrence. Some response pairs can occur simultaneously because their topographies make arrangements between them likely (e.g., writing and sitting). Other pairs simply cannot appear together because of their incompatible topographies (e.g., fighting and reading). In both cases, response structure would materialize through positive covariations in the former and negative covariations in the latter. While these structural properties are perhaps not as intriguing as those described in possibilities one, two, and three, they are nevertheless equally valuable from a clinical standpoint.

We consider the above concepts to be reasonable explanatory notions in the natural development of response structure. In addition, they offer useful guidelines in utilizing the structural phenomenon to produce clinical change in human problems. We now turn to a review of empirical investigations that yield data relevant to both of these issues.

Structural Characteristics of Child Behavior Repertoires

As should be evident from the preceding section, there are compelling theoretical reasons to expect organized response sets or structures in the behavior repertoires of children and adults. We briefly noted several research findings that support the notion of response structures in children's behavior. In this section we shall present a more extensive and detailed review of these empirical studies. Also, at the end of this section we will attempt to sum up what appears to be known about response structures—that is, the current state of the empirical base—before considering explanations. Before we begin the research review itself, however, several preparatory comments seem in order. First, the review is organized as a catalog of identified response structures. This seems to us a logical approach to presenting the empirical findings. Although some studies, as in imitation and language generalization research, appear to fit the general headings neatly, others do not. We recognize that other organizations of these studies are certainly possible; our organizing them into areas of response structure should not be mistaken for an attempt to catalog all possible response structures. Such a task is likely to be mammoth, if not impossible—somewhat akin to attempting to identify all possible reinforcing stimuli.

One must remember that our definition of response structure in terms of the observed correlation between two or more behaviors within a child's repertoire is rather wide-ranging. Within this framework we will be discussing a number of phenomena that have been variously labeled response classes, response induction, response generalization, behavior covariations, collateral effects, side effects, and multiple effects. In taking such an inclusive approach to these diversely described findings, we realize that some may contend we are lumping apples and oranges, since, for example, the controlling conditions of covarying behaviors of a response class and collateral effects may be quite different. Yet we think our approach is justified on two counts. On the one hand, response class, collateral effects, and so forth, share a common property—the covariation between behaviors in a child's repertoire—and thus fit our liberal definition of response structures. In this sense response structure is simply a more general, organizing term that makes no statement about the control dynamics of its various members. On the other hand, we will later suggest that there is perhaps more commonality among these sundry covariations than meets the eye, specifically in terms of the environmental mechanisms controlling these response structures.

The conditions under which response structures have been noted or studied are also wide-ranging. Some studies involve very "hard" observational data identifying specific covarying behaviors. Other studies provide a hard measure of some behaviors while providing "softer" measures (e.g., anecdotal reports) of their covariation. Again, some members of our audience may be concerned about the dependability of such verbal reports and consequently about the ultimate validity of the phenomenon. We share that concern, since the history of psychology has shown how beguiling, and ultimately erroneous, conclusions based upon such data can be. Yet the infant nature of the science of human behavior and the tenuous nature of our clinical technologies in regard to response structures warrant our attention to and later empirical verification of these purported relationships.

GENERALIZED IMITATION AND LANGUAGE RESEARCH

Perhaps two of the most visible and productive areas of research dealing with children's response structures have been those of generalized imitation and language training. At the risk of offending the technical and clinical innovativeness of the researchers we will cite in this section, we think it reasonable and helpful to first characterize the basic method of research in this area. In the typical study a specific set of imitative behaviors, verbal-vocal or motor-gestural or both, is taught to children who do not already possess an imitative repertoire. Such training is accomplished by having a model demonstrate a behavior and then verbally direct or physically prompt the child to immediately reproduce it. The model then provides the child with some positive consequence (e.g., food, praise) for imitative performance. This behavior (or set of behaviors) constitutes the trained behavior. To assess generalized imitation, the model also demonstrates another behavior or set of behaviors, but the child's performance of them is never reinforced. Thus, when the child's performance of nonreinforced behaviors begins to covary directly with his or her performance of those for which he has received reinforcement, generalized imitation is said to have occurred.

Baer and Sherman (1964) used a puppet to model three distinctive behaviors (head-nodding, mouthing, and nonsense statements) and to praise their imitation by subject children. In a second period the puppet also demonstrated a bar-pressing response, but its imitation was never praised. Seven of eleven subject children showed increases in bar-pressing as their other, reinforced imitative behaviors increased. Also, when praise was made noncontingent, imitation of both the reinforced and the nonreinforced behaviors decreased. Similarly, Metz (1965) and Baer, Peterson, and Sherman (1967) demonstrated that once imitation of one set of motoric behaviors had been established in severely handicapped children (childhood schizophrenics and severely mentally retarded youngsters) through modeling, cueing, and reinforcement procedures, the imitation of other nonreinforced and topographically different motor responses presented by an adult model also began to increase. Again, when the food reinforcement was made noncontingent, imitation of both the previously reinforced and the nonreinforced behaviors precipitously decreased.

Early studies of the establishment of imitative vocal-verbal behavior indicated similar response generalization. Lovaas, Berberich, Perloff, and Schaeffer (1966), through a lengthy shaping and modeling process, developed imitative word use in two previously mute schizophrenic children. Once imitation of English words was established in these children, the adult therapist model also interspersed nonreinforced Norwegian words between presentations of reinforced English words. The two children increasingly imitated the Norwegian words. A similar covariation was noted by Bringham and Sherman (1968) between children's imitation of modeled and reinforced English words and modeled but not reinforced Russian words.

More recently, dependencies have been demonstrated between complex aspects of verbal behavior. Garcia and DeHaven (1974) provided a review of generative response classes (in our terminology, response structures) in imitative and language behavior research, and a more extensive treatment of such research is available in that review. We might briefly point out several features of these findings: (1) Productive use of plural endings could be taught by training specific imitation on a select few words (Guess, Sailor, Rutherford, & Baer, 1968). (2) Modeling, direct prompting, and reinforcement of some instances of correct syntactical forms (the use of articles and auxiliary verbs) resulted in correct usage of the training-sentence items and also in the correct usage of non-training-sentence stimuli (Wheeler & Sulzer, 1970). (3) Acquisition of some receptive language was correlated with increments in other, nonreinforced sets of similar receptive skills (Whitman, Zakaras, & Chardos, 1971). (4) Training in receptive language skills facilitated children's later productive language skills (Mann & Baer, 1971).

SOCIAL BEHAVIOR/INTERACTION RESEARCH

One of the earliest behavior analytic studies to deal with childhood social withdrawal was reported by Allen, Hart, Buell, Harris, and Wolf (1964). The subject of this study was a 4-year-old preschool girl described as interacting freely with adults, rarely engaging peers in social exchanges, and not responding to peers' bids for her attention. In addition, her teachers reported that she frequently complained of minor nonexistent injuries and spoke almost inaudibly. Baseline levels of observed social behavior with peers were atypical, whereas adult-oriented behaviors were very frequent. To increase the girl's interaction with peers, Allen et al. had the classroom teachers ignore her periods of solitary play, give minimal attention during her self-initiated adult contacts, and praise her interactions with peers. Systematic shifts in the adults' attention from the girl's solitary and adult interaction to her peer interaction increased the frequency of her peer interaction and decreased her adult interaction. As peer interaction increased, the teachers reported fewer imaginary injuries and louder, more audible speech. That is, peer interaction appeared to be inversely related to injury complaints and positively related to louder speech. Unfortunately, no systematic measurement of these "apparent" behavioral correlates was conducted, nor were data presented to indicate whether adult attention to each of the behaviors (peer interaction, complaints, and speech volume) changed for peer interaction only or for all three behaviors simultaneously. Therefore it is not clear whether peer social interaction, complaints, and speech constituted a covarying set of behaviors, that is, a response structure, or whether adult attention contingencies changed simultaneously for each behavior.

A similar study was reported by Buell, Stoddard, Harris, and Baer (1968). Again a preschool-age girl in a nursery program displayed extremely low (near zero) levels in use of outdoor play equipment and in verbal and physical interaction with other children. The intervention in this case consisted of the classroom teacher's "priming" the girl's use of outdoor play equipment by placing the child on a particular piece of equipment, holding her there, and positively attending to her during these times. As expected, the girl's use of play equipment increased in frequency. Interspersed periods of noncontingent social attention were associated with decreases in use of play equipment. Concurrent with the initial increases in equipment use, the girl's approaches to and interactions with peers also increased. But this positive relationship was not maintained, since during other periods (the noncontingent attention probes) in which play equipment use decreased, peer social interactions continued to increase or to show no systematic decreasing trend. It appears, therefore, that this response covariation was short-lived, at least. It is likely that use of play equipment simply set the stage for the child to come in contact with peers and that the reinforcing attributes of peer interaction effectively controlled her subsequent social initiations.

A third social behavior study reported by Nordquist and Bradley (1973) suggests another instance of response covariation. Once more a preschool-age girl enrolled in a university nursery school program was the subject of an intervention to increase her cooperative play with peers. Teacher reports and baseline observation indicated extremely low frequencies of cooperative play and speech with peers. Owing to the extremely rare incidence of peer interaction, the teacher selected another child and prompted that child to initiate interactions with the withdrawn girl. She also dispensed positive attention to both children when such interaction occurred and ignored the withdrawn girl's initiations to the teacher. When cooperative play with the peer confederate and, later, other children increased under these conditions, concomitant increases and decreases were noted in the withdrawn child's speech frequency. Nordquist and Bradley argued that speech increases could not be "attributed to concomitant increases in the opportunity to speak to other peers because the percentage of speech scored during cooperative play increased even though the percentage of cooperative play across the treatment sessions remained relatively constant." Nor was it likely that the increases in speech were attributable to direct teacher reinforcement of speech, since the intervention procedure involved teacher attention only to nonverbal cooperative play. Although Nordquist and Bradley argued that for this girl cooperative play and speech formed a functional response class, they did acknowledge that speech may have been changed as a function of increased, contingent peer attention, citing a correlational relationship between increased peer approaches to the withdrawn child and increased speech.

Finally, Cooke and Apolloni (1976) reported an extremely interesting instance of response covariation in the development of positive social-emotional behavior in learning-disabled children. Four social behaviors—smiling, sharing, positive physical contact, and verbal compliments—were selected as targets of a modeling, prompting, and praising intervention that was successfully applied to each of those behaviors in a multiple-baseline design. Subject children's performance of the four behaviors was assessed during training sessions and during generalization sessions that immediately followed training sessions. When the intervention was applied only to children's smiling during the initial set of training sessions and baseline conditions were maintained for the other three behaviors, smiling increased while the other three behaviors remained at baseline levels. During this same phase, however, smiling, positive physical contact, and sharing also increased in the generalization sessions. Thus all four behaviors appeared to be functionally independent within the training setting but functionally interdependent during generalization sessions! The "functional variable" in this case is unknown. Possibly the generalization covariance was functionally related to the modeling, prompting, and praising implemented for smiling during training sessions. Lack of an immediately following withdrawal-of-treatment phase, in which those behaviors would be expected to increase concomitantly, precludes a causative analysis of this possibility.

OPPOSITIONAL SOCIAL BEHAVIOR

Much of the research on response structures in this problem area is an outgrowth of those classic, generalized imitation studies (e.g., Lovaas, et al., 1961) cited earlier. Our own work and that of others on the clinical treatment and empirical study of oppositional children has focused on the indirect control of one set of child problem behavior by direct intervention in another covarying set of behaviors. One of the earliest applied research examples of such indirect control was supplied by Wahler, Sperling, Thomas, Teeter, and Luper (1970). Here two young boys referred for disfluent speech (stuttering) also presented a second set of problem behaviors—opposition to parents' directions and high rates of activity shifting. Parents of the child who displayed opposition and stuttering were trained to use differential attention for cooperative (compliant) behavior and time out for opposition. Use of these procedures in the clinic and at home was associated with concurrent decrements in both the opposition and the untreated stuttering. Comparable results were obtained with the second child when the therapist employed differential attention to increase the amount of time the subject child spent interacting with a single specific object, person, or conversation topic. Again the application of differential attention procedures to one behavior (sustained interaction) was associated with improvements in that behavior and with concurrent reductions in stuttering. Further data analyses for both subject children established that: (1) stuttering and the secondary problem behaviors (opposition and activity shifts) rarely occurred close in time to each other; and (2) there was no shift across baseline and treatment phases in parental or therapist differential attention to stuttering. Thus changes in untreated disfluencies appeared to be the result of a functional relationship between disfluencies and the behavior targeted for intervention—opposition or activity shifting—rather than resulting from similar reinforcement control mechanisms, that is, differential attention.

A similar study was reported by Nordquist (1971), who investigated the direct contingency management control of a young boy's oppositional behavior as a means of indirectly eliminating the child's enuresis. Parents were taught to employ differential attention and time out to control the child's opposition, including his refusal to go to bed on time. The behaviors were first measured observationally, and parent reports of other tantrums and enuretic incidents were also systematically obtained. Successive phases of implementation and removal of the differential attention and time-out program were associated with reliable decreases and increases in opposition. Concurrently, reports of enuretic episodes were inversely related to compliance throughout all phases of the study. Parent instruction was maintained at a fairly constant rate across the time of the study. In sum, it was evident that cooperative behavior was controlled by application of the attention/time-out contingency and that "untreated" enuresis covaried inversely with cooperative behavior. Nordquist suggested that parents may have become more valuable or effective reinforcing agents through the use of time out and that they then were likely to have more effectively reinforced the child's self-initiated diurnal voiding.

An intensive and extensive study of the behavior of two young boys in their home and school environments was reported by Wahler (1975). The two boys, Fred and Carl, had been referred for psychological help. Fred's problems involved disruptive behavior in his classroom, while Carl's problems included oppositional behavior at home and self-stimulation and lack of social interaction at school. A multicategory behavior observation system was used to collect direct observational data on each boy's behavior at home and at school. Baseline behavior frequencies were intercorrelated and subjected to a cluster analysis to define sets of covarying responses for each child. For each boy a single response cluster was identified that was later found to recur across all experimental phases of the study and that included response members that were both positively correlated with some responses of that set and negatively correlated with others. Subsequent to the initial baseline phase and the identification of response clusters, contingency management procedures were instituted for Fred's behavior at school and Carl's behavior at home. Fred's school response cluster was composed of four behaviors—sustained schoolwork and self-stimulation, which were positively correlated with each other and negatively correlated with object play, which in turn was positively correlated with instances of noninteraction (correlations were calculated between behavior frequencies across observation sessions). A positive point system and social praise were applied to Fred's productive schoolwork, and time out was instituted for instances of object play, a disruptive behavior in the schoolroom. The general results of this study for both Fred and Carl were: (1) a single set of covarying responses was identified for each boy in the home and the school that continued to covary across all phases of the study; (2) some other response clusters were identified but were particular to only one or two phases of the study; (3) alternating phases of the application and removal of contingency management procedures to some members of the response class were associated not only with expected changes in the responses but also with their untreated covariates; (4) more fine-grained within-session analyses of both children's data failed to uncover any systematic changes in temporally proximal social stimulus category frequencies (e.g., adult or peer behavior directed to the subjects) that could otherwise explain changes in the response cluster members; and (5) there was no substantial across-setting consistency for either boy in terms of the identified response clusters. Thus Wahler (1975) identified naturally occurring response structures (covarying problem and appropriate behaviors) in two boys in two different settings and demonstrated that within-setting treatment of one response in these structures was associated with reliable changes in all response components.

In the preceding study (Wahler, 1975), an inverse relationship was identified between one child's problem, oppositional actions in the home, and the amount of his sustained toy play in that same setting. Several other studies (Wahler & Moore, Note 4; Wahler & Fox, 1980) replicated and extended the findings concerning this particular response cluster. Wahler and Fox (1980) reported on the within-home behaviors of four oppositional boys. The multicategory observation system used by Wahler (1975) was used again in this study, observations being conducted on target child and parent responses during 30-minute segments of the day that the subjects' parents characterized as problematic. In addition, the observer solicited parents' reports of their child's other, low-rate problem behaviors (e.g., fighting, property destruction, stealing, tantrums). After a series of baseline observations and measurements, interventions designed to increase specific child behaviors were instituted in the following order: (1) contingency contracting to increase cooperative social play episodes between the parent (mother) and the child; (2) contingency contracting to increase the child's sustained solitary play; and (3) continuation of the solitary play contract with a time-out procedure contingent upon instances of opposition. It is important to note that the contracts were in force only for a short period of time each day, typically just before the observation session but *never* during the session. The results indicated that: (1) during the baseline period, oppositional and social interactive behaviors were typically high, whereas toy play occurred at low frequencies; (2) when the social play contract was initiated, opposition and social interaction increased while toy play decreased; (3) when the social play contract was terminated and the solitary toy play contract initiated in its place, opposition and interaction decreased as toy play increased; (4) the toy play contract efforts were transitory in that in four to six weeks opposition and social interaction began to increase while toy play decreased; (5) addition of a time-out procedure for opposition was associated with decreased opposition and social interaction and increases in toy play; and (6) reductions in parent-reported, low-rate problem behaviors were concurrent with increased toy play and decreased opposition and social interaction. Not only do these data indicate some type of covarying relationship or response structure between relatively high-rate categories of child behavior such as opposition, social interaction, and toy play, but these dependencies extended to lower-incidence problem behaviors that occurred in other settings. Unfortunately, the controlling events of this apparent functional class of responses could not be isolated with any specificity. Certainly the response structure was affected by the particular type of contingency contract. But the level at which observer agreement on observational categories was achieved did not permit the type of within-session analyses performed by Wahler (1975). Thus it is unclear to what degree, if any, moment-to-moment changes in environmental social stimuli might have independently affected the occurrence of the individual behaviors of the apparent response class.

Perhaps the most practical demonstration of response structure phenomena is seen in the recent study by Ward, Cataldo, Russo, Riordan, and Bennett (1981). Reasoning that compliance appears as a dependable covariate with a good many deviant and desirable child behaviors, these investigators set positive reinforcement contingencies for this behavior in four problem children. Predictably, as compliance increased in frequency, a variety of disruptive behaviors, not under instructional control, decreased in frequency. The stability of these reductions marks this study as important for future clinical inquiry.

SELF-INJURY AND SELF-STIMULATION RESEARCH

Another area of research that has shed some light on the phenomenon of response structure has focused on a group of behaviors characteristic of severely developmentally delayed populations, that is, self-injury and self-stimulation in autistic and mentally retarded children.

Tate and Baroff (1966) reported one of the earliest instances of response covariation in this area. The subject was a 9-year-old blind, autistic boy who engaged in diverse, frequent, and severe instances of head-banging and head-hitting. Self-injury (SIB) occurred at various times of day but was systematically assessed during the child's daily 20-minute walk around the institution's campus with two research assistants. During control conditions, the two assistants simply held hands with the boy, guiding him and talking to him while ignoring any instance of SIB. In contrast, during experimental conditions they quickly and completely terminated any physical contact with the child contingent upon SIB. Data indicated that this latter punishment contingency was associated with considerable reduction in SIB. Also, anecdotal reports indicated that whining, crying, and hesitancy in walking, which ocurred frequently during control conditions, also decreased during the experimental phases. This decrement was obtained even though whining and such were not targets of the punishment intervention. Owing to the lack of additional data, however, it is not clear whether possible changes in physical or verbal adult attention behaviors could also have taken place in regard to these other problem behaviors and thus accounted for the collateral effects.

A more recent study of a different, life-threatening behavior—rumination—was reported by Becker, Turner, and Sajwaj (1978). A 3-year-old profoundly retarded girl, the subject of this study, exhibited chronic rumination, typically preceded by lip-smacking. After baseline observational assessment of rumination, stereotypic hand movements, object-touching, and crying, a procedure was implemented in which lemon juice was squirted into the girl's mouth whenever she ruminated. Reduction in rumination was associated with the lemon-juice procedure. Various "side effects" were noted concurrent with the decrease in rumination. Crying decreased, while object play and hand mannerisms increased over baseline levels. Several positive behaviors (babbling, toy play) and negative behaviors (head slaps, rocking, head-weaving) not seen during the baseline period also appeared during the treatment phase. Again, a clear explanation of the covariation between a treated behavior (rumination) and "untreated" behaviors (crying, stereotypies, etc.) could not be attempted, since data relevant to social and nonsocial environment changes other than the lemon-juice therapy were either not collected or not provided.

Simpson and Svenson (1980) combined the lemon-juice contingency with an overcorrection procedure (i.e., swallowing of the vomitus) in the treatment of rumination in a young schizophrenic boy. The combined procedure was implemented by the parents in the home and by the teacher in the classroom. Rumination, proximity to others, appropriate play, face-slapping, body-rocking and thumb-sucking were observationally assessed. Significant reductions in rumination, face-slapping, and rocking were obtained subsequent to the treatment of rumination only, while no significant differences were noted in proximity, play, or thumb-sucking.

A second behavior characteristic of severely impaired populations, self-stimulation, has attracted the interest of applied researchers both in terms of the effectiveness of certain interventions and in terms of its covariation with other responses. Risley (1968), in using several punishment procedures to eliminate the inappropriate climbing and rocking behavior of a 6-year-old brain-damaged, autistic girl, reported several anecdotally observed "side effects" of the procedure. Increases in eye contact and imitative behavior occurred after punishment-induced decreases in climbing and rocking respectively. Similarly, Stroufe, Stuecher, and Stutzer (1973) reported a package of skill-training procedures applied to a 6-year-old boy over a 12-week period preceded and followed by three-week and two-week no-treatment phases. Self-stimulation and hyperactive behavior, which were frequent during the baseline phase, decreased during treatment. Concurrent increases were noted in verbalizations, imitation, social behavior, and play as well as in self-help skills. Although no specific treatment was initiated for these diverse behaviors, the breadth of the "side effects" suggests that general or multiple environmental changes could have occurred that in turn could have effected the multiple behavior changes.

Punishment techniques for the suppression or reduction of self-stimulation and stereotypic behaviors have provided fertile ground for the study of response covariations. Since Risley's (1968) case report, cited above, a number of behavioral researchers have reported collateral behavior changes as a function of some punishment contingent upon self-stimulation. In a rather simple and straightforward procedure, Koegel, Firestone, Kramme, and Dunlop (1974) assessed the incidence of various self-stimulatory and appropriate toy play behaviors of an autistic boy and girl in a laboratory setting. Initially it was necessary to shape toy play, since neither child appeared to have this skill. Next, a baseline phase was conducted in which each child was simply placed in the experimental room with available toys and observed. In the next phase, self-stimulatory behavior was suppressed by having an adult shout "no!" and slap the child's hands whenever self-stimulation occurred. A second baseline and suppression condition followed. During baseline phases, self-stimulation was frequent and appropriate toy play was virtually absent. During suppression conditions, self-stimulation decreased and unreinforced toy play increased. Either or both behaviors could be scored simultaneously, and in some cases they were. Since this was the case, punishment occasionally coincided with both self-stimulation and appropriate play. Therefore appropriate toy play did not seem a likely avoidance response to punishment, and the increase in toy play could not reasonably be explained in this way. Physical incompatibility of the two responses was also ruled out as an explanation. Koegel et al. (1974) suggested that (1) the two responses then seemed functionally incompatible, or (2) both behaviors were maintained by their sensory effects upon the children and the rise in toy play served to provide the child with optimal stimulation that had been reduced in suppressing the self-stimulatory behavior. This latter hypothesis has received some support in a recent study by Rincover, Cook, Peoples, and Packard (1979) in which sensory reinforcement prameters of self-stimulation were empirically identified and then used to contingently shape appropriate toy play.

Side effects or response covariations have also been noted when other punishment techniques have been applied to self-stimulation. Epstein, Doke, Sajwaj, Sorrell, and Rimmer (1974) applied a hand overcorrection procedure to the inappropriate hand movements of two boys while initially leaving untreated the inappropriate foot movements of both boys and the inappropriate vocalizations of one boy. The overcorrection procedure reduced hand movements for both boys. Although one boy's reduced hand movements were not associated with reductions in untreated foot movements, the other boy showed increased appropriate toy play. Also, this boy's behavior was characterized by increased inappropriate foot movements when the overcorrection procedure was applied to hand movements. Thus, in this study one self-stimulating child displayed no response covariations while a second displayed both positive and negative response covariations.

A later study by Doke and Epstein (1975) further supported the idea of self-stimulation-related response structures. A young boy in a special day-care treatment program for disadvantaged children had previously been exposed to an overcorrection procedure (contingent toothbrushing) for thumb-sucking during language instruction. Although thumb-sucking had been suppressed in that situation, it persisted during naptime, when he also displayed other inappropriate object manipulation and gestural/verbal-vocal behaviors. Threats of overcorrection for thumb-sucking were then instituted during naptime, and the other inappropriate behaviors were simply measured. Decrements in thumb-sucking were accompanied by increases in other inappropriate behavior (kicking, rocking, arm-swinging) during the intervention on thumb-sucking. This inverse relationship was also apparent during the baseline phase. Only when overcorrection was applied to the "other inappropriate" category of behaviors did they also decline.

Finally, Simpson and Svenson (1980), cited above in regard to ruminating response covariations, also reported on the behavior of a second child whose self-stimulation involved repetitive vocalizations. In this case the parents and teachers employed a verbal command overcorrection procedure to reduce repetitive vocalizations. Concurrent with decreases in vocal repetitions there were increases in proximity to other people and reductions in hand-clapping and jumping.

Before ending this section on covariations involving self-injury and self-stimulation, let us point out that such response structures are not likely to be artifacts of punishment contingencies or "emotional behavior" generated by such punishment. Response covariations involving self-stimulation have been reported even when treatment techniques have a wholly or predominantly positive focus. For example, Flavell (1973) measured stereotypic and appropriate toy play behaviors in three severely retarded children in a laboratory setting containing various toys. Either behavior or both could be scored in an interval. Stereotypy (repetitive body or body part movements) was typically high and toy play typically low or absent during the baseline period. Once prompting and reinforcement for toy play were instituted, toy play increased as stereotypy decreased. No contingencies had been placed directly on stereotypic behaviors. Also, Herbert, Pinkston, Hayden, Sajwaj, Pinkston, Cordua, and Jackson (1973) taught differential attention procedures to the mothers of six children who displayed various referral problems (retardation, autism, learning disabilities, hyperactivity, and oppositional behavior). When the mothers implemented the differential attention procedures—ignoring inappropriate behaviors and praising task-oriented behaviors—in the clinic and the classroom, four of the children displayed substantial increases in a cluster of deviant behaviors concurrent with decreases in task-oriented behaviors. Also, more severe problem behaviors that had never been seen before in the clinic or the home (e.g., enuresis) began to occur.

BEHAVIOR COVARIATIONS
IN NORMAL CHILDREN

Except for those studies dealing with generalized imitation and language behavior, we have primarily reviewed response structures as they occur in deviant populations (oppositional, socially withdrawn, autistic, and retarded children). Yet there is evidence that response structures can also be found in normal children. For example, Kara and Wahler (1977) performed an intensive observational assessment and analysis of a preschool boy's behavior. The child was selected simply because of his acquaintance with one of those investigators. Prebaseline observations of the child's behavior were conducted in a laboratory playroom with various toys available and one of the investigators present. A multicategory observation system was used to observe the child's behavior during prebaseline, baseline, and experimental phases. Baseline behavior frequencies were submitted to statistical analyses to identify a set of correlated behaviors, some of which were positively correlated with each other and which were negatively correlated with others. A child response cluster of yelling, commands, laughing, playing, and talking was identified. During baseline conditions the adult attempted to make a specific response of his own—talking—100% contingent upon each behavior category of the child. The experimental manipulation consisted of withholding that adult attention from any instance of yelling by the child and assessing the effects of that manipulation on yelling and its untreated covariates. Manipulation of adult talk for the child yelling category led to decreases in yelling and concurrent changes in its covarying responses. Later baseline and manipulation phases reaffirmed the integrity of the yelling, laughing, command, play, and talk response cluster. As in all preceding studies, the covariations could not be related to systematic shifts in observed stimuli—in this case, the adult's behavior.

Some Structural Properties of Parents' Verbal Reports

Thus far we have reviewed little evidence on why child behavior repertoires are organized in covarying patterns. Neither have we seen much in the way of clinical utility based on monitoring these covariations. Certainly the latter consideration shows good promise of future development—particularly along the strategic lines mapped out by Ward, Cataldo, Russo, Riordan and Bennett (1981) and their colleagues. We turn now to another facet of response structure, this time emphasizing a specific set of covariations within the behavior repertoires of parents. Verbal reports by parents have always been considered significant components of the referral descriptions presented in child-parent relationship problems. As such, they serve at least two important functions with respect to the clinical change process: First, the verbal report is a measure of the parents' accuracy in describing the problem relationship. In this sense the report serves as an initial index of child deviance characteristics, the settings in which these characteristics are likely to be seen, and the parents' manner of dealing with the child. Second, these reports are indirect change targets regardless of their accuracy. In social learning treatment strategies, the direct change targets will typically be derived from discussions among therapist, parents, and child. But, regardless of what the direct targets turn out to be, parents' verbal reports are going to serve as a crucial "consumer satisfaction" assessment of the entire clinical process. Since parents are usually in charge of family functioning from a community legal standpoint, it is they who will ultimately provide validity judgments.

In the social learning process of treatment, parents' verbal reports will first become a direct target for accuracy shaping. It should come as no surprise that parents who report relationship problems with their children do so in vague or nebulous terms (Wahler & Afton, 1980). From the initial beginnings of parent-child behavior therapy, this assessment issue has been recognized and dealt with by teaching parents to pinpoint the relationship problems as concrete units of description (see Patterson, 1971). Thus, changing a parent's reports from a typically heard "he makes me be mean to him" to "he nags and then I yell," constitutes an important step in the clinical change process. Since it is the parent who must deal selectively with key aspects of problem and desirable behaviors in the child, that parent must be able to attend carefully to what the child does and does not do. It then stands to reason that a parent's continued success in using newly acquired parenting skills, such as response-contingent time out and approval, will depend on continued attention to the details of his or her relationship with the child. It is our contention that treatment failures are most likely to be caused by lack of maintenance in a parent's style of describing what goes on in these relationships. We will return to this maintenance issue later.

If parents' verbal reports are important treatment targets because they impede change in the child-parent relationship, one would wish to examine their structural properties in the same strategic sense as previously described probes into child behavior repertoires. Again, the same logic behind the search would prevail. A parent's description of his or her personal entrapment may be influenced by two factors: the stimulus pattern that constitutes the observed relationship problem (e.g., child whines—parent yells) and other responses within that parent's repertoire. If both factors exercise functional control over the parent's descriptive report, then both must be understood in order to plan an effective parent training program. It is clear that one can follow the traditional parent training format and simply teach parents to use a new descriptive report made up of molecular units. But, if the original vague and global reports are at least partially controlled by other covarying responses in that parent's repertoire, one must wonder how well the newly acquired report style will generalize across settings and over time. As we pointed out earlier, we believe that failures in parent training are most likely to be caused by nonmaintenance in parent styles of attending to and describing relationship problems.

Another complex parent response often seen in clinic referrals for child relationship problems concerns mother self-reports of *depression* (e.g., Patterson & Fleischman, 1979). These reports are usually based on psychometric test responses such as the Beck Depression Inventory (Beck, 1970) or the Minnesota Multiphasic Personality Inventory (published by the Psychological Corporation, 1948). For example, in Patterson's (1976) comparisons of clinic-referred mothers and mothers not reporting child relationship problems, the former were far more likely to endorse MMPI items describing themselves as being lonely, worthless, and unmotivated and having other characteristics summed under the rubric "depression." Since depressive reports are commonly associated with mothers who also report child relationship problems, a covarying association between these two reports seems likely.

Recently, Forehand and his associates (Griest, Wells, & Forehand, 1979) have presented data that indeed demonstrate correlational connections between a mother's reports of depression and her observational reports about her child's problem behavior. In this study Beck measures of mother depression were *better* predictors of mother-child behavior reports than were the actual child behaviors supposedly summarized by these reports. Thus we have here an instance in which the structural properties of a parent response appear to exercise greater influence on that response than do the relevant external stimuli. Griest, Forehand, Wells, and McMahon (1981) further demonstrated that this depression index does not covary with the observational reports of mothers who are adequately managing their children. In these cases the mothers' observational reports were accurate summaries of child behavior.

Finally, Ricard, Forehand, Wells, Griest, and McMahon (Note 3) extended the depression covariate research to instances in which child problem behavior was unlikely to serve a stimulus function for mothers' problem reports. Essentially, these investigators assessed three groups of mother-child dyads: those with no admitted problems; those with admitted problems confirmed by direct observation; and those with admitted problems in which direct observation showed no evidence of interpersonal problem exchanges. As expected, the depression index placed the last group of mothers apart from the other two groups. These mothers reported themselves to be more depressed than the others and, of course, they were also convinced that their children were behavior problems. Since the observational measures showed no differences between these children and the normal group, the depression factor appeared to be the only predictor of these mothers' observational reports.

Parent self-reports of depression also seem to be relevant in the success or failure of parent training interventions. Clear-cut predictors of such outcomes have yet to be substantiated, but, there are suggestions that parents who experience multiple problems in their day-to-day lives, and who are therefore depressed, are more likely to fail. This aspect of parent depression reports is relevant to our previously cited contention about the role of parent attending/ reporting styles in the therapeutic outcomes of parent training. Parents who report marked depression will tend to be poor observers of behavior interchanges involved in their own entrapment (Forehand et al., 1980). One would then expect that continued depression would compete with whatever attending skills such a parent might develop through parent training. If the depression reports are associated with (probably caused by) the child-parent relationship difficulties, one would expect parent training to reduce both problems. Without the attention-competing function of depression in operation, parent training ought to produce stable therapeutic out comes. But what if the depression reports are more obviously associated with adult relationship problems in that parent's life? Parent training could not be expected to reduce depression in these cases, and therefore the deleterious structural properties of this parent response would remain operational. In sum, the outcomes of parent training might not be favorable.

Treatment outcome findings in parent training programs support these contentions. Parents who describe themselves as harassed or coerced by adults as well as by their children are more apt to experience failure in parent training. In the failures reported by Reinsinger, Frangia, and Hoffman (1976), there were some likely connections between a parent's mismanageent of a child's behavior and that parent's coercive problems with the marital partner. In line with this finding, Wahler (1980) evaluated the parent training success of poverty-level mothers who reported consistent coercion problems with their own kinfolk and representatives of helping agencies. While these mothers were able to produce appropriate changes in their child relationship problems, the improvements were lost in a one-year follow-up. Reminiscent of Reisinger et al. (1976), Wahler found that the severity of mother-child relationship problems was greater on days marked by large proportions (80%) of contact between the mothers and their kinfolk or helping-agency representatives. That these poverty-level, harassed, and failure-prone mothers are also apt to report themselves depressed has recently been documented by McMahon, Forehand, Griest, and Wells (1981). Using dropout rate as their index of parent training success, these investigators found that Beck depression scores and mother's socioeconomic status were good predictors of this outcome measure: the lower a mother's socioeconomic status and the higher her depression score, the more likely it is that she will quit a parent training program before therapeutic outcomes are achieved.

We return now to our contention that parents' attending/reporting styles are instrumental in these treatment failures. Wahler and Afton (1980) devised a means of monitoring parents' verbal reports before and during parent training. Mothers who fit the poverty-level, multiply coerced pattern were compared with middle-income mothers whose coercion problems were restricted to their children. All the mothers were encouraged to describe their day-to-day coercive interchanges with their targeted problem children. These summary reports were videotaped and coded by professional observers into two categories reflecting the following qualities of each report: global versus specific, and presence versus absence of blame attribution. Assigning blame to the child and giving diffuse information were both considered signs of poor attentional tracking by a mother. In the first case, coercion is always a two-way exchange, and assigning blame to only one party is therefore an inaccurate reflection of the process. In the second case, we noted earlier that one's ability to alter the coercive process depends on specific information on what takes place. Findings in the study showed that both groups of mothers were equally diffuse and blame-oriented when they provided their child problem descriptions before parent training. During parent training, both groups demonstrated their ability to successfully change the coercion problems. But only the singly coerced, middle-income mothers altered their observational reports during the parent training phase. The multiply coerced mothers, despite their proved abilities to change child relationship problems, continued to describe these interactions in global, blame-oriented fashion. As expected from Wahler (1980), these mothers gradually returned to coercive interchanges with their children during a follow-up phase. The singly coerced mothers, however, maintained their therapeutic gains during this phase.

The Wahler and Afton (1980) study suggests a linkage between a mother's capacity to maintain the benefits of parent training and the quality of her attending/reporting style. In addition, since quality should have improved during parent training, one must wonder about the functional control of these reports. As we suggested earlier, a good bit of this control may be in the structural properties of such reports rather than in the mother-child interchanges to which the reports refer. As with the depressed mothers described by Griest, Wells, and Forehand (1979), these mothers' efforts to describe their children may have been influenced by maternal responses and experiences not directly relevant to their children.

Stimulus Control of Response Structure: Speculations

In the first section of this paper we outlined three reinforcement conceptions of response structure and one conception emphasizing the physical topography of responses. Some of the studies reviewed in the second section were geared to an examination of stimulus control in documented response covariations. While the topographic principle could account for some of the covariations obtained, none of the reinforcement models were very useful in this sense. Regardless of whether the observed covariations were inverse or positive, associated with planned interventions or with natural environmental conditions, the measured stimulus variables showed little systematic relation to the response patterns. However, although reinforcement principles could not account for these structural phenomena, this does not mean that other yet-unknown principles of environmental control were not operating.

An examination of laboratory-based studies of stimulus control offers a useful perspective on this issue. For some time, animal researchers have documented instances of stimulus control that make little sense on the basis of reinforcement principles. Skinner (1948), Morse and Skinner (1957), and Herrnstein (1966) showed repeatedly that it is possible to maintain durable response rates on the basis of noncontingent reinforcers. That is, once an animal's chosen response is developed to a stable rate through delivery of intermittent contingent reinforcers, that response rate can be maintained when reinforcement is shifted to a random schedule. This phenomenon, described by Herrnstein (1966) as "superstitious" behavior, is difficult to understand within an operant, or even a classical, conditioning paradigm. Either conception would lead one to believe that superstitious behavior cannot be durable in rate. If its stimulus associations are truly random, there is no conceptual basis on which to argue environmental support of the response rate. Eventually, extinction should occur. Certainly it is possible that the phenomenon will be shown to depend on some extraordinary intermittent reinforcement schedule. As of yet, however, superstitious behavior must be classified as an anomaly within operant and respondent frameworks.

Recently, several applied researchers have described phenomena that fit the criteria for superstitious behavior. Koegel and Rincover (1977) discovered that they could maintain the imitative behavior of autistic children by presenting food and social praise on a random basis. As in the Herrnstein (1966) model, the children's imitative responses were first developed through contingent reinforcement. Then, in a different setting, the same reinforcers were introduced noncontingently along with imitative prompts. This process was found to produce durable imitation, particularly if the previous training schedule of reinforcement was intermittently "thin." The authors reasoned that this maintenance outcome seemed to depend on reduced discriminability between the training and maintenance conditions. While this was undoubtedly the case, why should the children behave as if the randomly presented reinforcers were contingent? As in the superstition studies, extinction should be the rule of thumb. In a more naturalistic assessment of the same phenomenon, Fowler and Baer (1981) were able to produce stable sharing behavior in normal preschool children through superstitious stimulus control. In this fascinating demonstration, the children were told they could earn points for sharing behavior during an unspecified time span of their school day. One condition of the study entailed point tallies and their backup rewards immediately after a time span in which sharing responses led to contingent points. That time span (a morning free-play period) was the only setting in which sharing had a contingent relationship with the point reinforcers. In the second study condition, the feedback tally and backup reward session was delayed until the end of the day. Sharing behavior was measured by observers during the morning free-play period and an afternoon free-play period. Results showed stable increments in sharing responses in the morning period during condition 1 and no changes in sharing behavior during the afternoon period. During condition 2, however, sharing responses also increased in the afternoon even though they bore no relationship to the point reinforcers. By merely delaying the reinforcement delivery from morning to the day's end, superstitious stimulus control was achieved in the afternoon. Teacher approval was also measured in both periods and did not change over the course of the study. Thus the only feasible explanation for rate changes in the afternoon was the delay in reinforcer delivery. The reduced clarity of response-reinforcer contingencies during this delay condition was even reflected in the children's remarks ("Do I have to be good all day?"). These "superstitious" children were little different from Herrnstein's pigeons in terms of a reinforcement explanation for their behavior.

Ward, Cataldo, Russo, Riordan, and Bennett (1981) continued the inquiries into superstition, this time evaluating the phenomenon as a possible factor in response structure. Their clinical work with four deviant children was specifically addressed to the structural properties of these children's compliance with adult instructions. Findings clearly depicted such properties, in the sense that planned increases in compliance were shown to covary inversely with disruptive behaviors such as crying, kicking, and climbing. Since the investigators also monitored the delivery of available social and nonsocial reinforcers, it was possible to examine stimulus control of the response patterns obtained. As expected, the increments in compliance were found to depend on a systematic reinforcement contingency for that response. Then, as compliance rates increased, consistent decreases occurred in the disruptive behaviors. As far as stimulus control is concerned, one might expect that these decrements may have been due to reinforcer deliveries at times when the children were not engaged in disruptive behavior. However, while this association did materialize, there were also occasions marked by reinforcer delivery during occurrences of disruptive behavior behavior. Thus, if the lowered rates of disruptive behavior bore any functional connection to the available reinforcers, that connection was purely adventitious. In line with Koegel and Rincover (1977) and Fowler and Baer (1981), these children's covarying response patterns may have obtained their structural properties via superstitious stimulus control. This likelihood is enhanced by further observations showing that the children stopped most activity immediately after receiving compliance-contingent reinforcers. In essence, the children's heightened attention to the reinforcement source suggests their "anticipation" that further reinforcers might be forthcoming were they to continue their quiet, nondisruptive behavior.

Figure 1 outlines a superstition model for the maintenance of response structure. According to the model, one of the covarying responses is under contingent stimulus control of the environment. The other covariate members of that structure also share close temporal associations with that stimulus, albeit the associations are random. The features depicted in Figure 1 appear to fit the documented facets of superstitious behavior. Namely, contingent reinforcement appears to be necessary to developing the phenomenon. Once this step has occurred, that reinforcer may then exert "discriminative" control over the relevant response as well as over other responses that happen to occur in temporal proximity to the reinforcer presentations. But what looks like discriminative control is in fact superstitious control. That is, continued occurrences of the reinforcer need not signal any future contingencies. The reinforcer now functions as an instructional setting event—an instruction to perform specific responses that will lead only to randomly occur-

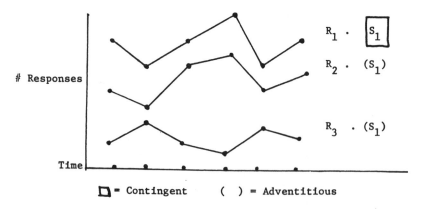

Figure 1. A schematic illustration of response structure comprising negative and positive covariations. Superstitious stimulus control of the structural properties is suggested.

ring payoffs. It seems probable that there are other, more long-term contingencies involved in superstitious stimulus control. At present, however, the model seems adequately described by those simplistic features of Figure 1.

The superstition model provides a particularly understandable account of covariations between parents reports of child problem behavior and the same parents' reports of depression. The point relevant to this structural phenomenon is the obvious role of parental attention. As the previously reviewed findings suggest, a parent may report that she or he is attending to a specific set of stimuli: the child's deviant social behavior. But it is also evident from the data that the parent's depression reports are good predictors of this child problem report. Since parent depression has been associated with (elicited by) that parent's coercive exchanges with adults as well as children, it is possible to view several sets of stimuli that bear close temporal relations to both depression and child problem reports. Following the superstition model, it is feasible to view parent depression as under the contingent stimulus control of adult and child coercive attacks. The depression response covariate, parents' reports of child problem behavior, might then fall under superstitious control of the adult coercive stimulus pattern in addition to its own relevant child stimulus pattern. Thus one would expect to hear multiply coerced parents sometimes describe their children's "bad" behavior in the absence of any such actions by the children. In such instances the parents' verbal reports would be described as purely superstitious. As in all instances of superstition, *attention* to a stimulus appears to be more relevant than how that stimulus actually functions as a response consequence.

In reference to the preceding statement, it is difficult to view superstition as contributing much to the typically lawful development of human behavior. If the developing child and the already developed parent are readily influenced by noncontingent, randomly occurring stimuli, one must wonder how it is possible to generate the organized behavior patterns that characterize families, schools, peer groups, and other natural groupings of most communities. The very existence of such stable group activity argues the powerful impact of contingent stimulus control. Superstitious control must be the exception rather than the rule. All that we know about its development is seen in the animal laboratory studies and in the two behavior control studies by Koegel and Rincover (1977) and Fowler and Baer (1980). That is, contingent reinforcement appears to be a prerequisite for the development of such stimulus control. These studies suggest a means of producing the phenomenon through planned manipulation of social and material reinforcers. Yet it is also possible, as suggested by Ward et al. (1981), that superstition may be at least partially involved in the natural development of social behavior. In fact, our own clinical experiences suggest that this sort of stimulus control may be more relevant to deviant social behavior than to normal behavior. To further continue our line of speculation, we would argue that developmental experiences that promote one's *attention* to stimuli will foster superstitious contingencies between these stimuli and responses; the stronger or more probable the attentional focus, the more likely it is that superstition can develop.

The strength or probability of child and parent attending to each other's actions is usually greater during aversive exchanges than during positive exchanges, particularly in clinic-referred dyads. This conclusion is based on naturalistic observations of child-parent interchanges by Patterson and his colleagues at the Oregon Social Learning Center. The use of aversive stimuli was found to be greater in deviant families than in normal families (Patterson, 1976). More important in this family comparison was the function of aversive stimuli to ensure a continuation of mutual attention between child and parent. In the deviant families, mutually aversive responses between child and parent markedly increased the likelihood that the dyad would continue the coercive exchange. In contrast, the non-clinic-referred dyads were likely to cease attending to one another after such an exchange. Aversive social responses do seem to "stand out" as figure in the content of nonaversive exchanges (Wahler & Leske, 1973). Also associated with this higher probability of aversive interchanges in deviant families is the finding that *noncontingent* aversive as well as neutral/positive social stimuli are more likely (Johnson, Wahl, Martin, & Johanssen, 1974). Troubled mothers, for example, were just about as apt to respond aversively to the children's prosocial behavior as to follow those child actions with positive reactions.

The conditions for establishing superstitious stimulus control appear most likely in those families marked by frequent and intense coercive relationships—presuming that the likelihood of noncontingent social stimuli is also high. Certainly the correlational connections between a parent's depression and that parent's reports of child behavior seem to develop within such conditions. The stable response structures seem in behavior repertoires of highly aggressive children (Harris, 1979; Patterson & Maerov, Note

1) appear to have similar developmental conditions. It is relevant here to recall Wahler's (1975) response structure finding with two coercive children: all of the stable patterns in home and school settings contained at least one response designated as deviant by the children's parents and teachers. Of course it is equally obvious the superstitious stimulus control and response structure can develop in normal children without any sort of coercive experiences as prerequisites. Our major point in this series of speculations has to do with possible relationships among three variables: coercive social interchanges, superstitious stimulus control, and response structure. Our argument that these variables may be part of a developmental and maintenance framework is crucial groundwork for the last section of this paper.

Implications for Family Therapy

Deviant, clinic-referred families are almost always characterized by coercive relationships among some of the dyads each family comprises. When child-parent interchanges are the basis for clinic referral, one would expect to see two features of the relationship: mutual coercion, in which the parties engage each other in manding episodes (e.g., nag-yell; cry-appease; hit-scream); and mutual statements of dislike about the other party's behavior (e.g., she's not fair; he's spoiled). In our experience these features are found in all such referrals but are seen most obviously in those involving child aggression or opposition, or both, as the child behavior complaint. As Patterson (1976) has documented, the child-parent coercive episodes in these families are significantly longer in duration than those in nonproblem families. Furthermore, Wahler, Hughey, and Gordon (1980) found that the length of coercion episodes differentiated more difficult to treat multiple-problem families from those whose problems were restricted to parent-child disputes. As expected, there were significantly more of the long episodes in the multiple-problem families. Thus the coercion factor represents part of the within-family process for parent-child clinic referrals— particularly when the problem descriptions entail child opposition or aggression or both.

The summary reports by troubled parents and children are also fairly typical in certain characteristic descriptions of one another. Both parties are apt to be "defensive" in the sense that each attributes blame to the other (Wahler & Afton, 1980). While each is also likely to express some semblance of dislike for the other's behavior, the mother is apt to offer derogatory views of herself as well (Patterson & Fleischman, 1979). As we noted earlier, maternal depression can interfere with the mother's capability to attend accurately to her troubled child's behavior (Griest, Wells, & Forehand, 1979).

Parent training in child management procedures has been shown to have fairly dependable therapeutic effects on both these features of child-parent relationships (Patterson & Fleischman, 1979). Here we have reference to the by now standard format of teaching parents to pinpoint molecular components of coercion, to use time out or response cost at the beginning of coercive episodes, and to use praise or token reinforcers or both for the child's noncoercive behaviors. Not only is coercion diminished and replaced by more positive child-parent interchanges, the two parties actually seem to enjoy each other and report greater self-satisfaction (Patterson, 1976; Wahler, 1969). However, as Patterson and Fleischman (1979) also point out, the therapeutic case for parent training has yet to be proved across the board for all families. Indeed, the bulk of research has focused on *mothers* as the parent training targets. In a practical sense this selective focus is justified because of the finding that a mother is the most typically entrapped parent in child-parent coercion episodes. But there are certainly instances in which mother-father coercion is an accompanying feature of the parent-child problem (Oltmanns, Broderick, & O'Leary, 1977). In addition, the coerced mother may also experience coercive relationships with her extended family and social service agents within the community (Wahler, 1980). It is in these cases when the mother suffers multiple coercive entrapment that parent training alone may prove insufficient as a means of altering her child relationship problems.

Figure 2 portrays a coercive relationship between child and mother that could be modified through parent training—were it not for the coercive input from other adults in the mother's family and community. For the moment, it is instructive to ignore this input to show what would happen in this schema through parent training alone. First, it should prove possible to alter response frequencies indirectly through helping the mother set new contingencies for her child's demands. When the mother's demands are replaced with a time-out contingency, the child's demands, as well as screaming and property destruction, ought to diminish. These systematic changes in the mother's behavior would completely alter the contingent and superstitious stimulus pattern for the child's deviant response structure. Likewise, the mother's appeasing, crying, and immobilization ought to become less likely through reductions in the child's screaming. Since the resulting stimulus patterns presented by both parties will become more *contingent*, the likelihood of accurate summary reports should also increase. The mother ought to note that her child's screaming is only part of his problem repertoire and that she has been most apt to handle that response through appeasement. The child, depending on age and intellectual development, may conclude that his screaming and property destruction have little to do with his mother's demanding behavior.

Figure 2, however, indicates that this mother's child-controlled response structure is also controlled by her coercive relationships

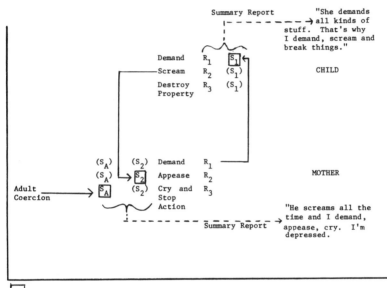

Figure 2. A schematic illustration of response structure relationships in a child-mother dyad. One three-component structure is depicted for the child and another for the mother. One response component in the child's structure is under the contingent stimulus control of the mother's demands, while the other two components are under superstitious control of this stimulus. Likewise, one of the mother's response components is under the contingent stimulus control of child's screaming, and the others are under superstitious control of this stimulus. In addition, another of the mother's response components is controlled by contingent coercive stimuli from other adults, leading to second-order superstitious control of her response components. As a result, both child and mother offer descriptive self-reports and other reports that are inaccurate.

with adults. Her contingent response to such input from spouse, kinfolk, and so on, is to cry, stop most of her activity, and perhaps comply with the manding input. Given the superstitious control that then develops, her child-directed responses, including her summary report, are also influenced by this second coercion trap. Her tendency to make demands on her child, appease his screaming, and erroneously describe her entrapment with him are at least partly influenced by her entrapment with the other adults. Unless this latter coercion problem is unraveled, it seems that its presence will compete with the therapeutic effects of parent training. Wahler (1980) provided correlational data in line with this assumption. In this study, the mother's self-reports of contacts with kinfolk, helping-agency representatives, and friends were correlated with her observed coercive interactions with her child. According to her reports, contacts with kinfolk and helping-agency people were apt to be aversive, while her friendship contacts were apt to be positive. Results showed that mother-child coercive interactions were significantly more frequent on days characterized by high proportions of kinfolk and helper contacts compared with days marked by high friendship contact. This study also revealed an absence of long-term therapeutic effects of parent training—possibly owing to the continued coercive relationships between the mothers and their kinfolk and helpers.

Given this problem with multiply entrapped parents, one could envision solving it through an expansion of parent training. Such an expansion along the lines of marital contracting (Weiss, Birchler, & Vincent, 1974) might help resolve coercive relationships between parents, between parents and kinfolk, and perhaps even between parents and helping-agency representatives. For two reasons, we believe such formal educational training must await completion of a relationship and attentional training step that could ensure success in parent training. We will present this step in a moment. First, consider the reasons formal educational training may not be a sufficient means of helping multiply entrapped parents. The most important of these centers on what we have found to be a pronounced tendency for multiply entrapped parents to become coercively entrapped with helping or change agents. A good many such parents are also described as poorly educated, living on marginal or poverty-level incomes, and dwelling in crowded, crime-infested areas of the city. As might be expected, these parents are far more likely to come in contact with social service or helping agencies than are middle-income parents. As Wahler (1980) documented, multiply entrapped "insular" parents tend to describe these contacts as manding or aversive. That is, the helper's efforts to "help" are viewed as little different from the coercive approaches of their children. While the insular parent may comply with these adult manding actions and thus complete the helper's mission, the compliance is purely escape-oriented. If the compliance process could be shifted to a positive reinforcement operation, the mand/countermand problems of coercive teaching would be eliminated (see Alexander, Barton, Schiavo, & Parsons, 1976). A second reason to mistrust a purely educational contracting approach to these parent-adult coercion problems has to do with the willingness of these second parties to become involved in treatment. Despite the "ideal" picture of family therapy outlined by Minuchin (1974), our experience with insular families has shown that kinfolk, boyfriends, and even husbands often refuse to become part of the contracting process.

MAND REVIEW: SORTING OUT STIMULUS CONTINGENCIES

One means of attenuating superstitious control involves making the controlling stimuli highly discriminable. This process is implemented in parent training by formal instruction on what to look at and how to report it. The same result can be achieved at a much slower pace by conversational shaping of a parent's summary reports about his or her coercion traps. The advantage of the latter clinical technique is twofold and, we think, critical with insular parents: First, initial acceptance of a parent's summary reports of personal coercion heightens the possibility of friendship. Therefore any further teaching might be accomplished through positive rather than negative reinforcement. Second, instead of preventing a parent's use of the initial summary reports, one can modify these usually long-standing reports. Assuming that the initial reports are under superstitious stimulus control, simply preventing them will not alter future occurrences once the suppressive contingencies of treatment are ended. We turn now to an elaboration of advantages—an elaboration considered under our descriptive label "mand review."

When a parent has the opportunity to simply talk about personal problem relationships, he or she will use global descriptors (Wahler & Afton, 1980). In describing that parent's personal coding taxonomy, it is worthwhile to note the metaphor consistently used by the parent in outlining coercion trap similarities (e.g., "He used to bring me a rose"; "He baits me and, like a fool, I rise to the bait"). In our experience these metaphors are stable, frequently used descriptors for particular trap situations. Their notation by a therapist will therefore dependably be followed by the parent's reference to specific people and description of some recent coercive interchange. Now, keeping the metaphor as the parent's personal cue, the therapist will begin to alter its discriminative properties: instead of cueing parent global descriptions, it must set the occasion for descriptors coded by the parent into more molecular, discrete units. In other words, the therapist still accepts the personal metaphor but now insists on specific information as its reference components. Notice that both parties are still conversing on the basis of some common global units—those metaphoric descriptors derived by the parent. But these labels must now come to summarize concrete events. Consider the following narrative from one of our mand review sessions.

> MOTHER (M): "He's still smothering me a lot of the time" [refers to child].
> THERAPIST (T): "Yes, I know, smothering you. How did that happen this week? When and where did it happen?"
> M: "Well, like when I was trying to talk to Ralph [boyfriend] yesterday. He just had to show off and hang on like he does."
> T: "Where were you and Ralph?"
> M: "Um, let's see. He was trying to tell me about his brother. We was sitting on the porch."
> T: "What did Mike [child] do?"
> M: "He was getting up in my lap and put his arms around my neck."
> T: "That's it?"
> M: "Well, it was hot and I told him to quit hanging on my neck. He did, but then he pouted."
> T: "Should that have been a time-out offense?"
> M: "I don't know. See, I was mad at Ralph because he lets his brother talk him into anything. He had his tail in a knot and said I was bitching. But I wasn't."
> T: "I guess I don't know what smothering means. I've heard you say you like to have Mike sit on your lap and hug you."
> M: "Yeah, but not when I'm mad."
> T: "So when you were mad at Ralph and Mike sat on your lap and hugged you—that's smothering?"
> M: "Yes."

Not only does this narrative exemplify a therapist's search for detail when presented with a parent's global reports of coercion, the search product also illustrates how a reported unit of parent-child coercion actually includes adult-adult coercion as well. This mother's metaphor "smothering" is a summary label for a broad spectrum of aversive events—only some of which involve her targeted problem child. Recall the earlier-cited efforts of Griest, Wells, and Forehand (1979) to predict mothers' summary reports about their children's coercive behaviors. These mothers' self-reports of depression were better predictors of their child-referenced reports than were the actual occurrences of child behavior. We, of course, interpret these findings within the rubric of superstitious stimulus control. The Griest et al. mothers, and the mother described above, appeared to have summarized depression-inducing experiences and child behavior into these personal codes that supposedly referred *only* to child behavior (see Figure 2). Parent training, with its emphasis on discouraging parents' use of such global reports, may not ensure disuse—at least with multiply coerced parents (Wahler & Afton, 1980). Thus we believe that the sort of search for clarity depicted in our "smothering" example might well bolster parent attention to the stimuli associated with coercive experiences; a sorting out of the specific stimuli into their appropriate summary reports. Conceivably, the parent-preferred metaphors will become discriminative for a set of contingent rather than adventitious stimuli.

Directly tied to this rather cumbersome shaping process is another hoped-for product—a parent-therapist relationship based on positive reinforcement. As we noted earlier, initial acceptance of a parent's summary reports of personal coercion heightens the possibility of friendship in the therapeutic relationship. In our experience, friendship development is at least partially related to the therapist's skill in respecting these initial parent reports while at the same time fostering the discrimination training just described. We have also discovered that this training proceeds a good deal more slowly for multiply entrapped parents—if one is to nurture and preserve the friendship relationship as well. Hollingshead and Redlich (1958) have argued an evident "mismatch" between the operating strategies of most (middle-class) therapists and their low-income, poorly educated clients. It is this mismatch in values, conceptions of behavior control, and so on, that supposedly results in a generally poorer prognosis for change in such clients. However, as Lorion (1974) has documented in his questionnaire study, there are virtually no differences in such attitudes and expectations about treatment as expressed by clients of middle and lower socioeconomic status (SES). Yet, in our experience, a mismatch can indeed exist for most low SES parents and their parent training therapists. That communication difficulty centers primarily on the therapist's expectations in promoting a search for detail in the summary reports parents offer. In our opinion, the multiply coerced, low SES parent may be under more extensive superstitious control than his or her middle-class counterpart. If so, one could expect a slower course of discrimination learning for multiply entrapped parents. While the therapist's efforts to rapidly induce such a parent's attention to contingent stimulus events might be feasible, the teaching process is apt to involve negative reinforcement principles. It should perhaps come as no surprise that dropout rates in traditional parent training are higher for low SES troubled parents (McMahon, Forehand, Griest, & Wells, 1980) and that parent training therapists tend to avoid working with them (Hargis & Blechman, 1979). In the following session narrative, this sort of therapist frustration and coercive press for detail are evident:

MOTHER (M): "He's just terrible! I don't know what I'm going to do with him."

THERAPIST (T):"What do you mean, he's terrible?"

(M): "He's just driving me crazy. It doesn't matter what I do, nothing pleases him."

(T): "Can you give me an example? What does Jimmy do?"

(M): "And another thing—if I can't get some peace of mind I don't know what's going to give first."

(T): "How is Jimmy terrible?"

(M): "He's just all over the place. He's terrible and nobody gives a damn!" [Mother begins to cry.] "I just wish daddy was alive."

(T): "Does Jimmy mind you when you tell him to do things?"

(M): "He won't do nothing! Don't you know how awful he is?" [Mother still crying.]

(T): "Look, I can help you with him, but you've got to tell me what he does."

(M): [Crying]. "I've told you."

(T): "Give me a for instance."

(M): "OK."

This session was the third in a baseline assessment phase. The therapist had already accumulated enough detailed information to instruct this mother in keeping a log of the boy's coercive actions and noncompliance with her instructions. However, the therapist continues to be "on task" and insists that the discussion center on the evident contingencies of mother-child coercive episodes. We would predict that this low SES, multiply entrapped mother would "quit" the parent training program in short order. In later sessions, however, the "slowed down" therapist discovered that "nobody gives a damn" was a wide-ranging summary term for three types of coercive episodes in this mother's day-to-day life: (1) those involving her aggressive/oppositional son; (2) those involving her husband's demands that she keep the house clean; (3) those involving her mother's critical remarks about her parenting style and her marital problems. Obviously the task of sorting out stimulus contingencies into their appropriate categories took considerable time—a good deal more time than we usually devote to singly entrapped parents.

Thus far, these anecdotes and speculations include a meager data base. We know that mand review sessions do reduce dropout rates with low SES, multiply entrapped mothers. We know that these sessions are associated with maintenance of parent training induced improvements in mother-child relationships. The components of mand review that account for these desirable outcomes are as yet unknown. In addition, when mand review sessions are terminated, the mothers return to baseline levels of coercive interchanges with their children. The "state of the art" has improved but it obviously leaves much to be desired.

REFERENCE NOTES

1. Patterson, G. R., & Maerov, S. L. A functional analysis of settings and children's coercive behaviors. Unpublished manuscript. Oregon Social Learning Center, Eugene, Oregon, 1977.

2. Voeltz, L. M., & Evans, I. M. Covariation of behavior in a preschool handicapped child with multiple behavioral problems. Unpublished manuscript. Department of Special Education, University of Hawaii, 1980.

3. Rickard, K. M., Forehand, R., Wells, K. C., Griest, D. L., & McMahon, R. J. An assessment of mothers of clinic-referred deviant, clinic-referred nondeviant and nonclinic children. Unpublished paper. University of Georgia, Athens, Georgia, 1980.

4. Wahler, R. G., & Moore, D. R. School-home behavior change procedures in a high-risk community. Paper presented at the meeting of the Association for Advancement of Behavior Therapy, San Francisco, December 1975.

REFERENCES

Alexander, J. F., Barton, C., Schiavo, R. S., & Parsons, B. V. Systems-behavioral intervention with families of delinquents: Therapist characteristics, family behavior and outcome. *Journal of Consulting and Clinical Psychology*, 1976, **44**, 565–664.

Allen, K., Hart, B., Buell, J., Harris, F., & Wolf, M. Effects of social reinforcement on isolate behavior of a nursery school child. *Child Development*, 1964, **35**, 511–518.

Allport, G. W. Traits revisited. *American Psychologist*, 1966, **21**, 1–10.

Baer, D. M., Peterson, R. F., & Sherman, J. A. The development of imitation by reinforcing behavioral similarity to a model. *Journal of the Experimental Analysis of Behavior*, 1967, **10**, 405–416.

Baer, D. M., & Sherman, J. G. Reinforcement control of generalized imitation in young children. *Journal of Experimental Child Psychology*, 1964, **1**, 37–49.

Beck, A. T. *Depression: Causes and treatment*. Philadelphia: University of Pennslyvania Press, 1970.

Becker, J., Turner, S., & Sajwaj, T. Multiple behavioral effects of the use of lemon-juice with a ruminating toddler-age child. *Behavior Modification*, 1978, **2**, 267–278.

Brigham, T. A., and Sherman, J. A. An experimental analysis of verbal imitation in preschool children. *Journal of Applied Behavior Analysis*, 1968, **1**, 151–158.

Buell, J., Stoddard, P., Harris, F., & Baer, D. Collateral social development accompanying reinforcement of outdoor play in a preschool child. *Journal of Applied Behavior Analysis*, 1968, **1**, 167–173.

Burton, R. V. Generality of honesty reconsidered. *Psychological Review*, 1963, **70**, 481–499.

Cooke, T., and Apolloni, T. Developing positive social-emotional behaviors: A study of training and generalized effects. *Journal of Applied Behavior Analysis*, 1976, **9**, 65–78.

Doke, L., & Epstein, L. Oral overcorrection: Side effects and extended application. *Journal of Experimental Child Psychology*, 1975, **20**, 495–511.

Epstein, L., Doke, L., Sajwaj, T., Sorrell, S., & Rimmer, B. Generality and side-effects of overcorrection. *Journal of Applied Behavior Analysis*, 1974, **7**, 385–390.

Flavell, J. E. Reduction of stereotypics by reinforcement of toy play. *Mental Retardation*, 1973, **11**, 21–23.

Forehand, R., Breiner, J., McMahon, R. J., & Davies, G. Predictors of cross setting behavior change in the treatment of child problems. *Journal of Child Clinical Psychology*, 1981. In press.

Fowler, S. A., & Baer, D. M. "Do I have to be good all day?" The timing of delayed reinforcement as a factor in generalization. *Journal of Applied Behavior Analysis*, 1981. In press.

Garcia, E., Baer, D., & Firestone, P. The development of generalized imitation within topographically determined boundaries. *Journal of Applied Behavior Analysis*, 1971, **4**, 101–112.

Garcia, E., & DeHaven, E. Use of operant techniques in the establishment and generalization of language: A review and analysis. *American Journal of Mental Deficiency*, 1974, **79**, 169–178.

Griest, D. L., Forehand, R., Wells, K. C., & McMahon, R. J. An examination of differences between nonclinic and behavior problem clinic-referred children and their mothers. *Journal of Abnormal Psychology*, 1980, **89**, 497–500.

Griest, D. L., Wells, K. C., & Forehand, R. An examination of predictor of maternal perceptions of maladjustment in clinic-referred children. *Journal of Abnormal Psychology*, 1979, **88**, 277–281.

Guess, D., Sailor, W., Rutherford, G., & Baer, D. An experimental analysis of linguistic development: The productive use of the plural morpheme. *Journal of Applied Behavior Analysis*, 1968, **1**, 297–306.

Hargis, K., & Blechman, E. A. Social class and training of parents as behavior change agents. *Child Behavior Therapy*, 1979, **1**, 69–74.

Harris, A. An emprirical test of the situation specificity/consistency of aggressive behavior. *Child Behavior Therapy*, 1979, **1**, 257–270.

Hartshorne, H., and May, M. A. *Studies in the nature of character.* Vol. 1. *Studies in deceit.* New York: Macmillan, 1928.

Herbert, E., Pinkston, E., Hayden, M., Sajwaj, T., Pinkston, S., Cordua, G., & Jackson, C. Adverse effects of differential parental attention. *Journal of Applied Behavior Analysis*, 1973, **6**, 15–30.

Herrnstein, R. J. Superstition: A corollary of the principles of operant conditioning. In W. K. Honig (Ed.), *Operant behavior: Areas of research and application.* New York: Appleton-Century-Crofts, 1966, pp. 35–51.

Hollingshead, A. B., & Redlich, R. c. *Social class and mental illness: A community study.* New York: John Wiley and Sons, 1958.

Johnson, S. M., Wahl, G., Martin, S., & Johanssen, S. How deviant is the normal child: A behavioral analysis of the preschool child and his family. In R. D. Rubin, J. P. Brady, and J. D. Henderson (Eds.), *Advances in behavior therapy.* Vol. 4. New York: Academic Press, 1974.

Kara, A., & Wahler, R. Organizational features of a young child's behaviors. *Journal of Experimental Child Psychology*, 1977, **24**, 24–39.

Kelly, E. L. Consistency of the adult personality. *American Psychologist*, 1955, **10**, 659–681.

Koegel, R., Firestone, P., Kramme, K., & Dunlop, G. Increasing spontaneous play by suppressing self stimulation in autistic children. *Journal of Applied Behavior Analysis*, 1974, **7**, 521–528.

Koegel, R. L., & Rincover, A. Research on the difference between generalization and maintenance in extra-therapy responding. *Journal of Applied Behavior Analysis*, 1977, **10**, 1–12.

Levitt, E. E. *The psychology of anxiety.* Indianapolis: Bobbs-Merrill, 1967.

Lichstein, K. L., & Wahler, R. G. The ecological assessment of an autistic child. *Journal of Abnormal Child Psychology*, 1976, **4**, 31–54.

Lorion, R. P. Social class, treatment attitudes, and expectations. *Journal of Consulting and Clinical Psychology*, 1974, **42**, 920.

Lovaas, O. I. Interaction between verbal and non-verbal behavior. *Child Development*, 1961, **32**, 329–336.

Lovaas, O., Berberich, J., Perloff, B., and Schaeffer, B. Acquisition of imitative speech by schizophrenic children. *Science*, 1961, **151**, 705–707.

Mann, R., & Baer, D. The effects of receptive language training on articulation. *Journal of Applied Behavior Analysis*, 1971, **4**, 291–299.

McMahon, R. J., Forehand, R., Griest,D. L., & Wells, K. C. Who drops out of therapy during parent behavioral training? *Behavioral Counseling Quarterly*, 1981. In press.

Metz, J. R. Conditioning generalized imitation in autistic children. *Journal of Experimental Child Psychology*, 1965, **2**, 389–399.

Minnesota Multiphasic Personality Inventory. New York: Psychological Corporation, 1948.

Minuchin, S. *Families and family therapy*. Cambridge, Mass.: Harvard University Press, 1974.

Mischel, W. *Personality and assessment*. New York: John Wiley and Sons, 1968.

Morse, W. H., & Skinner, B. F. A second type of superstition in the pigeon. *American Journal of Psychology*, 1957, **70**, 308–311.

Nordquist, V. M. The modification of a child's enuresis: Some response-response relationships. *Journal of Applied Behavior Analysis*, 1971, **4**, 241–247.

Nordquist, V. M., & Bradley, B. Speech acquisition in a non-verbal isolate child. *Journal of Experimental Child Psychology*, 1973, **15**, 149–160.

Oltmanns, T. F., Broderick, J. E., & O'Leary, K. D. Marital adjustment and the efficacy of behavior therapy with children. *Journal of Consulting and Clinical Psychology*, 1977, **45**, 724–729.

Patterson, G. R. *Families: Applications of social learning to family life*. Champaign, Ill.: Research Press, 1971.

Patterson, G. R. The aggressive child: Victim and architect of a coercive system. In E. Mash, L. Hamerlynck, and L. Handy (Eds.), *Behavior modification and families*. Vol. 1. *Theory and research*. New York: Brunner/Mazell, 1976.

Patterson, G. R., & Fleischman, M. J. Maintenance of treatment effects: Some considerations concerning family systems and follow-up data. *Behavior Therapy*, 1979, **10**, 168–185.

Raush, H. L., Farbman, I., & Llewellyn, L. G. Person, setting and change in social interaction. II. A normal-control study. *Human Relations*, 1960, **13**, 305–332.

Reisinger, J. J., Frangia, G. W., & Hoffman, E. H. Toddler management training: Generalization and marital status. *Journal of Behavior Therapy and Experimental Psychology*, 1976, **7**, 335–340.

Rincover, A., Cook, R., Peoples, A., and Packard, P. Sensory extinction and sensory reinforcement principles for programming multiple adaptive behavior change. *Journal of Applied Behavior Analysis*, 1979, **12**, 221–233.

Risley, T. R. The effects and side-effects of punishing the autistic behaviors of a deviant child. *Journal of Applied Behavior Analysis*, 1968, **1**, 21–34.

Sherman, J. A. Modification of non-verbal behaviors through reinforcement of related verbal behavior. *Child Development*, 1964, **35**, 717–723.

Simpson, R., & Svenson, C. The effects and side-effects of an overcorrection procedure applied by parents of severely emotionally disturbed children in a home environment. *Behavioral Disorders*, 1980, **5**, 79–85.

Skinner, B. F. "Superstition" in the pigeon. *Journal of Experimental Psychology*, 1948, **38**, 158–172.

Stroufe, L., Stuecher, H., & Stutzer, W. The functional significance of autistic behaviors for the psychotic child. *Journal of Abnormal Child Psychology*, 1973, **1**, 225–240.

Tate, B., & Baroff, G. Aversive control of self injurious behavior in a psychotic boy. *Behavior Research and Therapy*, 1966, **4**, 281–287.

Tharp, R. G., & Wetzel, R. J. *Behavior modification in the natural environment*. New York: Academic Press, 1969.

Wahler, R. G. Oppositional children: A quest for parental reinforcement control. *Journal of Applied Behavior Analysis*, 1969, **2**, 159–170.

Wahler, R. G. Some structural aspects of deviant child behavior. *Journal of Applied Behavior Analysis*, 1975, **8**, 27–42.

Wahler, R. G. The insular mother: Her problems in parent-child treatment. *Journal of Applied Behavior Analysis*, 1980, **13**, 207–219.

Wahler, R. G., & Afton, A. D. Attentional processes in insular and noninsular mothers: Some differences in their summary reports about child problem behavior. *Child Behavior Therapy*, 1980, **2**, 25–41.

Wahler, R. G., & Fox, J. Solitary toy play and time-out: A family treatment package for children with aggressive and oppositional behavior. *Journal of Applied Behavior Analysis*, 1980, **13**, 23–39.

Wahler, R. G., Hughey, J. B., & Gordon, J. S. Chronic patterns of mother-child coercion: Some differences between insular and non-insular families. *Analysis and Intervention in Developmental Disabilities*, 1980. In press.

Wahler, R. G., & Leske, G. Accurate and inaccurate observer summary reports. *Journal of Nervous and Mental Disease*, 1973, **165**, 386–394.

Wahler, R. G., Sperling, K., Thomas, M., Teeter, N., & Luper, H. The modification of childhood stuttering: Some response-response relationships. *Journal of Experimental Child Psychology*, 1970, **9**, 411–428.

Ward, E. M., Cataldo, M. F., Russo, D. R., Riordan, M. M., & Bennett, D. Child compliance and correlated problem behavior: Effects of contingent and noncontingent reinforcement procedures. *Journal of Applied Behavior Analysis*, 1981. In press.

Weiss, R. L., Birchler, G. R., & Vincent, J. P. Contractual models for negotiating training in marital dyads. *Journal of Marriage and the Family*, 1974, **36**, 321–331.

Wheeler, A., and Sulzer, B. Operant training and generalization of a verbal response form in a speech deficient child. *Journal of Applied Behavior Analysis*, 1970, **3**, 139–147.

Whitman, T., Zakaras, M., and Chardos, S. Effects of reinforcement and guidance procedures on instruction following behavior in retarded children. *Journal of Applied Behavior Analysis*, 1971, **4**, 283–291.

White, R. W. *The abnormal personality*. New York: Ronald Press, 1964.

Whitehurst, G. J. Generalized labeling on the basis of structural response classes by two young children. *Journal of Experimental Child Psychology*, 1971, **12**, 59–71.

The Abused Child: Victim, Instigator, or Innocent Bystander?[1]

John B. Reid, G. R. Patterson, and Rolf Loeber

Oregon Social Learning Center

*R*aising a child, even in the best of circumstances, is an extremely difficult task that places heavy psychological, social, and financial burdens on most parents. One of the most difficult facets of child-rearing is discipline. More than a third of the referrals to child guidance clinics are for "child management" problems (Patterson, 1964; Roach, 1948; Rogers, Lilienfeld, & Pasamanick, 1954; Woody, 1969). In our society, over 90% of parents either consistently employ or occasionally resort to spanking or other types of physical coercion to resolve discipline problems (Stark & McEvoy, 1970). Gelles (1979) reported on a probability sample of 960 fathers and 1,183 mothers who were interviewed about familial violence. The results showed that over the past year, 2.3% of the parents had thrown something at their children more than twice; 18.5% had pushed, grabbed, or shoved their children more than twice; 43.6% had slapped or spanked their children more than twice; 1.7% had kicked, bitten, or hit with a fist more than twice; and 9.8% had hit their children with objects more than twice. Given that hitting and spanking by parents commonly occur during discipline confrontations (and given that children are usually weaker than their parents, who are often quite angry at these times), it seems reasonable to assume that such episodes will occasionally escalate to such a level that children are

1. This research was supported by funds from Grant #1R01 MH 33067 and Grant #1R01 MH 31017 from the National Institute of Mental Health, United States Public Health Service. The Oregon Social Learning Center is an affiliate of the Wright Institute in Berkeley, California.

actually injured. This assumption is supported by Gil (1969, 1971), who found that over 60% of a sample of child-abuse incidents occurred in the context of discipline confrontations.

The position taken in this paper is that each time a parent finds it necessary to discipline a child there is a definite risk that violence or injury will be one of the outcomes. It is certainly true that the magnitude of this risk varies from one family to another and that the risk might be higher for families who suffer various types of disturbance or distress. Within a particular parent-child dyad, the probability of abuse will be associated with two interrelated factors: the frequency of aversive interactions between the parent and child that are likely to lead to discipline confrontations; and the parent's effectiveness in quickly terminating such confrontations. It is further assumed that these two variables can be affected in turn by a variety of background factors in which the parent-child interaction is embedded. The hypothesized interrelationships among these factors are depicted in Figure 1. Some examples are as follows. A

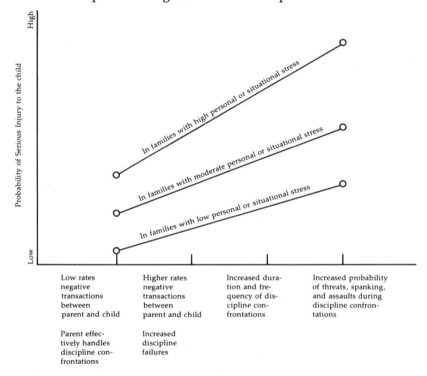

Figure 1. Proposed relations of parent-child interactional factors and background stress variables to the probability of child abuse.

child could instigate or raise the probability of abuse to the extent that he or she presents the parent with high rates of problem behaviors, or to the extent that he or she is unresponsive to discipline. A child's risk of being a victim of abuse could be increased by a parent's tendencies to issue commands that are age-inappropriate or excessive and to initiate aversive interactions with the child (e.g., nattering), or by an inability to use effective discipline procedures. A child's chances of being abused as an innocent bystander could be increased to the extent that marital conflict, emotional problems, and financial or other background stressors make the parents more irritable toward the child or less effective in quickly terminating misbehavior.

Summarizing to this point, the formulation presented here is that child abuse can be viewed as rooted in day-to-day transactions between parents and their children. Officially detected child abuse, as well as hitting or other "legal" assaults, are most likely in families where the parent and child are involved in high rates of aversive interchange and in which the parents' ability to quickly and successfully deal with discipline confrontations is minimal or impaired. Within any family, the likelihood of parental assaults on children is greatest on days when such aversive interchanges are highest and the parents' performance of child management skills are lowest. Although a number of variables undoubtedly can affect these factors, making child abusive episodes more likely in some families than in others, it is our position that the potential for child abuse exists to some extent in every parent-child relationship. In the rest of this paper we will review some literature and present some data that support the hypothesized relation between these two variables and parents' attacks on their children. We will then offer some ideas and pilot data that explore the relation of background variables to parent-child conflict and child abuse. Finally, we will present a case example that may have implications for clinical practice.

Relationship between Aversive Interchanges and Child Abuse

The idea that child abuse is most likely in homes where the rates of parent-child discipline confrontations and the level of day-to-day aversive behaviors of children and parents are high gains support from a large number of studies that have examined the background characteristics of victims and perpetrators of child abuse. A number of direct observational studies also support this idea.

Aversive Child Behavior

If one argues that a child's risk of physical abuse is increased to the extent that he or she irritates the parent, then child abuse should be more common in families with children who might be expected to present more discipline and child management problems or to be less responsive to verbal control or mild discipline. A number of studies are relevant to this issue: compared with nonabused children, victims of child abuse have been reported to demonstrate a higher incidence of general behavioral abnormalities (Gil, 1970), hyperactivity (Friedman, 1972; Green, Gaines, & Sandgrun, 1974), physical handicaps (Gil, 1970), and mental retardation (Elmer & Gregg, 1967; Sandgrun, Gains, & Green, 1975). A number of investigators have reported high incidence of abuse for children born prematurely or of low birthweight (Elmer & Gregg, 1967; Klein & Stern, 1971). Pasamanick and Knobloch (1966) found prematurity to be significantly related to subsequent mental retardation and behavioral and hearing disorders.

Home observation studies have recently been reported that provide more direct support for the idea that abused children present more management problems than those who are not abused. Burgess and Conger (1977) have reported that siblings in abusive families engage in significantly more conflict than do children in either nondistressed or neglectful families. Reid, Taplin, and Lorber (1981) reported the results of analyses of observational data collected in the homes of three groups of families: 61 referred for child management problems with no evidence of child abuse, 27 referred for child management problems but also demonstrating clear evidence of child abuse, and 27 nondistressed control families.[2] The children in the abusive families showed significantly higher rates of overall aversive behaviors than did the youngsters in the other two groups.[3]

2. Although not reported in that paper, observer reliability was assessed for 16% of the data collected. Mean entry-by-entry agreement was 78.4% (range = 51–100%).

3. It is tempting to speculate that children who demonstrate high rates of aversive behavior also engage in aversive sequences of long duration. Patterson (1979) conducted sequential analyses of home observational data collected on a small sample of children referred for child management problems. He reported a significant correlation of +.76 between the child's overall rate of aversive behavior and the probability that an aversive episode would include at least two negative behaviors.

These observational studies accord with the studies previously cited in suggesting that children who present high rates of discipline problems are more likely to be physically abused than those who do not. Is there also a relationship between a child's aggressiveness and the likelihood that he or she will be the focus of hitting, spanking, and threatening behavior by the parent? As a preliminary test of this idea, Reid (1981) analyzed observational data collected in the homes of 36 nondistressed families, 58 nonabusive families referred for child management problems, and 14 child-abusive families. For the whole sample as well as for the three subsamples, correlations were computed between the rates at which the children were observed to perform aversive/oppositional acts and the rates at which their parents were observed to engage in aversive behavior in general, to hit, and to threaten their children. As can be seen in Table 1, the correlations were highly consistent. Across all subsamples, there are significant and surprisingly high correlations between the rates of child aversive behavior and the rates at which the parents behaved aversively, hit, and threatened their children. Although the strongest relationships were found for the abusive families, high correlations were observed even in non-distressed families.

Finally, Patterson (1981) has carried out some pilot work that suggests that, within families, the rate at which children perform aversive acts on a given day is related to the rate at which their

Table 1

Relation between the Rate of Child Total Aversive Behavior (TAB) and the Rates of Parent TAB, Hitting, and Threatening

Correlations between child TAB and: [a]	Nondistressed sample (mothers: $n=36$; fathers: $n=25$)	Distressed, nonabusive sample (mothers: $n=58$; fathers: $n=32$)	Child-abusive sample (mothers: $n=14$; fathers: $n=8$)	Combined samples (mothers: $n=108$; fathers: $n=65$)
Mother TAB[b]	+.50***	+.24*	+.65**	+.40****
Father TAB	+.59***	+.27	+.49	+.38***
Mother hits	+.37**	+.21	+.53*	+.28***
Father hits	−.11[c]	+.24	+.74**	+.33***
Mother threats	+.38**	+.19	+.29	+.30***
Father threats	+.39*	+.29*	+.83**	+.30**

[a] Rate per minute scores for each variable were used in the correlations.
[b] Parents' TAB rates do not include hitting or threatening.
[c] Only one nondistressed father was observed to hit his child.
   * $.10 > p > .05$; ** $p < .05$; *** $p < .01$; **** $p < .001$.

mothers act in an aversive manner. Analyzing at least 21 days of home observation data for five families revealed significant correlations between rates of mother and child aversive behaviors in each case.

Taken together, these data offer broad support for one of the main hypotheses presented here: the probability that a parent will seriously abuse, hit, or threaten a child is in significant part a function of the rate at which the child presents the parent with behavioral problems. This is the case with nonabusive as well as abusive families. The previously noted tendency of this culture to endorse spanking or hitting as a parental reaction to child problem behavior, coupled with observational data showing that young children behave poorly on the average of three or more times an hour when they interact with their parents (Fawl, 1963; Minton, Kagan, & Levine, 1971; Forehand, King, Peed, & Yoder, 1975; Reid, 1978), suggests that most children are at serious risk of instigating their own abuse at some time during their development.

Aversive Parent Behavior

At the beginning of this paper we proposed not only that child abuse was related to the rate at which children act aversively, but that the same relation should hold between daily rates of parental aversive behavior and child abuse. Support for this hypothesis has been reported in a number of observational studies. In the previously cited analysis of home observational data by Reid et al. (1981), mothers in child-abusive families demonstrated significantly higher rates of overall aversive behaviors as well as significantly higher rates of hitting and threatening than did mothers in the nonabusive groups. The same trends were observed for fathers, but they were not statistically reliable. These results have some interesting implications. First, aggressive behaviors closely associated with child abuse (i.e., general parental aversiveness, hitting, and threatening) can actually be observed in natural settings. We had initially thought that parents concerned about, or in trouble for, abusing their youngsters might not demonstrate any aggressiveness in front of observers. Second, these results clearly support the hypothesis that child abuse is part of a pattern of increased aversive interaction between parent and child—not an occasional or unexpected breakdown in parental control caused by diffuse background factors such as stress or emotional collapse. Specifically, these data are in accord with the hypothesis that the more often a parent engages in aversive interchanges with a child, the greater the risk of an abusive episode.

These data provide support for the idea that high daily rates of parental aversive behavior are associated with serious child abuse. In the present formulation, we further assume that there is a positive relation between the rates at which parents demonstrate mildly aversive behaviors and the rates at which they hit and threaten their children. This relation should hold for nonabusive as well as abusive parents.

To test for this relation, Reid (1981) computed correlations among observed rates of mildly aversive behavior (total aversive behaviors minus threats and hits), hitting, and threatening for abusive and nonabusive parents.

As can be seen in Table 2, the rates at which parents are aversive are consistently and positively related to the rates at which they threaten or hit. Thus, the more frequently a parent engages in milder aversive behaviors (i.e., total aversive behaviors minus threats and hits), the more likely he or she is to engage in hitting or

Table 2
Relationships between Parents' Rates of Total Aversive Behavior (TAB)
and the Rates at Which They Hit and Threaten Their Children

Correlations[a]	Nondistressed sample (mothers: $n=37$; fathers: $n=26$)	Distressed, nonabusive sample (mothers: $n=58$; fathers: $n=32$)	Child-abusive sample (mothers: $n=14$; fathers: $n=8$)	Combined sample (mothers: $n=109$; fathers: $n=66$)
Mother TAB[b]x mother hit	+.66****	+.38***	+.59**	+.33****
Father TAB x father hit	−.13[c]	+.52***	+.78**	+.47****
Mother TAB x mother threaten	+.61****	+.44****	+.62**	+.51****
Father TAB x father threaten	+.33	+.46***	+.68**	+.43****
Mother hit x mother threaten	+.66****	+.53****	+.81****	+.55****
Father hit x father threaten	+.08[c]	+.67****	+.86****	+.52****

[a] Rate per minute scores for each variable were used in the correlations.
[b] TAB rates do not include hits or threats.
[c] Only one nondistressed father was observed to hit his child.
  * .10 > p > .05; **p< .05; *** p < .01; ****p < .001.

threatening. In addition, the more often the parents use threats, the more likely they are to escalate to hitting.

The data in Table 2 simply support the idea that as the parents' rates of aversive behavior increase, there is a *comparable* increase in the rates at which they hit and threaten their children. We are currently entertaining a frequency-aversiveness hypothesis that specifies that as the parents' total aversive behavior (TAB) increases, the *proportion* of TAB that is made up of hits and threats also increases (i.e., as the rate of aversive behavior increases, the rate of hitting and threatening increases exponentially). A preliminary analysis of home observation data recorded for nondistressed mothers interacting with their children (Reid, 1981) strongly supports this hypothesis. A correlation of $+.67$ ($df = 35; p < .0001$) was found between mothers' observed TAB scores and the ratios of hits and threats to less aversive behaviors that made up those scores.

At the beginning of this paper we argued that the most immediate variables accounting for child abuse and lesser parental attacks on children could be determined by analyzing the behavioral transactions that continually take place between parents and their children. Specifically, we hypothesized that the probability or frequency of such attacks is a function of two related interactional variables: the rate at which the parent is exposed to, or participates in, aversive interchanges and discipline confrontations with the child; and the parent's ability to quickly and nonviolently terminate such interchanges or confrontations. Up to this point, we have offered evidence in support of the first variable. To summarize, we have presented data to show that both parents and children in abusive families demonstrate higher daily levels of aversive, as well as assaultive, behaviors than do their counterparts in nondistressed or distressed but nonabusive families. Regardless of which historical, emotional, physical, parenting, or other background variables are involved from case to case, parents who abuse their children experience more negative encounters than those who do not. We have also presented data showing that this pattern not only is present in families who attack their children with such frequency or intensity that they are labeled child-abusive, but is evident in nondistressed or normal families as well.

Effectiveness of Parental Discipline

As we stated previously, the second aspect of parent-child interaction hypothesized to account for child-abusive or assaultive behaviors is the parent's ability to quickly and effectively resolve discipline confrontations. Young (1964) reported that over 90% of severely and moderately abusive families were characterized by inconsistent and ineffective parental discipline. In another study, Elmer and Gregg (1967) found a similar pattern of inconsistent discipline in abusive families.

In regard to the relation between abusive behaviors by parents and aversive or aggressive behavior by their children, a number of studies have pointed to a relation between aggressive child behavior and inconsistent discipline. A number of field studies have shown inconsistent discipline in the background of young delinquents (e.g., Glueck & Glueck, 1950; Jenkins, 1968; McCord, McCord, & Howard, 1961). In laboratory studies, Parke and Deur (1972) found that inconsistent parental punishment was less effective in controlling child behavior than punishment provided on a consistent schedule. The same investigators also found that children who were inconsistently punished showed the greatest resistance to extinction and the most persistence in responding in the face of a new schedule of consistent punishment (Deuer & Parke, 1970). Finally, in an observational study, Patterson (1976) found that parents of highly aggressive children were less effective when they punished their children than were parents of nonaggressive children. Moreover, there is increasing evidence that mothers in nondistressed families are able to resolve problems with their children through positive rather than aversive means. Loeber and Janda (1981) studied intervention in sibling conflict by mothers of normal and aggressive children. Mothers of normal children resolved such fighting more by means of positive interactions than did mothers of aggressive children, who used significantly more aversive methods.

More direct support for the relation between assaults on children and ineffective discipline was provided in the home observational study of abusive and nonabusive families reported by Reid, Taplin, and Lorber (1981), who studied the results of discipline confrontations between parents and children in abusive, distressed but not abusive, and nondistressed families. Specifically, they examined the immediate outcomes of all observed sequences in which the aversive behavior of a child at time 1 was followed by an aversive parental response at time 2 and calculated the probability that the child would continue to behave aversively at time 3. Mothers and fathers in the nondistressed group failed in terminating only about 14% of such sequences with one negative reaction. Parents in the distressed but not abusive families failed in immediately terminating significantly more sequences (a failure rate of about 35%). Fathers in the abusive families did not differ significantly from fathers in the other two groups in failure rates, but mothers in the abusive families were least effective of all groups in stopping aversive child behavior by reacting negatively to it (a failure rate of 53%). Their rate of failure in intervening in the aversive behavior sequences of their children was almost four times that of mothers in the nondistressed families. Also of interest was their finding that, within each nonabusive group, mothers and fathers had consistent and nearly identical success rates; in the abusive group, mothers failed twice as often as fathers. A concomitant of this failure is the incidence of threats. Threats usually refer to withdrawal of privileges or to impending punishment, including hitting. In the study by Reid (1981), father's threats correlated .83 with the child's TAB score in the abusive sample (see Table 1). For both parents the correlation between threats and hitting was over .80 (see Table 2). Rate of threats in the abusive sample, therefore, was the most evident predictor of hitting and probably of ultimate child abuse. The importance of threats as a precursor of interfamilial violence is also borne out in a study by the Detroit and Kansas City police (*Domestic violence* 1977). When threats were made in domestic disturbances, physical violence occurred in slightly more than half the cases; when family members used physical force, threats had been uttered in almost 80% of the disturbances.

These data provide strong support for the hypothesis that parents (particularly mothers) in child-abusive families have major difficulties in immediately and successfully resolving discipline confrontations with their children. Equally relevant was the finding that nonabusive parents of aggressive children also showed significantly more difficulty in handling conflicts than did the nondistressed controls. Taken together with the evidence presented earlier that nonabusive parents of aggressive children hit and threaten their children more often than do normals, it is reasonable to presume a relation between parental attacks and ineffective discipline in families that have not been traditionally labeled as abusive.

It is obvious that the data presented here do not help us decide whether the child is the instigator or the victim of abusive parent behavior. Both children and their parents are involved in escalating the rates of aversive behavior, as well as in prolonging the discipline confrontations that raise the likelihood of injury and abuse.

The Relationship between Background and Child Abuse

As the title of this paper suggests, we assume the distinct possibility that the escalating aggressive interactions that lead to abuse are not always a function only of the immediate, interactive effects of the victim's actions (e.g., rate of aversive behavior, response to discipline) and the perpetrator's actions (e.g., rate of aversive behavior, skillful use of child management skills). We assume there are variables that systematically affect the relevant interactional behaviors of parent and child (i.e., rates of aversive behavior, effectiveness of discipline attempts), creating the possibility that abused or assaulted children may be conceptualized as innocent bystanders. A large number of variables are reported in the survey and clinical literature that are commonly associated with child abuse. In the formulation presented here, we assume that stressful background factors increase the probability of child abuse, assault, or spanking to the extent that they systematically affect the day-to-day rates of aversive interactions between parents and child, the effectiveness of the parents' attempts to resolve discipline confrontations, or both.

Over the past two decades, a large number of such background variables have repeatedly been shown to be associated with child abuse: chronic financial hardship and unemployment (e.g., Gil, 1970; Light, 1973; Spinetta & Ringler, 1972); large family size (e.g., Gil, 1970; Light, 1973; Johnson & Morse, 1968); social isolation (e.g., Bennie & Sclar, 1969; Garbarino, 1977)[4] marital conflict or divorce (e.g., Green, 1976; Spinetta & Ringler, 1972; Zalba, 1971); and the density of stressful events to which families are exposed (Egleland & Brunnquell, 1977; Justice & Duncan, 1976).

There is more direct evidence to support the idea that such background variables are associated not only with child abuse, but

---

4. Comparable data from studies by Wahler and his associates (Wahler, Berland, Coe, & Leske, 1976; Wahler, Leske, & Rogers, 1978) have indicated that families with severe child management problems could be differentiated from nonproblem families by their rates and types of community contacts. It appeared that most contacts in the distressed families were initiated by outside agencies and were of a negative nature (e.g., school authorities or police complaining about child behavior). The high level of family disruption and the punishing aspects of outside contacts effectively isolated the families from positive influences of community involvement. It may be that such interactive aspects also function to isolate abusive families.

with the day-to-day level of aversive interactions between parent and child through which we think their effects are mediated. Reid, Taplin, and Lorber (1981), for example, found that parents who abused their children demonstrated several times the rate of aversive interspouse interactions during home observations as did parents in nonabusive families. In a recent study, Patterson, Forgatch, and Wieder (1981), using a laboratory problem-solving task, studied the relation between negative and insulting verbal behavior by mothers and the mothers' self-reported rates of environmental stress during the week preceding the study. Using families of adolescents, they found a positive and significant relation between number of reported stressful events and the rate of negative verbal behaviors by the mothers. In the same study, they reported a significant inverse relation between the rates of negative verbalizations by the mothers and the quality of problem resolutions reached, as judged by raters.

Although enough data have already been reported in survey studies to strongly support the relation of a large number of background stress variables to reported child abuse, much more work is needed to provide convincing and general support for the idea that such variables raise the day-to-day level of aversive interpersonal behaviors between parent and child or reduce the parents' ability to quickly and effectively deal with discipline confrontations. Given that further research supports this general relation, the next step is to determine how such variables are related to conflict and abuse. Are such stressors interchangeable, or is a given parent more affected by one than another stress variable? Do such variables have specific effects that are temporally related to the exchange of aversive behaviors between parent and child, or do they have more general effects? (For example, are parents in marital conflict generally aversive and ineffectual in dealing with their children, or do they show such behavior with their children only during or shortly after conflicts with each other?)[5]

Such questions have obvious theoretical importance in terms of understanding how the effects of background variables on child abuse are mediated. Such questions are also of immense clinical importance. In the clinical work we have been conducting at our center, we have found that many of our abusive clients demonstrate

5. Similarly, if impoverished parents are more likely to assault and abuse their children, is this a general state of affairs or is the aversive behavior more likely on those days when they directly experience intrusions on their lives related to poverty (e.g., being pressed for the rent, having the telephone disconnected)?

the high levels of aversive behaviors and the poor child management skills that our behavioral parent training was designed to correct. They also demonstrate some combination of the background factors discussed above, which complicates treatment. If one tried to work on all the background factors presented by these families, the time and cost of treatment would be impractical. Knowledge of which background factors are specifically relevant to abuse in a given case, as well as the specific way those factors aggravate the parent-child interaction, might well aid us in developing a more comprehensive treatment for these families.

Relevant to this issue, Patterson (1981) reported data from a pilot study of parent-child interaction with five aggressive, though not officially abusive, families (coded as Tofu, Pluto, Eclipse, Spring, and Pumpkin). For each family, home observations were carried out for at least 20 days. The mothers filled out Lubin mood ratings (Lubin, 1967) and the Community Interaction Checklist (Wahler, Leske, & Rogers, 1978) on each day when an observation was conducted. For each family, Patterson examined the daily covariation of mother's rate of observed aversive behavior (TAB) with her child's TAB rate, the number of crises she reported, the amount, frequency, and valence of her community contacts, and her mood. As can be seen from Table 3, the most consistent and powerful correlates of the mothers' daily TAB scores were the TAB scores of

Table 3

Variables That Covary with Mother's Day-to-Day Fluctuations in Rate of Total Aversive Behavior (TAB)

Family Code	Minutes of community contact[a]	Frequency of contacts[b]	Positive contacts[c]	Frequency of crisis[d]	Mother's Lubin score[e]	Child's TAB score[f]	Multiple R
Tofu	−.01	.02	−.11	−.23	.26	.49**	.59
Pluto	.32	.42*	.30	.43*	.26	.41*	.76
Eclipse	−.05	.12	.08	.40*	.60**	.58***	.82
Spring	.43*	.01	.26	.09	.22	.61***	.74
Pumpkin	−.14	−.16	.44**	.07	−.14	.42*	.61

Note. From Patterson, 1981.

[a] Number of minutes of interaction with people in the community each day.
[b] Number of interactions with people in the community each day.
[c] Number of positive interactions each day.
[d] Number of crises reported by mother each day.
[e] Mother's Lubin score each day.
[f] Total aversive behavior (TAB) observed for child each day.

*p < .10; **p < .05; ***p < .01.

their children. Also, the various background variables seemed to relate to mothers' TAB scores in different ways for each family. For Tofu, the mother's aversive behavior appears consistently related only to the behavior of her child. For Pluto, the mother's TAB seems to be affected by all the background factors in addition to her child's TAB rate. For Eclipse, the mother's TAB rate was related to her mood and to the frequency of crises. Spring and Pumpkin also show unique patterns of covariation.

Although tentative and exploratory in nature, data of these sorts should bring us closer to understanding the specific relationships between background variables and coercive interactional patterns that lead to abuse. From a clinical standpoint such data would be extremely useful (e.g., in Eclipse's family it would be appropriate to couple parent training with systematic work on mother's mood and crisis management skills). Finally, Passman and Mulhern (1977) have added support for the thesis that stress may influence maternal punitiveness toward children. In a laboratory study, the authors increased demands placed on the mother, which led to more intensive and speedy punishment of the child.

In summary, there is abundant evidence in the literature that a variety of stressful situational and interpersonal variables are associated with the incidence of child abuse and parental aversiveness. We presented preliminary data to suggest that various background stressors increase the probability that certain parents will behave more aversively toward their children (and possibly become less efficient in using child management skills). According to our formulation, the parents' increased aversiveness will be reciprocated by their children, increasing the probability of a confrontation that will escalate into physical abuse. We believe that a comprehensive theory of child abuse must specify both social interactional *and* background factors that relate to accelerated rates of parent-child aversive behaviors and to reduced child management skills by parents. A clinically useful theory of child abuse must specify how the effects are mediated.

Over the past 15 years we have been attempting to develop a consistent strategy for the family treatment of aggressive children (e.g., Patterson, Reid, Jones, & Conger, 1975). Based largely upon social learning theory, our approach has focused on teaching the parents to conceptualize their children's aggression in terms of specific, observable behaviors, to monitor those behaviors, and to react systematically to their occurrence with withdrawal of attention or mild punishment (e.g., time out or small chores). Similarly, the parents have been taught to define prosocial alternatives to their children's aggressive acts, to monitor them, and to systematically encourage their occurrence. For most families treated, the therapists have had to expend at least some effort on background factors such as situational and personal stress or marital discord that interfered with the parents' acquisition of these child management skills.

Using home observation data as the primary outcome measure, this approach has repeatedly been found effective in reducing aggressive child behavior (e.g., Chamberlain, Patterson, & Reid, 1981; Patterson & Fleischman, 1979; Patterson & Reid, 1973). In addition, a study by Arnold, Levine, and Patterson (1975) demonstrated a significant tendency for the siblings of referred children to show reductions in aggressive behavior as a function of the intervention.[6]

In a post hoc analysis of observation data for 27 child-abusive families, referred and treated because of oppositional child behavior, Reid et al. (1981) found a significant reduction in observed rates of aggressive behavior for the mothers.[7]

In work currently under way at our center, we are modifying our parent training techniques to focus more on the aversive aspects of the parents' behavior, and we are evaluating the procedures on a new sample of chronically child-abusive families. Although complete process and outcome data are not yet available, our early impressions are that the approach will be moderately useful for reducing the frequency of aversive parent-child interactions and for increasing the parents' skill in efficiently and nonviolently resolving discipline confrontations. However, it is also our impression that the intense background stressors described earlier in this paper are common in these families and must be dealt with if successful parent training is to be achieved.

A Case Example

The following case study illustrates the complexity of the interrelations among interactional variables, background factors, and parent-child conflict. A father and mother and their four-year-old

6. It is also the case that reliable reductions in parent-reported problem behaviors occur in about 75% of the treated cases.

7. At baseline, the fathers in this sample were observed to be no more aggressive than the nondistressed fathers.

son were referred to Reid for treatment because of the boy's "un-controllable" tantrums. He had been a severe management problem for the mother since he was about two years old, when he was diagnosed as hyperkinetic and placed on Ritalin. The mother had been agitated since his birth and was maintained on Valium. She reported beating her son severely on several occasions. Shortly before the referral, the family's doctors became concerned that the medication was being abused, and both mother and son were taken off medication.

Since this case was seen privately and the family was not affluent, it was not practical to obtain home observation data. Instead, the father agreed to observe the child for one hour each weekday (during or after dinner), simply recording the number of tantrum episodes. During a three-week baseline period, the father recorded an average of approximately seven tantrums per observational period (range = 4–9).[8]

After the baseline period, the parents were given about six weeks of straightforward child management training (e.g., Patterson, 1975; Patterson, Reid, Jones, & Conger, 1975). The training centered on teaching them to pinpoint and track the tantrums; to use social and consumable reinforcers contingent upon independent play, compliance to requests, and good table manners; and to use time out contingent upon temper tantrums. As can be seen in Figure 2, the training was not completely successful—in fact it exacerbated the problem.

The mother complained that she could not implement the proce-dures properly because she was continuously anxious and upset, and because the child misbehaved at a too high a rate and was too intense. Her husband fully agreed, and the family wanted to termi-nate treatment. Their physician was apprised of the problem and agreed to put the mother back on Valium temporarily. Parent training sessions were continued, and the rate of tantrums returned to about baseline level over the next three weeks. The parents still complained that the child's behavior escalated so quickly during his tantrums that the mother could not employ time out properly. At week 13 the boy's medication was restarted and parent training was continued. By the 16th week the parents reported genuine progress, corroborated by the data collected by the father. After continued progress, the mother was willing to stop taking Valium at the 22nd week. Although she had a number of difficult days with

8. He was observed to have eight high-amplitude tantrums during the 1½-hour intake interview.

her son over the next three weeks, the mean rate of reported tantrums stabilized at a low level. During the 28th week the boy was taken off Ritalin, and parent training was continued. After a few weeks of variable tantrum rates, the boy's tantrums again stabilized at a low level. Treatment was terminated at the 35th week, and follow-up continued for a month, during which the boy's tantrums remained at a low rate.

Although not an experiment, the case illustrates a number of points central to this paper. First, there appeared to be a strong relation between the personal characteristics of mother and child that served to maintain high rates of aversive child behavior and to interfere with the mother's effectiveness in dealing with this behavior. Child management training directed at reducing the aversive child behavior and developing child management skills was fruitless until the personal background characteristics of parent and child were dealt with. While the background variables were temporarily controlled, it was possible to teach the parents effective skills and to reduce the child's aversive behavior. During that respite from background pressures, it was possible for the mother to utilize the 32 weeks of parent training to perfect her skills to the point that she was able to neutralize the background variables.

This example describes our clinical strategy for dealing with conflict and child abuse in families (i.e., a consistent focus on aversive interaction and child management skills, attempting to deal with background variables when they clearly interfere with the parent training). The example also underlines the need for future research on the problem. On the one hand, more systematic and microscopic analyses should be carried out on aversive interchanges between parents and children and their resolution. Data on such transactions should be collected daily over weeks and months so that variations in, and relation between, the incidence of aversive behaviors and the effects of parental discipline strategies may be properly evaluated. On the other hand, individual background characteristics and macrosocial factors need to be further investigated to determine their aggregate effects (e.g., between individuals or groups) as well as their specific relation to the interactions between parent and child (e.g., relating day-to-day fluctuations in mood, economic stress, and environmental support to the daily frequencies, patterns, and outcomes of aversive interchanges). To the extent that we come to understand these functional relations, it will be possible to design specific interventions to reduce the rates of aversive interchanges and discipline failures in high-risk families and thereby lower the risk of child abuse and assault.

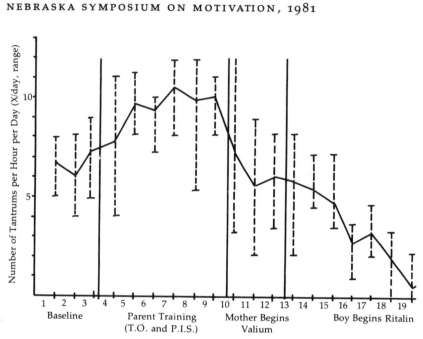

Figure 2. Mean number of tantrums per day as a function of treatment phases.

REFERENCES

Arnold, J., Levine, A., & Patterson, G. R. Changes in sibling behavior following family intervention. *Journal of Consulting and Clinical Psychology,* 1975, **43,** 683–688.

Bennie, E., & Sclar, A. The battered child syndrome. *American Journal of Psychiatry,* 1969, **125,** 975–979.

Burgess, R. L., & Conger, R. D. Family interaction patterns related to child abuse and neglect: Some preliminary findings. *Child Abuse and Neglect: The International Journal,* 1977, **1,** 269–277.

Chamberlain, P., Patterson, G. R., & Reid, J. B. A treatment comparison for families with antisocial children. Unpublished manuscript, Oregon Social Learning Center, 1981.

Deur, J. L., & Parke, R. D. The effects of inconsistent punishment on aggression in children. *Developmental Psychology,* 1970, **2,** 403–411.

Domestic violence and the police: Studies in Detroit and Kansas City. Police Foundation, 1977.

Egleland, B., & Brunnquell, D. An at-risk approach to the study of child abuse: Some preliminary findings. Unpublished manuscript, University of Minnesota, 1977.

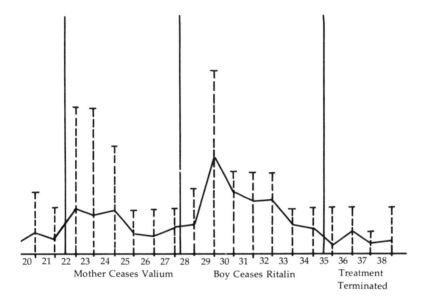

20 21 22 23 24 25 26 27 28 29 30 31 32 33 34 35 36 37 38

Mother Ceases Valium   Boy Ceases Ritalin   Treatment
                                                          Terminated

Elmer, I. E., & Gregg, G. S. Developmental characteristics of abused children. *Pediatrics*, 1967, **40**, 596.

Fawl, C. L. Disturbances experienced by children in their natural habitats. In R. G. Barker (Ed.), *The stream of behavior*. New York: Appleton-Century-Crofts, 1963.

Forehand, R., King, H. E., Peed, S., & Yoder, P. Mother-child interactions: Comparison of a noncompliant clinic group and a nonclinic group. *Behaviour Research and Therapy*, 1975, **13**, 79–84.

Friedman, S. B. The need for intensive follow-up of abused children. In C. H. Kempe & R. E. Helfer (Eds.), *Helping the battered child and his family*. Philadelphia: J. B. Lippincott, 1972.

Garbarino, J. The human ecology of child maltreatment: A conceptual model for research. *Journal of Marriage and the Family*, 1977, **39**, 721–735.

Gelles, R. J. *Family violence*. Beverly Hills, Calif.: Sage, 1979.

Gil, D. G. Physical abuse of children: Findings and implications of a nationwide survey. *Pediatrics*, 1969, **44**, 857–865.

Gil, D. G. *Violence against children: Physical child abuse in the United States*. Cambridge: Harvard University Press, 1970.

Gil, D. G. Violence against children. *Journal of Marriage and the Family*, 1971, **33**, 637–648.

Glueck, S., & Glueck, E. *Unraveling juvenile delinquency*. Cambridge: Harvard University Press, 1950.

Green, A. H. A psychodynamic approach to the study and treatment of child-abusing parents. *Journal of Child Psychiatry*, 1976, **15**, 414–429.

Green, A. H., Gaines, R. W., & Sandgrun, A. Child abuse: Pathological syndrome of family interaction. *American Journal of Psychiatry*, 1974, **131**, 882–886.

Jenkins, R. L. The varieties of children's behavioral problems and family dynamics. *American Journal of Psychiatry*, 1968, **124**, 1440–1445.

Johnson, B., & Morse, H. A. Injured children and their parents. *Children*, 1968, **15**, 147–152.

Justice, B., & Duncan, D. F. Life crisis as a precursor to child abuse. *Public Health Reports*, 1976, **91**, 110–115.

Klein, M., & Stern, L. Low birth weight and the battered child syndrome. *American Journal of the Disabled Child*, 1971, **122**, 15–18.

Light, R. J. Abused and neglected children in America: A study of alternative policies. *Harvard Educational Review*, 1973, **43**, 556–598.

Loeber, R., & Janda, W. Mother intervention in sibling fighting. Manuscript in preparation, Oregon Social Learning Center, 1981.

Lubin, B. *Manual for the Depression Adjective Checklist*. San Diego: Educational and Industrial Testing Service, 1967.

McCord, W., McCord, J., & Howard, A. Familial correlates of aggression in nondelinquent male children. *Journal of Abnormal and Social Psychology*, 1961, **62**, 79–93.

Minton, C., Kagan, J., & Levine, J. A. Maternal control and obedience in the two-year-old child. *Child Development*, 1971, **42**, 1973–1984.

Parke, R. D., & Deur, J. L. Schedule of punishment and inhibition of aggression in children. *Developmental Psychology*, 1972, **7**, 266–269.

Pasamanick, B., & Knobloch, H. Retrospective studies on the epidemiology of reproductive casualty: Old and new. *Merrill-Palmer Quarterly*, 1966, **12**, 7–26.

Passman, R. H., & Mulhern, R. K. Maternal punitiveness as affected by situational stress: An experimental analogue of child abuse. *Journal of Abnormal Psychology*, 1977, **86**, 565–569.

Patterson, G. R. An empirical approach to the classification of disturbed children. *Journal of Clinical Psychology*, 1964, **20**, 326–337.

Patterson, G. R. *Families: Applications of social learning to family life*. Champaign, Ill.: Research Press, 1975.

Patterson, G. R. The aggressive child: Victim and architect of a coercive system. In L. A. Hamerlynck, E. J. Mash, & L. C. Handy (Eds.), *Behavior modification and families. I. Theory and research. II. Applications and developments*. New York: Brunner/Mazel, 1976.

Patterson, G. R. A performance theory for coercive family interactions. In R. Cairns (Ed.), *Social interaction: Methods, analysis, and illustration*. Hillsdale, N.J.: Lawrence Erlbaum Associates, 1979.

Patterson, G. R. *Families of antisocial children: An interactional approach*.

Eugene, Oreg.: Castalia Publishing Co., 1981, in press.

Patterson, G. R., & Fleischman, M. J. Maintenance of treatment effects: Some considerations concerning family systems and follow-up data. *Behavior Therapy*, 1979, **10**, 168–185.

Patterson, G. R., Forgatch, M. S., & Wieder, G. The relationship between the aversiveness of communication and problem-solving in families. Manuscript in preparation, Oregon Social Learning Center, 1981.

Patterson, G. R., & Reid, J. B. Intervention for families of aggressive boys: A replication study. *Behavior Research and Therapy*, 1973, **11**, 383–394. (Also: In I. H. Strupp, A. Bergin, P. Lang, I. Marks, J. Matarazzo, & G. Patterson [Eds.], *Psychotherapy and behavior change*. Chicago: Aldine, 1974. Also: In D. H. Olson [Ed.], *Inventory of marriage and family literature*. Minneapolis: University of Minnesota Press, 1976.)

Patterson, G. R., Reid, J. B., Jones, R. R., & Conger, R. E. *A social learning approach to family intervention. I. Families with aggressive children.* Eugene, Oreg.: Castalia Publishing Co., 1975.

Reid, J. B. (Ed.) *A social learning approach to family intervention. II. Observation in home settings.* Eugene, Oreg.: Castalia Publishing Co., 1978.

Reid, J. B. Relationships between the frequency and aversiveness of confrontations between parents and children. Manuscript in preparation, Oregon Social Learning Center, 1981.

Reid, J. B., Taplin, P. S., & Lorber, R. A social interactional approach to the treatment of abusive families. In R. Stuart (Ed.), *Violent behavior: Social learning approaches to prediction, management, and treatment*. New York: Brunner/Mazel, 1981, in press.

Roach, J. L. Some social-psychological characteristics of child guidance clinic caseloads. *Journal of Consulting Psychology*, 1958, **22**, 183–186.

Rogers, M., Lilienfeld, A. M., & Pasamanick, B. *Prenatal and parental factors in the development of child behavior disorders*. Baltimore: Johns Hopkins University Press, 1954.

Sandgrun, R. W., Gaines, R. W., & Green, A. H. Child abuse and mental retardation: A problem of cause and effect. *Journal of Mental Deficiency*, 1975, **19**, 327.

Spinetta, J. J., & Ringler, D. The child-abusing parent: A psychological review. *Psychological Bulletin*, 1972, **77**, 296–304.

Stark, R., & McEvoy, J., III. Middle class violence. *Psychology Today*, 1970, **4**, 52–65.

Wahler, R. G., Berland, R. M., Coe, T. D., & Leske, G. Generalization processes in child behavior change. In B. Lakey & A. Kazdin (Eds.), *Advances in child clinical psychology*. New York: Plenum Publishing Corp., 1976.

Wahler, R. G., Leske, G., & Rogers, E. S. The insular family: A deviance support system for oppositional children. In L. A. Hamerlynck (Ed.), *Behavioral systems for the developmentally disabled. I. School and family environments*. New York: Brunner/Mazel, 1978.

Wolfgang, M. E. Overview of research into violent behavior. Paper presented at the Domestic and International Scientific Planning, Analysis, and Cooperation Subcommittee of the Committee on Science and Technology, U.S. House of Representatives, 1978.

Woody, R. H. *Behavioral problem children in the schools.* New York: Appleton-Century-Crofts, 1969.

Young, L. *A study of child neglect and abuse.* Princeton: McGraw-Hill, 1964.

Zalba, S. R. Battered children. *Transaction,* 1971, **8**, 58–61.

Determinants of Choice[1]

George H. Collier

Rutgers University

*T*o feed or not to feed, to defend the territory, trounce the subordinate, flee the predator, court the lady, build a nest, nurse the young, move, stay put, migrate, hibernate—these are some of the questions continually facing every animal. From an evolutionary point of view, the optimal allocation of time and/or energy to these fitness-related activities is the central problem of motivation. These choices govern the continuance, decrease, or increase of an animal's representation in the genetic pool. The ultimate (Wilson, 1975) determinants of these decisions lie in their contribution to the animal's fitness. Unfortunately I cannot offer a general theory of optimal allocation, which has only begun to be studied (Bernstein & Ebbesen, 1978; McCleery, 1978; McFarland, 1974, 1977; Pulliam, 1974), but must confine my analysis to a single activity, feeding. Even here, one cannot easily determine whether performance of a particular behavior is optimal. In a sense this is an unanswerable question, since costs and benefits are defined across the whole range of activities in which an animal engages. One can only ask, experimentally, whether behavior is efficient—that is, Is benefit maximized relative to cost? Efficient behavior requires choices between alternative courses of action. Thus choice is the central process in optimal behavior.

The Analysis of Choice

The concept of choice has had a long and parochial history in psychology. A wide variety of different, unrelated mechanisms

1. This research was supported by Grant HD–10588 from the National Institutes of Health and by a series of Biomedical Research Support Grants from Rutgers University. Much of the work on which the present ideas are based was contributed by many fine students, both graduate and undergraduate, over the past decade. In particular, the dissertations of Dr. Thom Castonguay and Dr. Lynn Kaufman formed the data base for our conjectures of the effect of cost on choices between behaviors and between dietary items. Finally, I thank my wife, Dr. Carolyn K. Rovee-Collier, for her contributions to both the form and the content of the manuscript.

have been invoked to account for choice behaviors. Underlying all these choice models is the assumption that choice involves pitting different, momentary behavior strengths against one another. There may be a fundamental error in this approach, arising from the constraints on time and activities necessary to compare response tendencies. In the cafeteria of earthly possibilities, the likelihood is seldom considered that an animal will indulge in many or all of the offerings, given the time and opportunities, distributing his time and effort among them.

There appear to be at least two loci of choice: choices of behaviors, and choices of items. In the early days of laboratory studies of choice behavior, psychologists most often tested animals in mazes and runways, using food and food deprivation to encourage the animal to traverse the maze in a particular direction. More recently, the use of such apparatus has been revived to study animal memory and cognition and optimal foraging (cf. Olton, 1979). Results obtained in the typical operant apparatus had suggested that rats, pigeons, and monkeys have very brief working memories and are highly stereotypic in their behavior. Now that the task has been changed to a spatial one, as in the maze, it is estimated that rats have a working memory of at least 12 items and that, given the opportunity, they will allocate time and effort to exploring the maze, employing alternative routes to the food once the maze has been learned (see Olton, 1979, for a review). Here we see that data and the theories they support are determined by the questions asked and by the situation in which they are asked.

A second approach to the study of choice in the laboratory has been to present the animal with a choice between items. Here again the setting has been important. Choices as studied in the laboratory have typically been demonstrated only when the duration and context of the observations are sufficiently constrained. For example, the well-known "sweet tooth" of the rat has been demonstrated by response rate (Collier, 1962), momentary preference (Young, 1961), distribution of time or responses on concurrent schedules, and choices between sucrose and salt, casein, or wheat in short sessions. If, however, one offers the rat a choice between a source of protein and a source of carbohydrate and then goes away, some time later one will find that the rat has consumed daily a constant ratio of protein to carbohydrate, the exact proportion being a function of the qualities of the two macronutrients, the state of the rat (e.g., growing, pregnant, lactating, exercising, freezing, etc.), and the relative costs and abundances of the two food items (Collier &

Hirsch, 1977; Hill, Castonguay, & Collier, 1980). Can we predict this proportion from the response rates for sucrose and casein, the relative rates on a concurrent schedule, or the percentage choices of a brief preference tester? No! The reason we have considered this possibility (i.e., that such prediction is possible) is that we have narrowly focused on the tongue, the gut, the brain, the vapors within, or the event(s) following a response. The alternatives are presented only briefly in terms of the subject's scale of time, and the opportunity to engage freely in other activities has been excluded. In fact, choice as it has been studied does not permit the psychologist or physiologist to understand the underlying process of choice solutions. It is this problem that I will consider in terms of the animal's solutions to survival-related problems. Only an analysis of choice that recognizes the time/energy allocation problem will suffice.

Errors in Approach

The fragmented character of the analysis of choice has resulted primarily from four investigator-imposed constraints.

THE FEEDING CHAIN

When a resource is continuously present (e.g., oxygen for land-dwellers or water for sea-dwelling animals), an animal's commerce with it is usually regulated continuously. However, when a resource is discontinuous or distributed in patches, commerce with the resource occurs in bouts interpolated between other activities. This occurs because the discovery and procurement of the resource diminishes or eliminates the possibility of engaging in other necessary activities. Thus most animals eat in meals. Their food items must be located, procured, and handled before consumption can begin. The first rigorous study of meal patterns was by Richter (1927). He found that rats ate approximately 9–10 meals a day, of 1–3 grams each, spending 1½–2 hours a day feeding. Seventy percent of the meals occurred in the dark. Figure 1 shows a schematic of such a pattern of feeding (Collier, Hirsch, & Hamlin, 1972).

Skinner (1932a, 1932b) saw in Richter's data the central problem of psychology—the discovery of the determinants of the initiation and termination of bouts of behavior. He approached the problem by attempting to analyze the internal dynamics of the meal, that is, the strength of the eating reflexes. His approach reflected the cur-

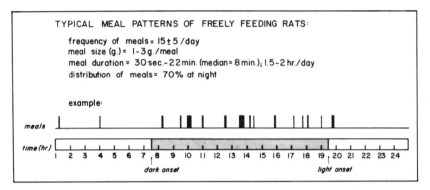

Figure 1. Schematic of the meal patterns of a freely feeding rat. Each meal is indicated by a black vertical column, the width of which indicates meal duration (based on Collier, Hirsch, & Hamlin, 1972).

rent Zeitgeist. With the successful example of physics before them, psychologists had sought to construct simple paradigms in which a few variables could be manipulated, all else being controlled, and the universal laws of behavior could be discovered. Pavlov had provided one paradigm, Thorndike the other. In each case the fact that food-deprived animals engage in feeding behavior when presented with food was exploited. These paradigms permitted investigators to study, respectively, the signals that indicated that food was present and the contingencies between responses and the presentation of the ingestant.

With the exception of the bad manners exhibited by animals who swallow their food (prey item) in one gulp, ingestion is a recurrent response (chewing, licking, sucking, etc.) with a relatively fixed repetition rate. It was this feature of feeding that attracted Skinner, particularly when he discovered that an "arbitrary initial reflex" (the bar-press), appended to the front portion of the chain of ingestive reflexes, "behaved" in the same way as the other reflexes in the chain. It provided a simple and direct measure of reflex strength: *the rate of responding*.

Figure 2 shows Skinner's original eating data, a cumulative curve of the number of pellets eaten by a deprived rat in Skinner's eatometer (Skinner, 1932a). Each time the rat pushed open a small door with its nose, it could seize a single pellet. Figure 3 shows a similar curve based on performance of the arbitrary initial reflex, when the rat had to bar-press for each pellet (Skinner, 1932b). Figure 4 illustrates Skinner's conjecture. Recall that his interest was in the discovery of the initiators and terminators of a bout of

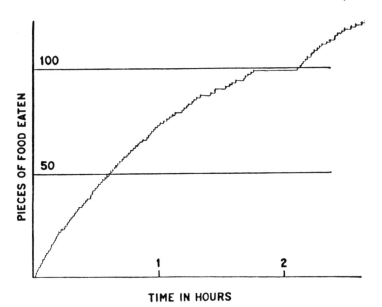

Figure 2. Cumulative food intake during a single meal lasting 2 hours taken by a deprived rat (from Skinner, 1932a).

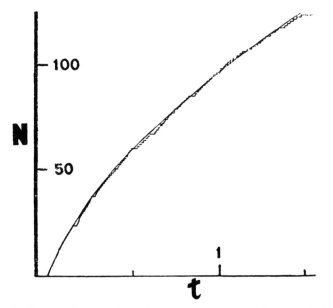

Figure 3. Cumulative number of bar-presses (N) made for pellets in a single meal lasting 1½ hours taken by a deprived rat (from Skinner, 1932b).

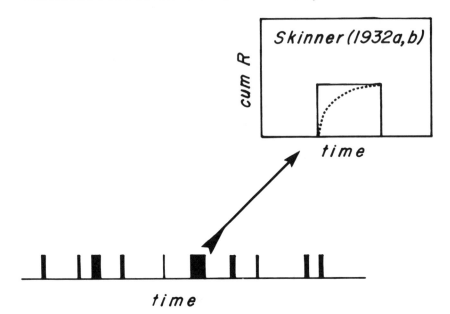

Figure 4. The conjecture made by Skinner that the initiation and termination of a meal could be predicted from the rate of responding within a meal. This satiety function is illustrated by the dotted line.

feeding. He argued that a knowledge of the strength of the feeding reflexes, as indexed by the rate of bar-pressing, would predict the onset and offset of feeding. That the rate at which these reflexes occurred was a function of the degree of deprivation provided an easy method of manipulating reflex (response) strength. The experimenter could initiate the meal and then step back and watch the changing response strength in the hour or so following its onset. By using short sessions, small portions, and schedules that spaced the portions (reinforcers) in time, it was possible to obtain an eating curve (segment) that was linear. The study of feeding was reduced to the study of a meal, and the science of operant psychology became the science of chaining ingestive responses within a meal. This has become an interesting exercise, since Skinner's original discovery that an arbitrary initial reflex behaves in the same way as the ingestive reflexes has proved true for almost any behavior (schedule) interpolated *between bites*, with the recurrent property being preserved.

The generality of operant psychology depends, however, on our being able to generalize its principles to other behaviors—

principles derived from the recursive property of ingestive responses and the resulting sequence of recurrent responses for which rate is a presumed measure of response strength. In particular, can the initiation and termination of bouts of behavior be predicted from the rate at which behavior occurs within a bout, as Skinner conjectured? This approach has led psychologists to focus their attention and efforts almost exclusively on the internal dynamics of a meal. In fact, this original conjecture has not been tested. Moreover, studies of freely feeding animals suggest that the *likelihood of initiating or terminating a meal is uncorrelated with the rate of eating within a meal.*

It might be argued that use of the runway avoids this problem. One objection to the runway expressed by operant psychologists is that it does not provide a measure of recurrent responses, but only of speeds and latencies. This objection arises from a lack of imagination or understanding. An animal traversing any tunnel, runway, or such, will ultimately encounter either a meal or a portion of a meal at the "goal." The behavior is quite different depending upon the nature of the "reward" in the two cases. If the animal is provided only a portion of a meal, and if a continuous runway (circular, square, running wheel, etc.) is used so that the subject can repeat the behavior for the next bite, the behavior is, in fact, recurrent. The cumulative trips around the runway will have the same character as cumulative bar-presses and will reveal the same schedule effects (cf. Skinner, 1956, pp. 224–225). This is not observed in most runway and maze studies because the experimenter must intervene to transport the subject from goal to start box, and he is not on the same schedule as the animal. On the other hand, the subject who discovers a *meal* at the end of the maze or runway consumes it and goes about his business. As we shall see, how often he returns for more and the size of the meal he takes depend on other factors, such as the cost of getting there. If one wishes to observe *recurrent* behavior in a runway or maze, then one must observe the subject during the course of a single meal.

One principle of operant psychology that has contributed to its viability is that *present consequences influence future performance.* One version of this principle is the concept of reinforcement, that is, that *responses are strengthened and weakened by their contingent consequences.* The first principle is hard to deny. The second is simply a version, almost unquestioned since the time of Thorndike, of how the first principle works. Adaptive behavior is viewed as constructed out of successful responses. The unasked question, since the time of Descartes (cf. Skinner, 1931), is whether either the reflex or the response is the appropriate unit of analysis. I have argued (cf. Collier, Hirsch, & Kanarek, 1977; Collier & Rovee-Collier, in press) that, in the study of feeding behavior, the *meal* is a better unit of analysis than the within-meal responses or reflexes in terms of predicting total daily intake or diet balance, and that meal frequency and size cannot be predicted from ingestive response rates. My argument is based on the premise that selection pressure is on the *biological system and the principles incorporated in it* rather than on single responses. While schedules extend the range of responses controlled by a reinforcement, they do not obviate the problem. A strong case can be made that schedule performance is a joint function of the economy as well as the local contingencies (Collier, in press; Hursh, 1980). *Reinforcement is not a universal principle*. It describes only a very limited set of behavioral relations within a meal.

To study feeding, one must study the whole feeding chain, including the means by which the animal discovers and gains access to a meal, the means of consuming it, and finally how the animal processes and utilizes it. Foraging is neither a recursive behavior nor a recurrent one in the usual sense. One cannot predict its occurrence from counting responses. In addition, I will demonstrate that the rate at which ingestive behavior occurs also does not predict its strength or its likelihood of occurrence. The use of the recursive property of ingestive responses in an attempt to get an accurate and sensitive measure of behavior strength has been a mistake.

ECONOMICS

A second failure was not to consider the various economies within which animals operate. Psychologists early learned that rats and other creatures would press bars, trot down runways, or peck keys for little bites of food, and that the longer they had been without food and the more weight they had lost, the faster they would press, run, or peck. This was easy to explain, since Cannon (1932) had pointed out that many behaviors were instigated by perturbations of the internal milieu and terminated by its restoration (homeostasis), the strength of the behavior varying as a function of the size of the perturbation. This explanation was later buttressed by the finding of a structure in the brain of which one portion presumably excited feeding and one presumably inhibited feeding (cf. Brobeck,

1955). The elegant simplicity of this concept has charmed our be-
liefs. No one doubts that we eat because we are depleted (*physiologically* hungry) and stop because we are repleted (*physiologically*
satiated). Someone less familiar with Cannon, however, might ask
whether this is the best of all strategies. Should one wait to replace a
resource until a disturbing loss has occurred? Might it not be safer
in this world of uncertain resources to eat in anticipation of our
needs, using various organs to store the food and thus to buffer the
potentially deleterious effects of varying intermeal intervals? For
example, Figure 5 shows the growth curves of chicks reared under a
12:12 light:dark cycle. The upper curve is for birds fed only during
the light period, and the lower curve is for birds fed only in the
dark. These data show the weight loss occurring between periods of
access to food. Chickens usually undergo a self-imposed fast at
night; they are diurnal feeders. Would it not be a good strategy for a
bird with such a high metabolism and a diurnal habit to load its
crop in the period preceding the onset of darkness and the accompanying overnight fast (see Figure 6), thus mitigating or even
eliminating the attendant body weight loss? (Cf. Kaufman &
Brashier, 1978; Squibb & Collier, 1979.) Similarly, the freely feeding
rat never, at least in the laboratory, has an empty gut (Armstrong,
Clarke, & Coleman, 1978). Numerous animals use the anticipatory
strategy in a wide variety of circumstances. On the other hand,
many animals have strategies of either self-imposed excesses of
intake that lead to substantial obesity (e.g., hibernators and mi-
grators) or self-imposed periods of starvation when allocating their
time and energy to other activities (e.g., Collier, 1980; Collier &
Rovee-Collier, 1980; Katz, 1974; Mrosovsky & Sherry, 1980). The
determinants of intake lie not in the internal milieu, which is highly
buffered by many mechanisms, but in the solutions to the problem
of optimal allocation of time and energy to survival-related activities and the corollary requirement for efficient feeding selected
for across generations or acquired during an animal's lifetime.

Many animals are able to defend total daily intake under a wide
variety of conditions (for example, under various schedules or
combinations of schedules) when they control the initiation and
termination of their own meals (Collier, in press; Hursh, 1980).
When the total intake and the pattern of intake are controlled by the
animal, it is operating in a *closed economy*; when the experimenter
controls the total intake and/or the pattern of intake, it is operating
in an *open economy* (cf. Hursh, 1980). It can be shown that feeding
behavior (as well as other behavior) is very different in these two

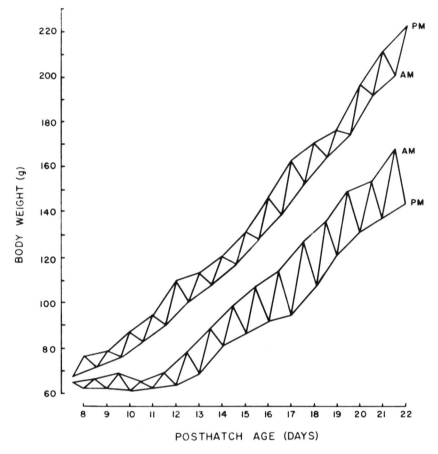

Figure 5. The pattern of weight gain over successive 12-hour periods for chicks raised on a 12:12 light:dark cycle. The upper curve is for chicks eating only in the light, the lower curve is for chicks eating only in the dark (from Rovee-Collier, Clapp, Collier, & Raabe, 1981).

types of economies. For example, the relations between rate of responding and the simple interval and ratio schedules are reversed in the two economies. Similarly, the relation between the size of the reinforcer and the rate of responding is an increasing one in an open economy (the classic magnitude of reinforcement relations) and a decreasing one in a closed economy (Collier, 1980; Collier, in press; Hursh, 1980). Many other economies can be designed with different constraints in them and, as a result, yield different relations between the same variables (cf. the conservation model of Allison, Miller, & Wozny, 1979).

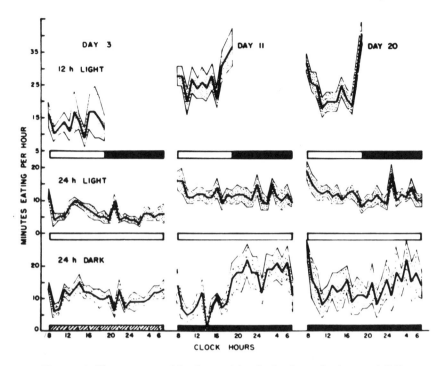

Figure 6. The pattern of feeding of freely feeding chickens of different days of age as a function of lighting conditions (from Squibb & Collier, 1979; reproduced by permission).

Our preoccupation with the deprivation paradigm and, as a result, the open economy has obscured a central problem for the animal from the point of view of fitness, namely, the defense of total intake. The period over which defense occurs depends on many factors, such as the animal's size, metabolic rate, and niche. When the experimenter assumes the burden of this problem, providing the animal with its daily bread in amounts, in kinds, and at times dictated by his (superior) conception of the animal's needs, desires, and capabilities, he denies himself the possibility of observing the animal's (or the species') hard-won solution(s) to this conundrum.

TEST ENVIRONMENTS

The failure to construct test environments that parallel the animal's representation of its environment has further jeopardized the analysis of choice. In the ideal test environment, if we were to follow Skinner's original prescription (Skinner, 1938), the animal would be floating weightless in the void of outer space with only the bar, the magazine, and the discriminative stimulus present; no other inputs or response opportunities would be available. It is traditionally assumed that these circumstances would yield the simplest, least variable functions relating the variables of interest. This conception of the ideal experimental paradigm originated with the refinement experiment, which was so successful in early physics. It views the organism as a collection or library of reflexes, modified across phylogeny or ontogeny (e.g., Skinner, 1932a, 1932b, 1938, 1956), rather than as a biological system whose behavior and morphology have been selected to gather food energy (or perform other activities) most efficiently in a given environment (cf. Schoener, 1971). Considering the fragmentary and degraded information that an animal receives from the environment and the limited exposure the animal has to the environment, I think that an animal must possess both a *representation of its environment* and a *schema of efficient behavior* which accounts for the precision with which it acts. There appears to be much information concealed behind its tabula rasa (cf. Oatley, 1978). In fact a test environment must simulate the essential features of this representation and yield the consequences that its schema would predict if we are to assess its capacities and discover laws of behavior.

THE NICHES

The fourth omission has been a consideration of the species' niche and the problems a given species has evolved to solve. Every elementary textbook in ecology points out that species have specialized in the exploitation of food resources; in fact, one of the major niche dimensions is feeding (Hutchinson, 1959). Figure 7 presents a simplified version of energy flow within a community. Animals have further specialized within trophic levels. This specialization involves both morphology and behavior. While all animals share the needs for the same macro- and micronutrients, their means for obtaining them vary widely. Food resources vary in abundance, availability, quality, and caloric density. Each food niche is some compromise between these four factors.

The primary consumers (herbivores) have taken advantage of the abundance and availability of plants. Because plants have variable amino acid profiles, low caloric density, low and variable mineral content, obstructive carbohydrates in their cell walls, and secondary compounds that are toxic (an antipredator strategy), they pre-

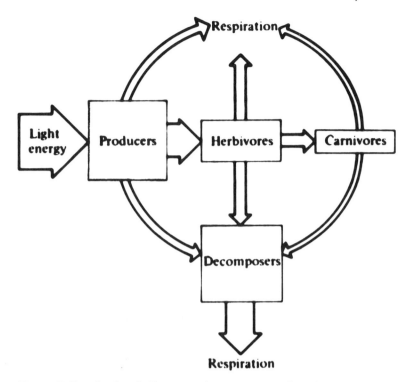

Figure 7. Trophic levels (from Pianka, 1978; reproduced by permission).

sent special problems to their consumers. Bell (1971) has shown that
the herbivores of the Serengeti specialize in particular portions of
plants, some eating only the tips (new growth), others consuming
the old leaves and stems, and still others feeding only on the seeds,
shoots, or berries. Some herbivores are ruminants and must rely
upon symbiotic microorganisms to prepare their food for utilization. They feed the grasses and such to these organisms in their
rumens, and these in turn convert the food into the necessary
volatile fatty acids, sugars, and proteins. Other herbivores are
monogastric herbivores and obtain a balanced diet through selective absorption from the gut. The ruminant is highly efficient,
utilizing almost everything it eats, and is selective; the monogastric
herbivore is inefficient, requiring a large-volume intake of which it
utilizes only a small fraction, and is unselective. These animals form
a continuum ranging from those that maximize food value per
given meal to those that maximize food processed per unit time
(Milton, 1981). Each is adapted to a particular niche (Bell, 1971;
Milton, 1981). Their requirements are very different, and their
feeding strategies determine their size, activity levels, social life,

and so forth. Some herbivores specialize even further, exploiting only a single part of a single plant. The koala, for example, specializes in eucalyptus leaves.

Each of these feeding strategies requires the animal to choose among a variety of potential food items. Some herbivores have a very large number of taste buds, suggesting an ability to discriminate among a wide variety of food items. The dimensions along which these choices are made also vary widely. The ruminant must choose the menu for the flora and fauna inhabiting its rumen carefully in order to ensure their, and thus its own, well-being. The monogastric herbivore, on the other hand, places its bets on volume, with little regulation of intake (witness the foundering of horses on rich pastures), letting its gut do the choosing. Carnivores lead a simpler life in that they have simpler digestive tracts and eat food that is highly similar to themselves in composition (e.g., amino acid profile) and caloric density. For the carnivore, the choice among food items for their nutritive value is not an important problem, but finding and catching the food items is. Little work has been done on the food selection behavior of carnivores (cf. Kanarek, 1975). Because the food items differ so little in important nutritive dimensions, however, there would be little selection pressure operating, and as a result, the carnivore's ability to select a diet on the basis of nutritional value should not be highly developed. Omnivores, being catholic in their taste and opportunistic in their foraging, face a more difficult problem than either herbivores or carnivores. Their food may vary widely in both caloric density and nutritional quality. They must choose dietary items in such a fashion that over some relatively short time (perhaps over a 24-hour period), they both balance their diet and defend body weight (or grow) by consuming a sufficient number of calories. It is interesting—perhaps fortuitous, perhaps foresightful, perhaps ironic—that psychologists have focused on the behavior of the rat in studies using food reward, insofar as the rat is one of the greatest generalist omnivores of all time (Canby, 1977). Most of our ideas about diet balancing, caloric regulation, and preference have also come from the study of the rat.

The comparative study of ingestive, digestive, and absorptive physiology reveals a great diversity of feeding mechanisms. An ethological and ecological study of feeding behavior reveals a similar diversity. The generality of the principles of choice behavior, both within and across species, must take this diversity into account, both in experimental techniques and in theory.

The Feeding Chain

A schematic of the chain of events involved in feeding behavior is presented in Figure 8. These divisions are *functional* in the sense that the behaviors constituting each subdivision relate to independent variables differentially and in a specific fashion, but the boundaries between the subdivisions may be more or less sharp for different species and food items. It is my thesis that there are certain choice rules or decision rules that determine behavior at each point in the feeding chain.

Foraging is the means by which animals gain access to food and prepare it for consumption. The major problem of a foraging animal is to maximize both encounter rate and value with respect to foraging cost. *Consumption* is the means by which animals ingest food (i.e., eat a meal) once they have gained access to it. The consumption component is the *gate* (Davis, Collins, & Levine, 1976) for including or excluding dietary items. Consumption cost as well as the sensory properties of the food and the physiological state of the organism are the important variables at this level of the feeding chain. *Utilization* is composed of a long chain of processes, from the

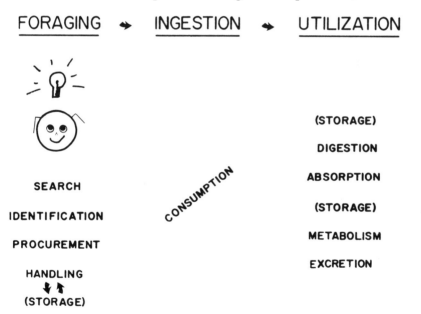

Figure 8. The major divisions and subdivisions of the chain of feeding behavior.

initial mechanical degradation of food to the final cellular utilization or storage of nutrients. Of particular interest to behaviorists is
the way these processes provide feedback for behavior. This problem has been the preoccupation of physiological psychologists for
the past 30 years.

The discussion of the feeding chain and the definition of its
components have arisen from the work of ecologists on optimal
foraging (see Emlen, 1966; MacArthur & Pianka, 1966; Pyke,
Pulliam, & Charnov, 1977; Schoener, 1971 for reviews) and resulted
from their attempts to relate environmental structure to animal
behavior.

Utilization

For purposes of this paper, utilization will be considered only
briefly (cf. Collier, in press; Collier & Rovee-Collier, in press). Most
of the interest and attention of physiological psychologists inves-
tigating feeding behavior has been organized by two hypotheses:
(1) the *depletion-repletion hypothesis* of the instigation and termination of meals; and (2) the *deficit hypothesis* of choice between food
items. Stemming directly from Cannon (1932), but steadily moving
from peripheral to central events in the quest for explanatory
variables, the depletion-repletion hypothesis has been the major, if
not the only, hypothesis of the control of food intake. Following
Cannon, it is assumed that as the result of metabolism the organism
undergoes a constant decline in "internal resources" until a
threshold is crossed, at which point behavior is instigated and
continues until the balance is restored. The nature of these internal
resources (circulating metabolites, hormones, fats, proteins or
peptides, etc.) and the structure(s) that meter them remain an
unsolved problem (cf. Novin, Wyrwicka, & Bray, 1976). Opinions
are strong, but agreement is weak. A similar hypothesis, with some
variations (cf. Rozin & Kalat, 1971), has been set forth to describe
the means by which animals balance their diets (i.e., between
protein, carbohydrates, and fats) and consume the proper quan-
tities of micronutrients. Again it is assumed that some momentary
deficit, this time in the required nutrients, is reflected in the choice
of food items. In neither case, however, has the hypothesis been
strongly entertained that animals are preprogrammed to meet their
requirements and never, when their "system" is working, undergo
substantial depletion or deficit (cf. Novin et al., 1976). Here I will
show that animals will work to maintain a balanced and sufficient

diet, and that they are flexible about their requirements when the cost of feeding changes.

Consumption

Let us first consider the consumption component in a *closed economy*. Our paradigm will consist of a rat pressing a bar for pellets in a free-feeding situation. The rat lives continuously in the experimental chamber, obtaining all its food, water, and amusement there. An adult rat will eat approximately 500 45-milligram Noyes pellets per day (22.5 g or 81 Kcal). The number of meals per day (approximately 25) is somewhat greater, and their size (20–30 pellets or 1–1.4 g) is somewhat smaller than the meal characteristics of the same rats eating powdered chow. If the rat behaves *economically*, then three variables must be considered: cost, value, and income. If the rat behaves *efficiently*, it will maximize benefits relative to cost. In this paradigm, cost refers to the time and effort required to obtain the daily intake and is defined operationally in terms of the number of bar-presses required to obtain a single pellet. Value is held constant.

The rat in this paradigm can exploit one of two strategies. First, it can reduce cost by reducing its income (i.e., total number of pellets), thereby controlling the time and effort required to feed. If the rat chooses to reduce income, it can do it by reducing meal frequency, meal size, or both. A second cost-control strategy, which affects the time it takes to feed, is to alter response rate. The greater the ratio of responses to pellets, the more behavior that is interpolated *between* successive pellets, and therefore the longer it takes to complete a meal (i.e., to obtain the 20–30 pellets composing the single meal). The results of such an experiment are summarized in Figure 9.

It is clear that the rats use *both* strategies. Their total daily number of responses increased linearly (except at cost extremes) as a function of the ratio requirement. However, the rate of increase was insufficient to defend total intake on a fixed ratio (FR) 20 schedule of reinforcement, and intake fell linearly as a function of ratio size. After FR 20, the rats sacrificed one pellet of income for each additional response required per pellet. If a scale transformation is performed, converting the abscissa to responses per gram of food consumed ("unit price" in economic terminology), then income remains a decreasing function of the number of responses per gram. This reduction in pellet intake reduces both the total effort ex-

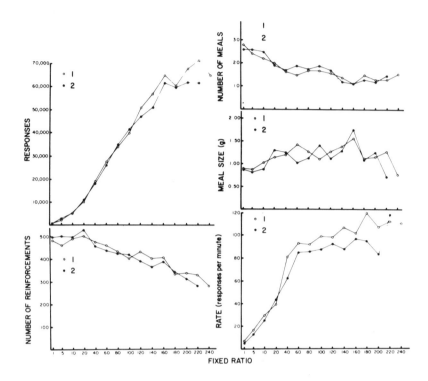

Figure 9. The effect of consumption cost ("fixed ratio") on meal size, meal frequency, rate of consumption, number of 45-milligram Noyes pellets consumed per day ("reinforcements"), and total number of bar-presses per day of two freely feeding rats living in a closed economy (from Collier, Hirsch, and Hamlin, 1972; reprinted by permission).

pended and the time spent expending it. In effect, the rats traded food (income) for time and energy (cost). Food intake was reduced through a decrease in meal frequency; meal size remained relatively constant.

The second strategy was to conserve time spent feeding by increasing the rate of responding. The response rate increased from 5 per minute at the lowest FR to approximately 110 per minute (6,000–7,000 bar-presses per hour) at the highest FR. The meal durations increased from approximately 10 minutes per meal to 50 minutes per meal over the same range of FR values. At FR 200, it took approximately 10–12 hours to obtain the 300 pellets that were consumed.

These two strategies of lowering intake and increasing response rate as cost increased were successful. If the rats had continued to take 500 pellets per day at 110 responses per minute at FR 200, it would have taken 100,000 responses and a minimum of 17 hours to obtain this intake. If the rats had continued to respond at 5 responses per minute under these conditions, it would have taken 333 hours per day to obtain their 500 pellets. Clearly these strategies conserved time and effort at but a small cost to potential growth. During the course of the experiment, one experimental rat gained 22 grams and the second lost 30 grams. However, because food intake was reduced by 40%, we see that there was a substantial increase in feed efficiency. Control animals gained 75 grams over the same period. Similar results have been obtained guinea pigs (Hirsch & Collier, 1974a, 1974b).

These results differ from those usually obtained in an *open economy* where the animal does not control either the initiation and termination of its meals or its total intake. Here there is an inverted U-shaped function between rate of responding and ratio size, with the maximum rate usually occurring at a very low ratio size (cf. Barofsky & Hurwitz, 1968). The position of the maximum is influenced both by portion size and by concentration (Collier & Jennings, 1969; see also Hursh, 1980, for a review). In other words, the size of the ratio an animal can tolerate in an open economy is a function of the *rate of calorie flow*. In a closed economy, where the animal controls meal initiation and termination as well as total intake, rate of calorie flow also influences rate of responding, but in the opposite fashion. In the latter situation, any factor that slows the rate of caloric intake would be predicted to increase the rate of responding. For example, smaller portion sizes (e.g., smaller pellets) should yield higher response rates than larger ones, if the rat defends rate of intake. The results of two such experiments are shown in Figures 10 and 11.

In the first experiment, either 22-milligram or 97-milligram Noyes pellets were used. In the second experiment, feeder duration was varied (.5 minutes to 64 minutes). In both experiments, ratio size was varied. In each instance, rate of responding was a decreasing function of portion size; that is, the larger the "reinforcement," the slower the rate.

In this paradigm, with our present equipment (e.g., bar weight, cage size, etc.) and rat strain, 60,000–80,000 responses per day and 7,000–10,000 bar-presses per hour appear to define the upper limits of the rat's capacity. Rats working for 22-milligram pellets have to

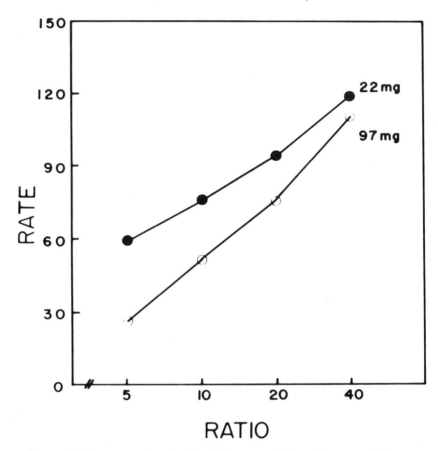

Figure 10. Response rates for 22-milligram and 97-milligram pellets as a function of the cost of consumption ("fixed ratio") for rats living in a closed economy (from Hill & Collier, 1978).

make 4.4 times as many responses as those working for 97-milligram pellets. It is obvious that rats working for the 22-milligram pellets will reach this ceiling more rapidly. What is interesting about this is not what the upper limits are but, rather, the fact that it is *the boundary conditions set by total daily intake that are controlling the behavior rather than the relation between pellet size and the contingent responses.*

Figure 12 presents an analysis of the pellet experiment in terms of the time required to obtain 10 grams of food at different ratio sizes. The dashed curve reflects the assumption that the rat continues to respond at the FR 5 rate on the higher ratios. The dotted curve

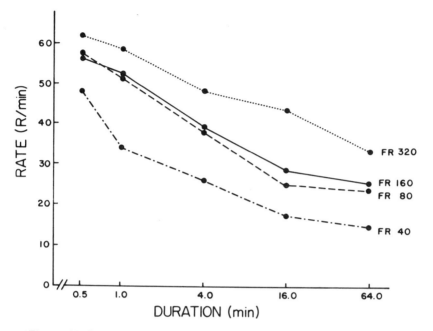

Figure 11. Response rate as a function of magazine durations ranging from .5 to 64 minutes and the cost of consumption (fixed ratios ranging from 40 to 320 bar-presses) for rats living in a closed economy. Duration of feeder access simulated prey size and reflects the same "magnitude of reinforcement" function as seen in Figure 10 (from Collier & Kaufman, 1977).

reflects the assumption that it compensatorily increases the rate of responding in such a fashion that meal duration remains constant. The solid curve depicts the observed performance.

These data, along with those of the previous experiment, suggest that the animal maximizes the net energy yield relative to feeding time (Schoener, 1971) when it can control the pertinent variables. The rat is not maximizing the momentary rate of reinforcement but is minimizing the time spent getting its total daily intake, which it controls. To understand this we must return to Richter's original observations (Richter, 1927). He pointed out that the pattern of meals was random, that is, that one could not construct a sequence of prior meals that would predict the next meal. A number of people have labored over this problem (e.g., deCastro, 1975; LeMagnen, 1971; Panksepp, 1973), attempting to obtain significant pre- and postprandial correlations. Their results have been disappointing

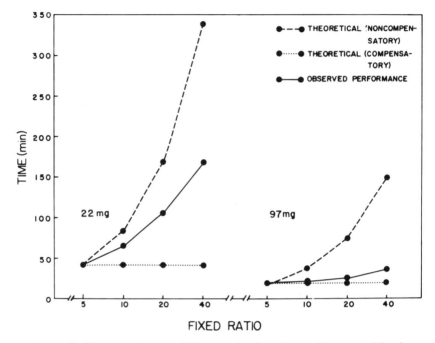

Figure 12. The time that would be required to obtain 10 grams of food at different consumption costs and for different pellet sizes (22- or 97-mg pellets) if the rat maintained the *same rate of responding* over all consumption costs (*dashed line*) or if the rat *increased response rate* as consumption cost increased in a fashion that conserved meal duration (*dotted line*). The actual meal time as a function of consumption cost ("fixed ratio") is indicated by the solid line. The rat was able to conserve meal duration better with the larger pellets (from Hill & Collier, 1978).

and controversial. Using the *size* of the previous meal as a factor, one can, perhaps, improve the prediction of the time of the next meal. Increasing the number of predictors (meal size, number of meas, successive intermeal intervals, etc.), however, does not improve the correlation (deCastro, 1975; Panksepp, 1973). An alternative possibility is that meal-taking is a path-independent process, the outcome of which is determined by the boundary conditions. This would suggest that within-meal rate of responding is a function of these boundary conditions (for example, of the rate of calorie flow in the environment) rather than of any momentary contingencies. I will return to this problem later.

It is clear from data like these that in an economy in which the animal controls the initiation and termination of its bouts of eating as well as its total intake, response rate and total intake are *strategies*, not measures of response strength or of regulatory processes.

The theories and laws of classic psychology are based on observations of a deprived animal eating a meal. The data consist of rate of responding within a meal. In the experimental paradigm, a deprived animal is allowed to respond for small portions (i.e., "bites") of a meal. The experimenter determines the initiation and termination of the meal and, usually, the total intake. In this open economy there are, or appear to be, strong relations between rate of responding and degree of deprivation, the sensory properties of the ingestant, and the schedule of delivery. Figure 13 shows the rate of responding on an interval schedule for food and for water as a function of percentage weight loss. Figure 14 shows rate of responding for sucrose solutions of different concentrations under two conditions of deprivation.

Enumeration of all of the schedule effects that have been obtained in this reinforcement paradigm would fill a multivolume Ferster and Skinner (1957). The reproducibility and power of these functions has encouraged the view that the immediate contingencies between responses and their consequences (or between responses and responses) determine the rate of responses. But let us consider these relations from a different perspective. Why should an animal eat a meal faster when it is depleted? What is the utility of this behavior? Why should an animal respond faster for a larger portion or for a more concentrated sweet solution? What is it maximizing? Why should an animal decrease response rate as the rate of delivery of the ingestant declines? Is it simply that these operations make the effect of the ingestant upon the preceding ingestive response stronger or weaker? Why is it that these relations exist only in an economy in which the animal is deprived and has no control over when, where, what, or how much it can eat? Why are the relations so very different, even if the animal is not deprived, if it can control the parameters of its own intake and bouts of feeding?

To answer some of these questions, we must consider the implications of three facts concerning the consequences of deprivation for the behavior of animals living in a closed economy. First, when a freely feeding animal is deprived of food (or water) for a relatively brief period and then allowed free access to the withheld item, the amount the animal consumes in the very first bout (e.g., meal) approximates the deficit that was incurred, if it was not too great.

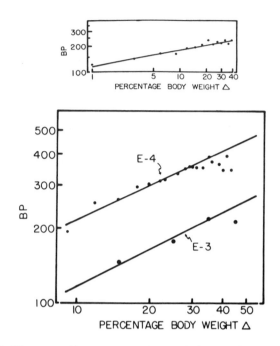

Figure 13. The rate of bar-pressing by food-deprived rats for food as a function of body weight loss (*upper panel*: Collier, Levitsky, & Squibb, 1967; copyright 1967 by the American Psychological Association; reprinted by permission) and the rate of water-deprived rats for water as a function of body weight loss (*lower panel*: Collier & Levitsky, 1967; copyright 1967 by the American Psychological Association; reprinted by permission).

Some animals undershoot, a few overshoot, but most of them approximate the deficit within a few percentage points (Adolph, 1950, 1980). Second, more severely deprived animals also eat a large first meal after the return of the withheld item, but they do not consume a sufficient amount in that meal to make up for the deficit incurred during the deprivation phase. Thereafter, these animals eat meals that are equivalent in size to those of nondeprived control animals, yet they ultimately exhibit "catch-up." Because the cumulative total intake of the animals who were severely deprived is less than that of the nondeprived animals over the recovery period (Levitsky, Faust, & Glassman, 1976), it is clear that their recovery from the deficit was not by replacement but by increased efficiency of utilization. This fact has been exploited in animal husbandry for thousands of years (Brody, 1945). And, third, the

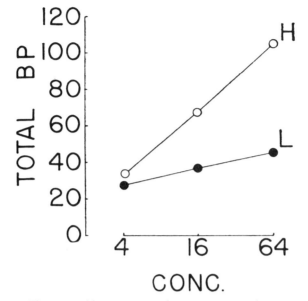

Figure 14. The rate of bar-pressing for sucrose as a function of sucrose concentration and degree of deprivation (high, H; low, L) (based on data in Collier & Willis, 1961).

latency of the first response is shorter, and the rate of responding is higher, in the first meal following deprivation (Bolles, 1975). Yet in subsequent meals (in the freely feeding animal) the rate of responding of deprived and nondeprived animals is the *same*, even if the former have not recovered body weight (Tang & Collier, 1971). A parallel phenomenon can be observed in running-wheel activity (Collier, 1969; Hamilton, 1969; Messing & Campbell, 1971). To observe high rates of responding, one must repetitively deprive and refeed the animal. In essence this maintains its first-meal-following-deprivation performance and ensures the robustness of the observations obtained during brief sessions in which the animal works to obtain food following, for example, 23-hour deprivation periods. But *the functions relating behavior to deprivation apply only to "first meals."* This striking fact has not been appreciated, perhaps because psychologists fail to realize that they are observing the animal eating a meal. Yet it casts a new light both on the effects of deprivation and on the results of experiments performed within the deprivation paradigm. For example, we now see that *the classic magnitude of reinforcement function is an instance of the "first meal" phenomenon*. That is, deprived animals observed during a brief session following a period of nonaccess to food respond at higher rates for larger pellets and at slower rates for smaller ones. In contrast, nondeprived animals living in a closed economy are solving different problems (e.g., regulating the rate of caloric intake) and respond at lower rates for larger pellets and vice-versa.

An interesting aspect of the "first meal" phenomenon is the declining rate at which eating (responding) occurs within a meal. This satiety function (see Figure 2) can be observed only in a repetitively deprived animal. Figure 15 presents the within-meal behavior of a freely feeding animal. Note that the rate of eating does not decline as the meal progresses. Freely feeding animals do not satiate in the usual sense; they simply stop eating (i.e., terminate the meal). This is not predicted by response rate.

Why do animals eat faster, and satiate, in first meals? The phenomenal experience is described by the word "ravenous" and exemplified by the frenzied activity of a partially starved animal in the presence of food. One can conjecture that in an uncertain world it may be adaptive to "get it while you can." However, this strategy it not necessarily efficient. Rather, it appears to be an *emergency strategy* and may relate to the replacement of a critical short-term deficit. This deficit may possibly be measured in terms of the rate of eating (responding).

The important point here is that our current models of learning and motivation are based on the "first meal" phenomenon, which is very restricted. In natural settings deprivation is either an accident or a time/energy allocation strategy; it is not an inevitable and invariable consequence of normal living. It is not clear what the dynamic properties of the recursive, recurrent ingestive responses are that make them sensitive to the rate of caloric flow (i.e., schedule effects).

Let us turn to the question of why consumption responses are sensitive to the sensory properties of the ingestant. Rats, for example, respond at high rates for sugars. The rate is a linearly increasing function of log concentration, the slope of which is a function of the degree of deprivation (see Figure 14). Data such as these are the source of the myth of the "sweet tooth" in rats (Collier & Hirsch, 1977; Hill, Castonguay, & Collier, 1980). The explanation for these data has traditionally been that rats "prefer" sweet tastes and find them highly palatable. The circularity of this logic is obvious. It is true that some substances are repeatedly chosen over others. Also, some substances are more efficacious reinforcers than others. However, the consumption of some substances (e.g., salt) is explained in

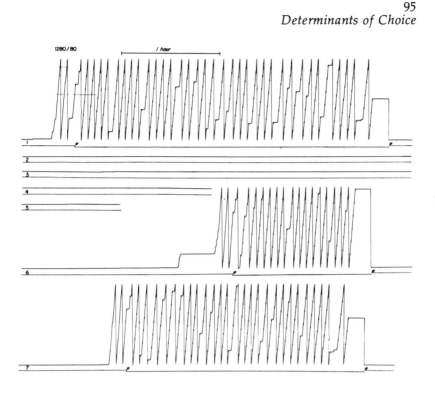

Figure 15. The complete 24–hour record of a rat required to complete 1,280 bar-presses to gain access to the feeder (procurement cost) and 80 bar-presses for each pellet within a meal (consumption cost). In this record the animal ate three meals; the onset of the consumption component is indicated by the downward deflection of the pen on the second channel. Arrows indicate the onset and termination of the consumption phase of the meal. The feeder remained accessible until the animal had not responded for 10 consecutive minutes. (Note the abruptness with which a meal is terminated.)

terms of deficit-induced threshold changes (Richter, 1942), and the consumption of others (e.g., vitamins) is attributed to learned effects associated with recovery from illness induced by the initial deficit (Rozin & Kalat, 1971). Might an analogous nutritional effect be hypothesized for sugar consumption? Here again we must turn to the example of the freely feeding animal and consider its typical diet. What does it contain, and what components are likely to be missing? The food in which many animals specialize meets all or almost all of their daily nutritional requirements, hence one would not expect them to have evolved any specialized mechanisms for diet-balancing. The diets of ruminants, as we have seen, are balanced by the microorganisms in their rumens. Only minerals are likely to be missing from their diets, and these they obtain by eating mineral-rich soils. The diets of most carnivores are likewise nutritionally adequate (most consume the entire carcass) and require no highly specialized mechanism for diet-balancing. The diets of generalist omnivores such as the rat, however, consist of items varying in caloric density and nutritional quality. Does a rat change its diet *after* a deficiency has developed? Does it balance its diet by simply eating a large quantity and variety of items, "hopeful" that the requisite dietary components will be obtained in the process? Or does the rat anticipate its dietary needs?

Rats offered sources of protein, carbohydrate, and fat on an ad libitum basis will balance their diets, consuming most of their calories from the carbohydrate source (Collier, Leshner, & Squibb, 1969; Musten, Peace & Anderson, 1974; Richter, 1942). If any components are diluted, the rat compensates by increasing meal frequency (Collier & Hirsch, 1977; Kanarek, 1976). Attempts to observe predictive sequences of ingestion of fats, carbohydrates, and protein have failed (Sunday, 1977), suggesting that rats do not develop momentary deficits that they correct by choosing that component in a subsequent meal.

An interesting feature of the rat's diet-balancing is the robust effect of consumption cost on choice. Using our consumption paradigm, we offered rats ad libitum access to either a 32% sucrose solution (the carbohydrate source) or Noyes pellets (the protein source) and required them to bar-press for the alternative component (pellets or sucrose, respectively). When the cost of obtaining pellets was increased (i.e., a larger FR was instituted), the number of responses also increased, but not compensatorily. Here the rat defended its caloric intake by increasing the intake of sucrose. As a result, the proportion of protein to carbohydrate dropped from 16% protein to 6% protein. At this point the rats stopped consuming either item. The values at which the rats stopped eating pellets ranged from 60,000 to 80,000 responses per day. Even though the sucrose was available ad libitum, response rate for pellets increased as a function of pellet cost in the fashion I have previously described. Thus the rats were willing to pay the price of eating protein even though sucrose was free! The same result was obtained when the cost of the sucrose was varied. However, the maximum response value for sucrose was 30,000 responses per day. Moreover, the rat continued to eat the free pellets even after he refused to pay the price for sucrose (Hirsch & Collier, 1975; Castonguay, Phillips, & Collier, unpublished data). Thus the choice of dietary items is determined jointly by the animal's nutritional requirements and the cost of consuming the items.

In summary, the relations between response rate and number and the cost (schedules) and value of the food items in a closed economy are described in terms of the defense of caloric intake and dietary balance, and by the maximization of the cost of consumption relative to the benefits. Consumption acts as a *gate* that controls the amount and kind of food ingested. The "system" appears to work in such a fashion that the animal is neither depleted nor deficient except in emergency situations or as a specific adaptive strategy. The classic within-meal paradigm involving deprived animals in an open economy is a special case and does not model natural feeding patterns. Rather, the paradigm appears to model the behavior of an animal taking its first meal after a repetitive period of deprivation. The rate of consumption, the change in the rate of consumption (i.e., satiation), and the amount consumed appear to reflect the degree of depletion or deficit. The schedule effects are reflected in the recursive, recurrent properties of the ingestive responses and may in turn reflect the flow of calories within a meal.

Foraging

Foraging is the behavior by which an animal gains access to food. It is a *non*recursive behavioral chain. The major dimensions of foraging are the path or route, encounter rate, availability, meal frequency, meal size, distribution of meals, and choice of dietary items. The components of foraging are depicted in the first portion of the feeding chain in Figure 16.

SEARCH

Efficient search behavior maximizes the rate of encounter with potential prey items and minimizes search cost. For the most part, the pattern of search is highly species-specific and has been extensively studied in the field (for reviews see Curio, 1976, and Krebs, 1978). Recently there have been attempts to manipulate the setting to study, for example, revisiting rates (Kamil, 1978; Olton, 1979, Pyke, 1981).

2-ITEM CHOICE MODEL

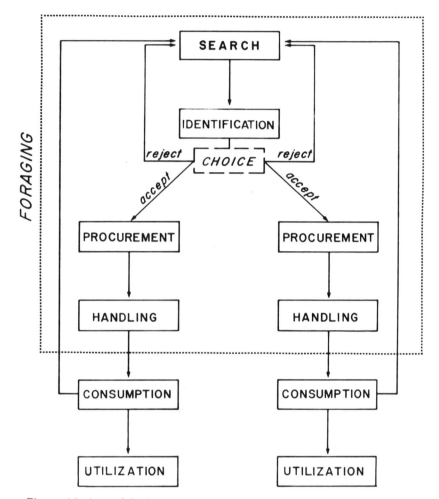

Figure 16. A model of the feeding chain showing the components of foraging for choices between two items that are successively encountered as a result of search.

IDENTIFICATION

Once a potential prey item has been encountered, it must be identified, and the animal must deide whether to include the item in its diet. The historical origin of optimal foraging theory was in this problem (Emlen, 1966; MacArthur & Pianka, 1966). Search cost and pursuit costs were seen as the major determinants of the choice. Cost was defined in terms of time, and value was a constant in the original models. MacArthur and Pianka proposed that if all dietary items were ranked in terms of profitability (i.e., value/cost), then the animal would include any given item if the decrement in search time resulting from the addition of a particular item were greater than the resulting increment in pursuit time (see Figure 17). Every item to the left of the intersection of the two functions in Figure 17 should be included in the diet, and all the items to the right should be excluded. It is clear that profitability is a complex term. Value can vary along many dimensions, as can cost. Many different tests of these optimal choice models have been devised (cf. Krebs, 1978).

In our analyses, we have modified the terminology of MacArthur and Pianka, separating "search" into two components, "search" and "identification," and "pursuit" into two components, "procurement" and "handling." These divisions are functional in that they are based on different classes of behaviors that are functions of different sets of variables.

PROCUREMENT

Once the animal chooses to include an item in its diet, the next step is to procure it. This is often an energy-intensive process. It can vary from the spectacular chase of a wildebeest by a cheetah to a cow's prosaic trip to the pasture.

HANDLING

Having procured, captured, or otherwise gained access to the food item or source, the animal must prepare it for consumption. The handling component can vary from killing the prey to shelling a nut. On occasion, as a result of the variety of species-specific behaviors, the feeding chain components will shade one into the other. Handling is often difficult to differentiate from consumption. However, the recursive property of an ingestive response is taken here to be the defining characteristic of consumption.

A LABORATORY MODEL OF FORAGING

We have attempted to develop a laboratory model of foraging that simulates some of the essential characteristics of the animal's niche (Collier & Rovee-Collier, 1980). The major characteristic of our

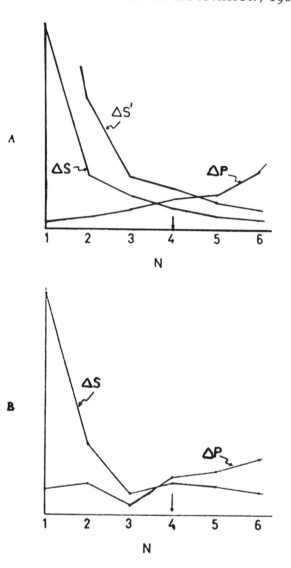

Figure 17. Figure 17A illustrates the MacArthur & Pianka (1966, p. 605) decision rule for adding to the diet equally abundant items that vary in profitability. On the x-axis, N items are ranked from most (1) to least (6) profitable. Adding a less profitable item to the diet would decrease mean search time (ΔS) and increase mean pursuit time (ΔP). The item ($N + 1$) should be added only if the increase in pursuit time resulting from enlarging the diet does not exceed the resulting decrease in search time ($\Delta S'$). Figure 17B illustrates the same relation for the case in which items are not equally abundant. (Copyright 1966 by the University of Chicago Press; reprinted by permission.)

model is that the initiation and the termination of bouts of feeding are under the control of the animal, who lives in the apparatus around the clock. In our first apparatus, we have not attempted to simulate species-specific foraging routines; rather, we have used operant technology to simulate the time and energy costs associated with foraging.

Figure 18 shows one version of our apparatus. It contains a "search bar" and two "procurement bars." Completion of the FR requirement on the search bar turns off the cue light over that bar and produces a visual cue at the other end of the apparatus that indicates the cost or value (or both) of the prey that the animal has encountered as a result of its search. The animal must identify the meal opportunity (i.e., prey item) and decide whether to procure it. If it decides to procure it, it can gain access to the item by completing an FR requirement on the appropriate procurement bar. Once the magazine operates, it stays in position until the animal has remained out of the feeder for 10 consecutive minutes, terminating a meal. (The 10-minute meal criterion is shown clearly at the conclusion of each meal in Figure 15.) Once the meal is completed, or if the animal chooses to reject the meal opportunity initially (i.e., by waiting for the procurement cue to disappear), the light over the search bar is once more illuminated, and the animal can initiate another meal whenever it wishes. It should be noted that various schedules can be imposed on the search and procurement bars to simulate availability, abundance, and predictability. Different numbers of magazines can be used to present foods of different values or quality. The apparatus is simplistic; the results are interesting.

THE EFFECT OF PROCUREMENT COST
ON MEAL PATTERNS

In the following experiment the search component was eliminated and only one procurement bar was used. Instead of seeking the determinants of meal patterns in the internal state of the animal, we sought to explore the effects of the cost of procurement on the size and frequency of meals. In Figure 19 data are presented for three rats bar-pressing to gain access to a meal. These rats ate 10–15 meals per day before the introduction of the bar-press requirement. As the number of bar-presses required to gain access to the feeder increased from 1 to 5,120 presses, meal frequency decreased from 10–15 meals to 1 meal per day. Meal size increased compensatorily,

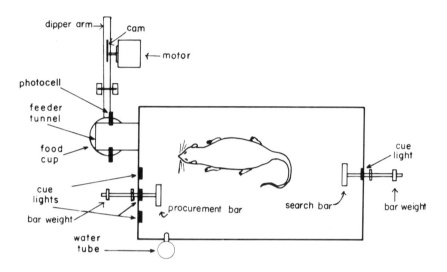

Figure 18. The experimental cage in which an animal lives around the clock. The animal searches for a food item by completing the operant requirement on the "search bar," which is active when the cue light mounted above it is on. That a food item has been encountered as a result of search is indicated by the illumination of a pattern of cue lights at the opposite end of the cage, the particular pattern of lights signaling to the animal the cost of procuring that particular item. The animal identifies the nature of the prey item in terms of its procurement cost and either procures it by completing the prescribed number of presses on the "procurement bar" or, after a 30-second wait (or, in some cases, a bar-press on a "reject bar"), returns to the "search bar" to complete another search, which may result in the encounter of a less costly food item. When an item has been procured, the feeder operates and the animal is free to eat a meal of any size (i.e., for as long as it "wishes"), with the feeder retracting only after the animal has remained out of the feeder tunnel for 10 consecutive minutes. Water is continuously available. Weights can be placed on the bars in order to manipulate the energetic cost of foraging independently of the time required to complete the bar-press requirement. It is important to note that the animal controls both the initiation of each foraging bout and the size of the meal taken.

and total intake was defended. Similar data have been obtained from cats observed in the same paradigm (Kanarek, 1975). The savings in time and energy that result from this strategy of increasing meal size and decreasing meal frequency are illustrated in Figure 20, based on the cat data. This strategy has been observed in a variety of animals tested in this paradigm in the laboratory (e.g.,

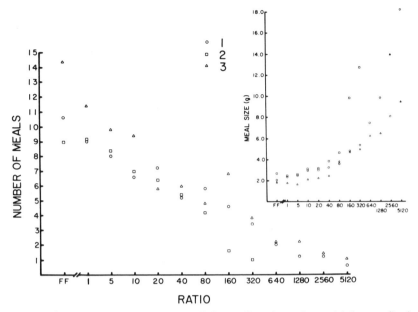

Figure 19. Daily meal frequency (*left panel*) and meal size (*right panel*) of three rats as a function of procurement cost (ratio = number of bar presses required to gain access to the feeder). A meal was terminated when the animal had not entered the feeder for 10 consecutive minutes; thus both meal initiation and meal termination (i.e., meal size) were under the animal's direct control. Meal frequency and size were compensatory, resulting in constant food intake except at extreme ratios. "FF" indicates the free-feeding meal frequency and meal size when there was no bar-press requirement (from Collier, Hirsch, & Hamlin, 1972; reproduced by permission).

rats, chickens, cats, ferrets, mice, degus, agoutis, guinea pigs, wild rats, wild guinea pigs) and has also been observed in home-raised free-ranging cats and in a number of animals observed in the wild (cf. Collier & Rovee-Collier, 1980). These functions are highly reproducible within and across individuals and species and are not affected by practice. The rate of responding on these schedules appears to be a function of variables other than the schedule parameters (Collier & Rovee-Collier, 1980; Sunday, 1981).

If, instead of a feeder that delivers Purina chow, completion of the procurement ratio activated a pellet feeder that could then be operated on an FR schedule, we could observe the procurement-consumption sequence. Figure 15 presents a typical cumulative record for a rat that had to press 1,280 times to gain access to the

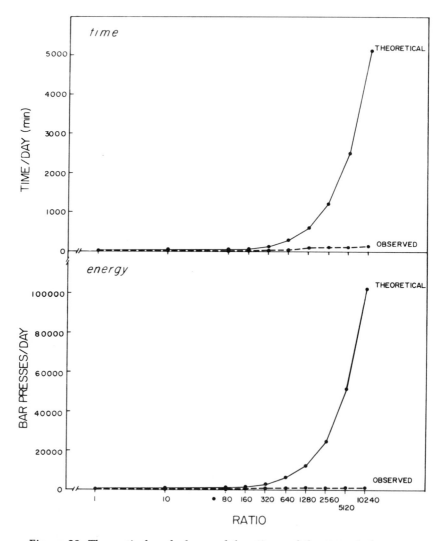

Figure 20. Theoretical and observed functions of the time and energy required for a cat to feed each day as a function of procurement cost (fixed ratio), that is, the cost of gaining access to the feeder. The theoretical values are based on the cat's free-feeding meal frequency and eating rate; the observed values reflect the cat's solution to the cost increase. (These curves were interpolated from data of Kanarek, 1975.)

feeder (procurement component) and 80 times for each pellet that composed the meal (consumption component). The record, taken from a 24-hour period, shows that the rat initiated and consumed three meals that day, each of which was several hours long. The requirements on these two components did not interact. Procurement costs affect meal frequency and size; consumption costs affect rate of responding within the meal and total intake.

THE EFFECT OF SEARCH COST AND PROCUREMENT COST ON THE CHOICE OF DIETARY ITEMS

Figure 15 illustrates the schedule used in these studies. The search key was available (indicated by the cue light over it) ad libitum except during the actual procurement and consumption of the meal. Upon the completion of a self-initiated search, one or the other of the cue lights signaling what prey item had been encountered in terms of cost would come on. The order of cue lights was semirandom ($p = .5$ chance of one or the other prey items being encountered), with the restriction that no more than four of the same cues would be encountered in succession. If the animal chose to exploit the prey item it had encountered, it simply initiated procurement. Once having done so, however, the animal was required to complete the procurement fixed ratio, which was always followed by a meal presentation, before being allowed to renew search. If the animal chose to reject the meal, it could wait 30 seconds (or in some cases it could press a "reject bar") and then return to search again, presumably in "hopes" of encountering a less costly meal opportunity.

Figure 21 presents a model of this problem. If we consider first the example in which the search cost is fixed at 20 responses and the procurement costs of the two prey items that will be randomly encountered when a search is completed are fixed at 5 responses for the low-cost item and range from 5 to 160 responses for the high-cost item, then we can see that there are two strategies available to the animal in making its choice of whether to accept (include in the diet) or reject (exclude from the diet) successively encountered prey items. It could either take only the low-cost items that its search turned up (TOL strategy) or take both items (TB strategy) irrespective of their costs. Let us assume that the animal typically eats 6 meals per day. If it were to follow the first strategy (TOL), then it would have to initiate, on the average, 12 meals at a total search cost

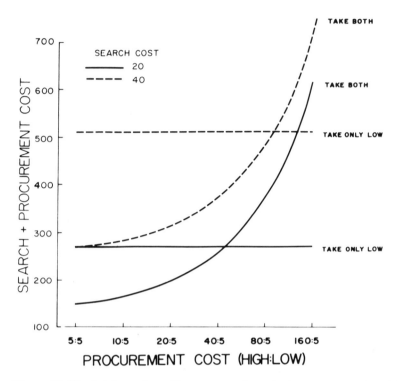

Figure 21. The total number of bar-presses (search + procurement costs) that an animal eating an average of six meals per day would have to perform if it chose to procure all items encountered as a result of search ("take both") or to procure only the low-cost item of pairs of items successively available, on the average, 50% of the time ("take only low"). The optimal strategy, that is, to minimize total cost, shifts at the point of the intersection of the pair of solid (or dashed) lines. This strategy is shown for two examples in which search cost is either 20 or 40 responses.

of 240 bar-presses. It would encounter on the average of 6 low-cost items (five bar-presses each), for a combined foraging (search + procurement) cost of 270 bar presses. If the animal followed the take-both (TB) strategy, it would have to initiate only 6 meals at a total search cost of 120 bar-presses. If both prey items cost only 5 responses to procure (5:5; low cost:high cost), the total procurement cost for this strategy would be 30 bar-presses, and the total foraging cost of this strategy would be 150 bar-presses. As the cost of the high-cost item increased from 5 to 160 responses, the total cost of foraging would increase from 150 to 615 responses.

Following the MacArthur and Pianka (1966) logic, the TB strategy would initially be the optimal choice. As the cost of the high-cost item increases, however, the cost of the TB strategy also increases, and it exceeds the cost of the TOL strategy between pairs of procurement costs of 5:40 and 5:80 (see Figure 21). Thus, for item costs greater than 40, the animal should follow the TOL strategy. The MacArthur and Pianka formulation also predicts a *discontinuous* choice function. That is, the animal should choose to include both items in the diet up to the point at which including the high-cost item would increase the total cost above the cost of the TOL strategy. If now you increase search cost to, for example, 40 barpresses, it can be seen that the point of the switch should shift to the right; that is, the animal should now include higher-cost items in its diet. Thus a high search cost makes animals less finicky.

A representative set of results from a series of experiments by Kaufman (1979) is shown in Figure 22. In the bottom panel we see that, as the cost of the high-cost item increases, the percentage of high-cost meal opportunities the animal accepts continuously decreases. In the upper panel we see that, as search cost increases, the percentage of high-cost meal opportunities the animal accepts also increases until, at the highest search costs, all opportunities encountered are included in the diet. Clearly, item choice is affected by search costs and procurement costs. But how are these costs scaled by the animal? Figure 23 shows that the *relative rather than the absolute difference* between costs determines choice (i.e., is constant). This may explain why we do not observe a discontinuous function. In this choice situation, costs are on a psychophysical rather than a purely physical scale. This is supported by data from procurement cost experiments in which we find that meal frequency declines linearly as a function of *log cost* (cf. Figure 19).

In the same choice paradigm, however, when procurement cost is held constant and the size of the meal or prey item is varied in terms of the duration of feeder presentation (1 versus 5 minutes), the rat chooses the larger prey item for the majority of its meals as long as the search cost is low and rejects the smaller prey. However, when search cost increases, this preference disappears, and the rat procures whatever prey (size) it encounters (see Figure 24). Thus choices between prey items are made on the basis of cost and value.

For as long as choice behavior has been studied, investigators have been puzzled by the problem of *exclusive choice*—that is, when

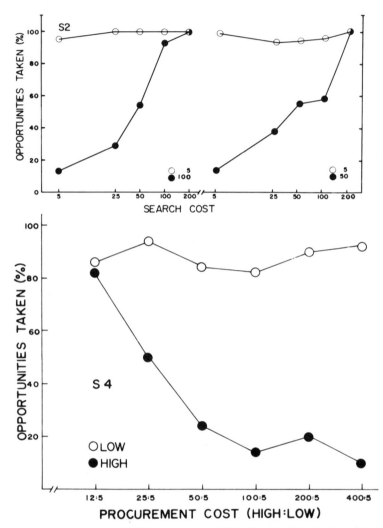

Figure 22. *Lower panel:* The percentage of high-cost (12, 25, 50, 100, 200, or 400 responses) and low-cost (5 responses) items or meal opportunities procured by rat 4 (S4) as a function of pairs of procurement costs encountered successively during six different series of costs. Search cost was fixed at 10 responses. *Upper panels:* The percentage of high-cost (100 responses) and low-cost (5 responses) items or meal opportunities procured by rat 2 (S2) as a function of search cost (5, 25, 50, 100, or 200 responses; *upper left curves*). The percentage of high-cost (50 responses) and low-cost (5 responses) items or meal opportunities procured as a function of search cost (5, 25, 50, 100, 200 responses; *upper right curves*). (Data from Kaufman, 1979; reproduced by permission.)

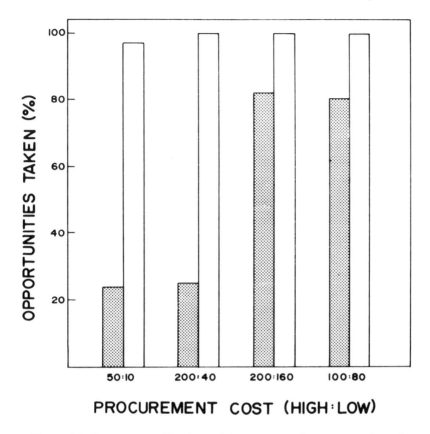

Figure 23. Percentage of high- and low-cost meal opportunities taken when meal costs differed as a constant ratio of each other (1:5 in left half of figure; 4:5 in right half of figure); search cost was always fixed at 10 responses (from Kaufman, 1979; reprinted by permission).

the animal shows an exclusive preference for a single item. These cases are sometimes described as side preferences, fixations, and such. Most procedures have incorporated a forced-choice design so that the animal does not develop an exclusive preference. We have also observed the development of exclusive preferences in the search-procurement paradigm. Once the animal chooses the low-cost item exclusively (100% of the time), it becomes insensitive to search cost. It takes extensive retraining to recover the usual relations (Jensen, 1980).

At this point, I should note an important difference between the present results and those typically obtained in studies of "self-

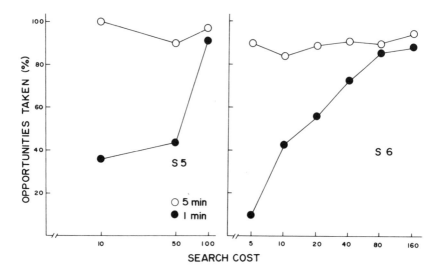

Figure 24. Percentage of meal opportunities taken by two rats (S5, S6) from a pair of magazine durations (5 minutes or 1 minute) encountered in a random sequence ($p = .5$) as a function of search cost (from Kaufman, 1979; reprinted by permission).

control" or "delay of gratification" within the concurrent-chain paradigm (Fantino & Navarick, 1974; Rachlin & Green, 1972). In the self-control version a delay is introduced between the final link and the reinforcement. The animal is given a choice between a short-delay, small reinforcement and a long-delay, large reinforcement. Reinforcement size, duration of delay, and duration of the first link are the major variables. If the difference in delays is large and the difference in reinforcement size small, the animal chooses the short-delay, small reward. In this paradigm the choice is made at the outset of the first link (rather than following the "search" link, as in the foraging model; see Figure 16). Performance is "improved" by displacing the choice further in time from the reinforcement; this is accomplished by increasing the duration of the first link. The pigeons used in these experiments apparently find delay of gratification a very difficult task, and a long period of training, often lasting many months, is required (Mazur & Logue, 1978). In the foraging paradigm, animals find it quite easy to defer gratification. If the relative procurement cost of the high-cost item is high, the animal readily rejects the high-cost option by waiting 30 seconds or by pressing a reject bar and then typically begins the search requirement once more. Following initial magazine training, this routine is usually learned in a few days. Moreover, rats do not appear to be in a hurry when rejecting a meal opportunity. Their response rates are low. From yet another perspective, we see that animals choose to procure a single large meal after intervals as long in some instances (e.g., chickens, cats) as three to four days, rather than pay the high procurement price and eat a smaller meal more often. It should be recalled, however, that the animal determines both the size of its own meal and the "delay" interval and does not lose weight even if eating infrequently except at the highest procurement FRs. The difference in the types of results obtained in the concurrent-chain paradigm and in the foraging paradigm is probably a function not of the reinforcement schedules but, rather, of the *test economies*.

If the animals in the delayed gratification experiments were tested in a closed rather than an open economy, we think they would learn the problem (i.e., to delay gratification) easily. Moreover, we think their choice would reflect a solution to the problem of maximizing calories gained relative to the time spent gaining them. Hungry animals, as we have seen earlier in this presentation, find it difficult to "wait" in the presence of food (cf. Bolles, 1975, pp. 200–210). It appears to be difficult for animals to make optimal decisions when they are hungry and when they cannot control their pattern of feeding and their total intake.

When diet-balancing is studied as a function of procurement cost, we see results different from those reported for the effects of consumption cost. For example, if a rat is presented with a choice between an item that is 60% protein and a 32% sucrose solution (adequate minerals and vitamins being provided elsewhere), an adult will consume these two items proportionally so that its diet contains 10% to 14% protein. If the cost of the protein component is now increased by increasing the number of bar-presses required to gain access to the 60% protein item, but the cost of the carbohydrate component remains low (or is free), the rat will decrease its frequency of protein meals and increase meal size compensatorily. At the same time, the meals taken from the carbohydrate source are unaffected, as is the ratio of protein to carbohydrate in its diet (see Figures 25 and 26; Castonguay, 1978). The rats will tolerate very high fixed-ratio schedules to maintain their protein intake. In fact, some rats procured a single large protein meal costing 10,000 bar-presses only once every two days. If instead the cost of gaining access to the 32% sucrose solution were increased while access to

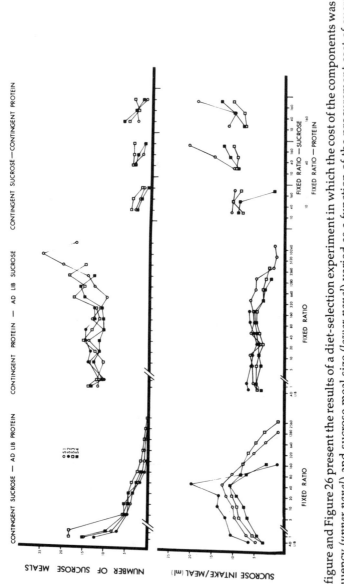

Figure 25. This figure and Figure 26 present the results of a diet-selection experiment in which the cost of the components was varied. Sucrose meal frequency (*upper panel*) and sucrose meal size (*lower panel*) varied as a function of the procurement cost of sucrose (*left panel*) or protein (*middle panel*). Protein was available ad libitum in the experiment presented in the left panel; sucrose was available ad libitum in the experiment presented in the middle panel. The cost of both the sucrose and the protein components was varied in the right panel. In all cases, sucrose meal frequency declined and sucrose meal size increased as procurement cost increased (from Castonguay, 1978; reproduced by permission).

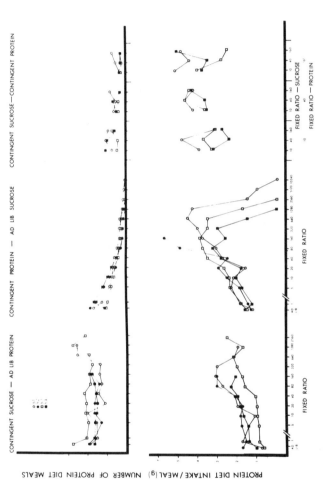

Figure 26. Protein meal frequency (*upper panel*) and protein meal size (*lower panel*) as a function of the cost of procuring either sucrose (*left panel*) or protein (*middle panel*). Protein was available ad libitum in the experiment depicted in the left panel. Sucrose was presented ad libitum in the middle panel. The procurement costs of both dietary components were varied in the right panel. Again, frequency of protein meals decreased and protein meal size increased as procurement cost increased (from Castonguay, 1978; reproduced by permission).

the protein component was either free or fixed at a low cost, rats decreased their frequency of carbohydrate meals and increased the size of those meals. It is interesting to note that the rats did not tolerate as high an FR requirement for the sucrose, given the alleged "preference" of rats for sucrose. Here again we see important differences between foraging and consumption behavior.

THE EFFECT OF HANDLING COST ON DIETARY CHOICE

Considering now the final component of foraging, we varied the cost of preparing an item for consumption. In this instance we explored the preference of rats for seeds with and without hulls (Kaufman & Collier, 1981). When rats were offered two cups of sunflower seeds containing either hulled or unhulled seeds, as expected they chose the unhulled seeds, thus avoiding the cost of hulling them. Starch was always offered along with the seeds as an alternative source of calories, because the protein level of the seeds exceeds the rat's normal requirement. In fact, the rats chose sufficient starch to maintain their characteristic protein:carbohydrate ratio. In a subsequent study the two types of seeds were mixed in different proportions so that the rat had to search for the seeds without hulls. When the proportions were equal (1:1), most of the rat's intake was from the hulled seeds (see Figure 27). However, as the proportion of hulled:unhulled seeds decreased (i.e., the encounter rate of hulled seeds decreased) and the rat had to spend more time searching for the hulled seeds, it chose increasingly more unhulled seeds, paying the price of hulling them. Here again, cost determines choice.

The determinants of the choice of dietary items are clearly multiple. I have shown in the preceding examples that in a simple situation, both cost and value affect choice behavior. These variables are just the beginning of a long list of variables that determine choice. For example, consider the relation between anatomy and prey size. Holling (1964) showed that the relation between the percentage of prey attacked by mantids and prey diameter was an inverted U-shaped function. The predicted optimum prey size was calculated from the geometry of the mantid's foreleg. "More" is not always "better". Even more complex relations may obtain when the niche, the social structure, competition, predation, and such, are considered. In many species the nocturnal, diurnal, and crepuscular patterns of feeding can be modified by

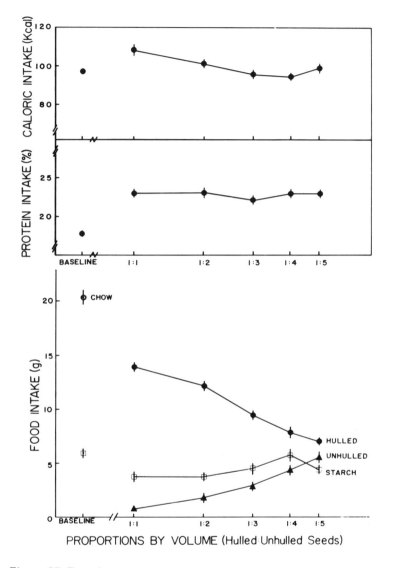

Figure 27. Data from an experiment in which rats were presented with mixtures of hulled and unhulled sunflower seeds on a 24-hour ad libitum basis. Dextrinized starch was also available. The lower panel shows the intake of starch and of each seed type as a function of the ratio of the two types of seeds in the mixture. The upper two panels show that the proportion of protein taken and the daily total caloric intake remained constant (from Kaufman, 1979; reproduced by permission).

varying either the cost or the value of feeding under a given lighting condition (Curio, 1976, p. 36; Rovee-Collier, Clapp, Collier, & Raabe, 1981; Wilets, 1981). Consider also bees' choice of flowers: how far to fly, the pattern of search, and the flower type on which to specialize (dilute versus concentrated nectar in big versus small amounts, difficult or easy to reach, etc.) are determined by the solution to the problem of maximizing benefits relative to feeding costs. Heinrich (1979) has presented a fascinating discussion of this problem. His landmark book is the first complete analysis of the multiple determinants of choice for a single species. Once we begin to consider the determinants of choice from an ecological perspective, the vacuousness of such concepts as "magnitude of reinforcement" and even "reinforcement" per se becomes obvious.

Schemata, Representations, and Reinforcement

That animals maximize nutritional benefits over a wide range of foraging, consumption, and utilization costs raises a number of interesting questions. How do they accomplish this worthy objective? In some fashion, both the phylogenetic history and the ontogenetic history of the animal must contribute to this efficient behavior, the latter history adapting the wisdom acquired across generations to current circumstances.

Historically, organisms have been conceived of as possessing some mechanism(s) that renders a current account of the deviation of their momentary nutritional state from some ideal state defined in terms of the milieu of the cells (Cannon, 1932). Associated with this homeostatic model has been the concept of reinforcement: Any responses that lead to the reparation of this internal state are strengthened (phylogenetically or ontogenetically), and any stimuli associated with these responses are conditioned to them. These concepts continue to form the base of all current accounts of the regulation of intake and of the acquisition and performance of behavior.

A major shortcoming of these accounts, however, is their failure to consider the structure of the environment and, more important, the biological information contained in this structure. A biological description of this structure has been supplied by ecologists (cf. Pianka, 1978) and is embodied, in part, in the concept of the niche (Hutchinson, 1959). If animals have been selected on the basis of maximizing profitability (Pulliam, 1974; Pyke, Pulliam, & Charnov, 1977; Schoener, 1971), then it is likely that the information contained in the structure of the animal's environment, which served as the basis of this efficient behavior, would be incorporated into its adaptive repertoire. In a nonlaboratory world, the abundance, distribution, seasonality, availability, and quality of resources vary widely *but not randomly*. By discovering the rules of this variation, a species can either be specialized and efficient or deploy an armamentarium of strategies appropriate to the various facets and phases of its niche, sacrificing some degree of efficiency for greater flexibility in range of feeding opportunities. The more stable the environment or the narrower the niche, the more rigid and preprogrammed the strategies can be. At one extreme, for example, is the efficient, stereotyped feeding behavior of the panda, which specializes on bamboo shoots. At the other extreme is the generalist—a jack-of-all-trades, master of none. For example, the rat sorts garbage, dives for mussels and fish, shells seeds, cracks nuts, catches insects, kills mice, sucks eggs, and presses bars for a bite to eat (Canby, 1977).

At the core of all of these feeding strategies is a complex of species-specific, stereotyped behavior, suited to the morphology of that species and its prey, that is relatively unaffected by niche variation. Within trophic levels and within individuals, feeding behavior is progressively more stereotyped as one progresses through the feeding chain. It is this stereotypy, most clearly seen in the ingestion (consumption) and utilization components, that has been the focus, respectively, of psychologists and of physiologists.

A second shortcoming of the classical accounts is their failure to consider the nature and flow of information in feeding activity. For many animals, the time from the point at which foraging is initiated to the point at which a nutrient reaches its final resting place (the "consequences" of behavior) is quite long, ranging from hours to days. In some ruminants the process may even require many days; and in the case of hoarding or deposition in the adipose tissue the consequences may not be realized for weeks or even months. Further, the degradation of information about the food items from the point of consumption to the point of absorption must be considered. The mouth and the stomach are mixing-and-diluting devices. The resulting product is metered into the gut in such a way as to maintain a constant volume and concentration. Thus, specific information about the texture, concentration, amount, and quality of the food item is lost long before the food is digested and absorbed. The *consequences* of a meal, thus, are ponderous, and the *stimulus events* preceding it are fleeting and highly articulate, temporally distant, and delicately tuned to the current status of the habitat. It is hard to imagine *realistically* how the former can shape and strengthen the latter.

A third shortcoming of the classical accounts is their reliance on deprivation or depletion or both as instigators of feeding activity. It would be the height of folly to begin the often protracted, energy-intensive, and unsuccessful search, identification, handling, and procurement routine only after reaching a state of negative energy balance, particularly if such a critical condition were avoidable. A more efficient strategy would be to anticipate nutritional require-ments by exploiting the predictability of resources. Although intermeal intervals are highly buffered by various storage mechanisms (e.g., hoards; mouth pouches; the crop, gut, and adipose tissue), these are only short-term devices that ameliorate the grain of the environment. In fact, naturalistic observations have confirmed that prudent predators exploit the information in the structure of their environments to feed in such a fashion as to prevent physiological depletion except when depletion is a specific biological strategy or adaptation. Although we all subjectively ex-perience "hunger" and "satiety," the question is whether these are the result of physiological depletion and repletion respectively, or whether they are part of the feed-forward strategy. We have shown that one major determinant of meal patterns is the current cost/ benefit relations in the animal's habitat. Numerous other studies have shown that animals learn to anticipate any regularly occurring event (cf. Marwine & Collier, 1979; Squibb & Collier, 1979), thereby improving their efficiency.

A fourth shortcoming is the failure of classical accounts to con-sider the competition of feeding with other activities for time and energy. When, where, what, and how much to eat are determined not only by opportunities and requirements but also by priorities. For example, many species allocate feeding to a time of maximal food resource density or quality and engage in other survival-related activities at other times (cf. Collier, 1980). Thus, defense of status or territory, courting, parental care, nest-building, anti-predator behavior, and other survival-related activities may pre-empt feeding or may be preempted by it.

What, then, determines the pattern of feeding? The present re-sults elucidate a few of the factors. In freely feeding animals operating in a closed economy, the frequency, size, rate of con-sumption, and choice of items are determined in large part by the cost and value of the items. These results appear to be analogous to those obtained from observations of animals in their natural habitats. In what way do animals exploit the information contained in the structure of the environment? It is clear that they cannot go to school to learn their economics, geology, nutrition, climatology, biology, predator-and-prey behavior patterns, and energetics. In some fashion this information must be stored, but obviously not in any great detail, considering its potential variety. In fact, the more variable the environment, the greater should be the variability in the behavioral repertoire.

Consider, for example, the very strong inverse relation between meal frequency and meal size. This relation appears to be neither learned nor a matter of a momentary deficiency (i.e., a long inter-meal interval does not predict a large meal). In addition, the same relation has appeared in all the species thus far observed both in the laboratory and in seminatural settings (cf. Collier & Rovee-Collier, 1980). I conclude, therefore, that this relation is an *economic rule* that must be stored in the animals' repertoires (cf. Collier, 1980). As I previously noted, a similar rule was observed for the choice between dietary items varying in profitability. These rules are *schemata* that the animal brings to its pursuit of a living. A number of such schemata are reviewed in Schoener (1971). He has suggested, for example, that some species are time-minimizers and others are energy-maximizers. The terms of these schemata appear to be quite open. In the preceding example, for instance, when procurement cost is simulated by the number of bar-presses, or revolutions in an activity wheel, or key-pecks, or chain-pulls, the relations between procurement cost and meal size and frequency are similar to those of lions feeding in the wild (Schaller, 1972) or those of animals living at various distances from a waterhole (cf. Marwine & Collier, 1979).

Another determinant of patterns of feeding is the defense of caloric and nutrient intake. This defense appears to occur over the circadian cycle, at least in small animals such as the rat, while it may occur over days in larger animals such as chickens and cats. One should recall that meals occur randomly when animals control the initiation and termination of their own feeding bouts. Prediction of either the occurrence or size of a meal is not improved by knowledge of either the previous sequence of meals or their size. Total intake is defended by the correlation between meal frequency and meal size, not by the correlation between meal size and intermeal interval or between intermeal interval and meal size. Animals optimize the costs of feeding by adjusting meal frequency and defend intake by correlating meal size with meal frequency. If, as I have argued, feeding is a path-independent process whose outcome is determined by the boundary conditions (e.g., cost, value, abundance, light cycle), then the initiation and termination of meals is the result not of homeostatic perturbations but rather of random events occurring with probabilities determined by some representation of either intake or body size, or both.

Computer models of such a process have been developed by Oatley (1978, pp. 123 ff.) and others. Although the Oatley model is based on intake of animals suffering a water deficit, it can easily be adapted to anticipatory drinking (cf. Collier, 1980). Another model in which animals are presumed to have a representation of intake has been developed for the growth process (Tanner, 1964; Weiss & Kavanau, 1957). Rearing animals under a standard set of conditions on a nutritionally adequate diet yields a standard growth curve that expresses their genetic potential for size. If, however, their access to food is limited, they grow at a slower rate; and if the restriction of food is severe, they lose weight. After a period of time, if they are again given access to food, they will (if not stunted) recover body weight and return to the normal growth curve. Two aspects of their recovery are interesting. First, their body weight recovers to the value *expected at that point in time on the uninterrupted growth curve*; and, second, the momentary rate of recovery is proportional to the *momentary deviation from the expected value*. The implications of this model are that the animal has a representation of its expected size at a given point in time on its growth curve and that it can measure the distance between its actual size and the expected size. While both these models reflect a homeostatic assumption, they differ from the classic accounts in that they introduce the assumption that an animal has a *representation* of expected intake and/or size that guides its behavior. These models predict feeding behavior equally well for animals who are "on target," with no perturbation, and animals who deviate from the expected value. Classic accounts address only the latter. Finally, for both models the means by which the animal's representation of its intake and/or size is reflected in its behavior remain a mystery.

Thus far we have considered some of the economic rules that are embedded in a species' behavioral repertoire by its phylogenetic history. Next we will briefly consider the niche. Species have specialized in the exploitation of resources. Successful exploitation of a niche requires a detailed knowledge of a small portion of the animal's environment. Here again efficiency requires that the animal possess a representation of its niche that has been acquired over the history of the species. The more specialized the animal and the more stable the environment, the more detailed this representation can be. In most cases, however, only the most general relationships in the niche can be represented; the details of the structure of the environment must be filled in by the individual history of the animal. Two obvious examples of this are seen in the problems of prey identification and "homing" behavior. In the first instance, animals must acquire a search image for the prey particular to their habitat. In the second case, both transitive location rules that define a map and distance must be part of the homer's phylogenetically determined repertoire; the details of the particular features of the local terrain must be filled in. If we can simulate, in the laboratory, the *general relations that define the species' niche,* we may be able to discover the nature of the animal's representation of its niche and what schemata it uses in exploiting it.

A final question raised by the ecological approach, and one I will not answer, concerns the nature of learning. Psychologists have usually been satisfied with two types of learning, classical and instrumental, though there has been some dissension in the ranks on the part of those who would reduce the "two" to "one" and others who would increase the list. What is clear from the present analysis is that animals do *not* learn specific S-R or R-R associations. What, then, do they learn? There are maps to be filled in, motor skills to be acquired or sharpened, information about the abundance, distribution, availability, and quality of prey to be uncovered, contingencies to be discovered, rank in a status hierarchy or the boundary of a territory to be established, predator and prey idiosyncrasies to be uncovered, mothers and offspring to be identified, potential escape routes or hiding places to be determined, and so on. To a greater or lesser degree, the animal brings to these tasks its schemata and representations, out of which its knowledge, skills, tactics, and strategies are formed through the interaction of the animal with the structure of its environment. Thus what the animal learns is how to *translate its schemata and representations in terms of the particulars of the current status of its habitat.* The consequences of behavior in some way guide this learning process, but certainly not in terms of strengthening or chaining reflexes, as in classic accounts of learning.

Once we have understood the function of an animal's performance in a given situation—that is, "what" it must learn and "why"—we can return to the two central questions: (1) What is the nature of the animal's schemata and representations? and (2) What are the proximal mechanisms by which the phylogenetic heritage and experience interact?

Conclusions

The classical theories of choice have assumed that choice results from pitting different momentary response strengths against each other. A variety of proximal mechanisms, such as the state of the organism, its reinforcement history, and the properties of the ingestant, have been investigated. It is our thesis that the problem of choice can best be understood from the perspective of the animal's economy.

To investigate the determinants of choice that reside in the animal's economy, we have studied choice behavior and item selection in a simple feeding environment based on the chain of events that normally are involved in the discovery, procurement, and consumption of food in a closed economy, where the animal determines the initiation, termination, and rate of execution of its own bouts of feeding (i.e., meals). This has allowed us to observe the interplay among costs, values, and quantity and quality of intake. The boundary conditions in this path-independent economy appear to be time, energy, and total income. The animals choose those behaviors and items that maximize calories and nutritive quality relative to the time and energy spent performing or obtaining them. While it was not possible to demonstrate that these choices were the most efficient, it was possible to show that they were efficient in the sense that they were less expensive or more valuable than the measurable alternatives.

To study feeding behavior as the model of choice behavior more generally, one must recognize that choice of either behaviors or items cannot be understood without examining the entire feeding chain of the animal being studied. Moreover, one must recognize that animals have specialized both morphologically and behaviorally for the exploitation of available resources. A complete understanding of the determinants of choice requires an understanding of the evolutionary history of the organism—its physiology, its ecology, its nutritional requirements, and its behavioral adaptations—and of the current status of its habitat. Finally, one must recognize that animals must continually choose from among a variety of survival-related activities "which" to perform, "when," and "for how long." Feeding is only one of the activities requisite for fitness. What motivates an animal is the evolutionary requirement that time and energy be allocated optimally among the various survival-related activities in which it must engage. From this we conclude that choice is best understood in terms of the function it serves in assuring the animal's fitness within the niche it occupies.

REFERENCES

Adolph E. F. Thirst and its inhibition in the stomach. *American Journal of Physiology*, 1950, **161**, 374–386.

Adolph, E. F. Intakes are limited: Satieties. *Appetite*, 1980, **1**, 337–342.

Allison, J., Miller, M., & Wozny, M. Conservation in behavior. *Journal of the Experimental Analysis of Behavior*, 1979, **25**, 185–198.

Armstrong, S., Clarke, J., & Coleman, G. Light-dark variation in laboratory rat stomach and small intestine content. *Physiology and Behavior*, 1978, **21**, 785–788.

Barofsky, I., & Hurwitz, D. Within-ratio responding during fixed ratio performance. *Psychonomic Science*, 1968, **11**, 263–64.

Bell, R. H. V. A grazing ecosystem in the Serengeti. *Scientific American*, 1971, **225**, 86–93.

Bernstein, D., & Ebbesen, E. B. Reinforcement and substitution in humans: A multiple response analysis. *Journal of the Experimental Analysis of Behavior*, 1978, **30**, 243–253.

Bolles, R. *Theory of motivation* (2nd ed.). New York: Harper & Row, 1975.

Brobeck, J. Neural regulation of food intake. *Annals of the New York Academy of Sciences*, 1955, **63**, 44–55.

Brody, S. *Bioenergetics and growth*. New York: Reinhold, 1945.

Canby, T. Y. The rat: Lapdog of the devil. *National Geographic*, 1977, **152**, 60–86.

Cannon, W. B. *The wisdom of the body*. New York: Norton, 1932.

Castonguay, T. W. The effects of acquisition cost on dietary component selection in the rat. Ph.D. diss., Rutgers University, 1978.

Collier, G. Consummatory and instrumental responding as functions of deprivation. *Journal of Experimental Psychology*, 1962, **64**, 410–414.

Collier, G. Thirst as a determinant of reinforcement. In M. J. Wayner (Ed.), *Thirst—First international symposium on thirst in the regulation of body water*. New York: Pergamon Press, 1964.

Collier, G. Body weight loss as a measure of motivation in hunger and thirst. *Annals of the New York Academy of Science*, 1969, **157**, 594–609.

Collier, G. An ecological analysis of motivation. In F. Toates & T. Halliday (Eds.), *Analysis of motivational processes*. London: Academic Press, 1980.

Collier, G. Life in a closed economy: The ecology of learning and motivation. In M. D. Zeiler & P. Harzem (Eds.), *Advances in analysis of behavior*. Vol. 3. *Biological factors in learning*. London: Wiley, in press.

Collier, G., & Hirsch, E. Nutrient factors as determinants of sucrose ingestion. In J. M. Weiffenbach (Ed.), *Taste and development: The genesis of
sweet preference.* Washington, D.C.: Superintendent of Documents,
Government Printing Office, 1977.

Collier, G., Hirsch, E., & Hamlin, P. The ecological determinants of reinforcement in the rat. *Physiology and Behavior,* 1972, **9,** 705–716.

Collier, G., Hirsch, E., & Kanarek, R. The operant revisited. In W. K. Honig
& J. E. R. Staddon (Eds.), *Handbook of operant behavior.* New York:
Prentice-Hall, 1977.

Collier, G., & Jennings, W. Work as a determinant of instrumental performance. *Journal of Comparative and Physiological Psychology,* 1969, **68,**
659–662.

Collier, G. H., & Kaufman, L. W. The economics of magnitude of reinforcement. Paper presented at the meeting of the Psychonomic Society,
Washington, D. C., November 1977.

Collier, G., Leshner, A. I., & Squibb, R. L. Self-selection of natural and
purified dietary protein. *Physiology and Behavior,* 1969, **4,** 83–86.

Collier, G., & Levitsky, D. Defense of water balance in rats: Behavioral and
physiological responses to depletion. *Journal of Comparative and Physiological Psychology,* 1967, **64,** 59–67.

Collier, G. H., Levitsky, D., & Squibb, R. L. Instrumental performance as a
function of the energy content of the diet. *Journal of Comparative and
Physiological Psychology,* 1967, **64,** 68–72.

Collier, G., & Rega, F. Two-bar sucrose preference. *Learning and Motivation,* 1971, **2,** 190–194.

Collier, G. H., & Rovee-Collier, C. K. A comparative analysis of optimal
foraging behavior: Laboratory simulations. In A. C. Kamil & T. Sargent
(Eds.), *Foraging behavior: Ecological, ethological, and psychological approaches.* New York: Garland STPM Press, 1980.

Collier, G. H., & Rovee-Collier, C. K. An ecological perspective of reinforcement and motivation. In E. Satinoff & P. Teitelbaum (Eds.), *Handbook of behavioral neurobiology: Motivation.* New York: Plenum, in press.

Collier, G., & Willis, F. N. Deprivation and reinforcement. *Journal of
Experimental Psychology,* 1961, **62,** 377–384.

Curio, E. *The ethology of predation.* New York: Springer-Verlag, 1976.

Davis, J. D., Collins, B. J., & Levine, M. W. Peripheral control of meal size:
Interaction of gustatory stimulation and postingestinal feedback. In D.
Novin, W. Wyrwicka, & G. Bray (Eds.), *Hunger: Basic mechanisms and
clinical implications.* New York: Raven Press, 1976.

deCastro, J. M. Meal pattern correlations: Facts and artifacts. *Physiology and
Behavior,* 1975, **15,** 13–15.

Emlen, J. M. The role of time and energy in food preference. *The American
Naturalist,* 1966, **100,** 611–617.

Fantino, E., & Navarick, D. Recent developments in choice. In G. H. Bower
(Ed.), *The psychology of learning and motivation* (Vol. 8). New York:
Academic Press, 1974.

Ferster, C. B., & Skinner, B. F. *Schedules of reinforcement.* New York: Appleton-Century-Crofts, 1957.

Hamilton, C. L. Ingestion of nonnutritive bulk and wheel running in the rat. *Journal of Comparative and Physiological Psychology,* 1969, **69**, 481–484.

Heinrich, B. *Bumblebee economics.* Cambridge: Harvard University Press, 1979.

Hill, W., Castonguay, T. W., & Collier, G. Taste or diet balancing? *Physiology and Behavior,* 1980, **24**, 765–767.

Hill, W. L., & Collier, G. H. The economics of response rate as a feeding strategy. Paper presented at the meeting of the Eastern Psychological Association, Washington, D.C., April 1978.

Hirsch, E., & Collier,G. The ecological determinants of reinforcement in the guinea pig. *Physiology and Behavior,* 1974, **12**, 239–249. (a)

Hirsch, E., & Collier, G. Effort as a determinant of intake and patterns of drinking in the guinea pig. *Physiology and Behavior,* 1974, **12**, 647–655. (b)

Hirsch, E., & Collier, G. Motivational control of dietary selection in the rat. Paper presented at the meeting of the Psychonomic Society, Denver, November 1975.

Holling, C. S. The analysis of complex population processes. *Canadian Entomology,* 1964, **96**, 335–347.

Hursh, S. R. Economic concepts for the analysis of behavior. *Journal of the Experimental Analysis of Behavior,* 1980, **34**, 219–238.

Hutchinson, G. F. Homage to Santa Rosalia; or, Why there are so many kinds of animals. *The American Naturalist,* 1959, **93**, 145–149.

Jensen, G. Optimality models of choice: Laboratory simulations. Master's thesis, Rutgers University, 1980.

Kamil, A. C. Systematic foraging by a nectar-feeding bird, the Amakihi (*Loxops virens*). *Journal of Comparative and Physiological Psychology,* 1978, **92**, 388–396.

Kanarek, R. B. Availability and caloric density of the diet as determinants of meal patterns in cats. *Physiology and Behavior,* 1975, **15**, 611–618.

Kanarek, R. B. Energetics of meal patterns in rats. *Physiology and Behavior,* 1976, **17**, 395–399.

Kanarek, R. B., & Collier, G. Patterns of eating as a function of the cost of the meal. *Physiology and Behavior,* 1979, **23**, 141–145.

Katz, P. L. A long-term approach to foraging optimization. *The American Naturalist,* 1974, **108**, 758–782.

Kaufman, L. W. Foraging strategies: Laboratory simulations. Ph.D. diss., Rutgers University, 1979.

Kaufman, L. W., & Brashier, D. Optimal feeding in chickens. Paper presented at the meeting of the Eastern Psychological Association, Washington, D.C., March 1978.

Kaufman, L. W., & Collier, G. The economics of seed handling. *The American Naturalist,* 1981, **118**, 46–60.

Krebs, J. R. Optimal foraging: Decision rules for predators. In J. R. Krebs &

N. B. Davies (Eds.), *Behavioral ecology.* Sunderland, Mass.: Sinauer Associates, 1978.

LeMagnen, J. Advances in studies on the physiological control and regulation of food intake. In E. Stellar & J. M. Sprague (Eds.), *Progress in physiological psychology* (Vol. 4). New York: Academic Press, 1971.

Levitsky, D. A., Faust, I., & Glassman, M. The ingestion of food and the recovery of body weight following fasting in the naive rat. *Physiology and Behavior,* 1976, **17**, 575–580.

MacArthur, R. H., & Pianka, E. R. On the optimum use of a patchy environment. *The American Naturalist,* 1966, **100**, 603–610.

Marwine, A. G., & Collier, G. H. The rat at the waterhole. *Journal of Comparative and Physiological Psychology,* 1979, **93**, 391–402.

Mazur, J. E., & Logue, A. W. Choice in a "self-control" paradigm: Effects of a fading procedure. *Journal of the Experimental Analysis of Behavior,* 1978, **30**, 11–17.

McCleery, R. H. Optimal behaviour sequences and decision making. In J. R. Krebs & N. B. Davies (Eds.), *Behavioral ecology.* Sunderland, Mass.: Sinauer Associates, 1978.

McFarland, D. L. Time-sharing as a behavioral phenomenon. In D. S. Lehrman, J. S. Rosenblatt, R. A. Hinde, & E. Shaw (Eds.), *Advances in the study of behavior* (Vol. 5). New York: Academic Press, 1974.

McFarland, D. L. Decision making in animals. *Nature,* 1977, **269**, 15–21.

Messing, B. R., & Campbell, B. Effect of nonnutritive bulk and food deprivation on wheel-running activity of vagotomized rats. *Journal of Comparative and Physiological Psychology,* 1971, **77**, 403–405.

Milton, K. Food choice and digestive strategies of two sympatric primate species. *The American Naturalist,* 1981, **117**, 496–505.

Mrosovsky, N., & Sherry, D. F. Animal anorexias. *Science,* 1980, **207**, 837–842.

Musten, B., Peace, D., & Anderson, G. H. Food intake regulation in the weanling rat: Self-selection of protein and energy. *Journal of Nutrition,* 1974, **104**, 563–572.

Novin, D., Wyrwicka, W., & Bray, G. (Eds.). *Hunger: Basic mechanisms and clinical implications.* New York: Raven Press, 1976.

Oatley, K. *Perceptions and representations.* New York: Free Press, 1978.

Olton, D. S. Mazes, maps, and memory. *American Psychologist,* 1979, **34**, 583–596.

Panksepp, J. Reanalysis of feeding patterns in the rat. *Journal of Comparative and Physiological Psychology,* 1973, **82**, 78–94.

Pianka, E. R. *Evolutionary ecology* (2nd ed.). New York: Harper & Row, 1978.

Pulliam, H. R. On the theory of optimal diets. *The American Naturalist,* 1974, **108**, 59–74.

Pyke, G. H. Humming-bird foraging on artificial inflorescences. *Behavioral Analysis Letters,* 1981, **1**, 11–15.

Pyke, G. H., Pulliam, H. R., & Charnov, E. L. Optimal foraging: A selective review of theory and tests. *Quarterly Review of Biology*, 1977, **52**, 137–154.

Rachlin, H., & Green, L. Commitment, choice and self-control. *Journal of the Experimental Analysis of Behavior*, 1972, **17**, 15–22.

Richter, C. P. Animal behavior and internal drives. *Quarterly Review of Biology*, 1927, **2**, 307–343.

Richter, C. P. Total self-regulatory functions in animals and human beings. *Harvey Lectures*, 1942, **38**, 63–103.

Rovee-Collier, C. K., Clapp, B. A., Collier, G., & Raabe, J. The economics of food choice in domestic chicks: When or what to eat? Paper presented at the meeting of the Eastern Psychological Association, New York City, April 1981.

Rozin, P., & Kalat, J. W. Specific hungers and poison avoidance as adaptive specializations of learning. *Psychological Review*, 1971, **78**, 459–486.

Schaller, G. B. *The Serengeti lion: A study of predator-prey relations*. Chicago: University of Chicago Press, 1972.

Schoener, T. W. Theory of feeding strategies. *Annual Review of Ecology and Systematics*, 1971, **2**, 369–404.

Skinner, B. F. The concept of the reflex in the description of behavior. *Journal of General Psychology*, 1931, **5**, 427–458.

Skinner, B. F. Drive and reflex strength. *Journal of General Psychology*, 1932, **6**, 22–37. (a)

Skinner, B. F. Drive and reflex strength, II. *Journal of General Psychology*, 1932, **6**, 38–48. (b)

Skinner, B. F. *The behavior of organisms*. New York: Appleton-Century-Crofts, 1938.

Skinner, B. F. A case history in scientific method. *American Psychologist*, 1956, **11**, 221–233.

Squibb, R. L., & Collier, G. H. Feeding behavior of chicks under three lighting regimens. *Poultry Science*, 1979, **58**, 641–645.

Sunday, S. A meal pattern analysis of dietary self-selection in the developing rat. Master's thesis, Rutgers University, 1977.

Sunday, S. Feeding strategies in five hystricomorph rodents. Ph.D. diss., Rutgers University, 1981.

Tang, M., & Collier, G. Effect of successive deprivations and recoveries on the level of instrumental performance in the rat. *Journal of Comparative and Physiological Psychology*, 1971, **74**, 108–114.

Tanner, J. M. Relationships of different bodily tissues during growth and in the adult. In G. E. W. Wolstenholme & M. O'Connor (Eds.), *Diet and bodily constitution*. Boston: Little, Brown, 1964.

Weiss, P., & Kavanau, J. L. A model of growth control in mathematical terms. *Journal of General Physiology*, 1957, **41**, 1–47.

Wilets, I. F. Moonlighting: Is eating in the dark necessary? Paper presented at the meeting of the Eastern Psychological Association, New York City, April 1981.

Wilson, E. O. *Sociobiology*. Cambridge: Harvard University Press, 1975.

Young, P. T. *Motivation and emotion*. New York: John Wiley, 1961.

Absolute and Relative Consumption Space[1]

Howard Rachlin

*State University of New York
at Stony Brook*

T his article summarizes and extends a psychological theory of behavior based on maximization that, unlike classical theories of behavior, is not reducible to physiological terms. Because psychology, especially behavioral psychology, has roots in reflexology and association, theories of learning have generally been both physiological and associational. Like the prototypical associationist David Hartley, the learning theorists in the early part of this century seemed unsatisfied with a theory unless it was paralleled by (or reducible to) a mechanism, usually a physiological mechanism. An exception to this trend was Tolman, who avoided physiologizing (or "neural mythology"), but who also avoided, it seems, postulating any coherent theory, being satisfied with rebuttals to Hull and an eclectic viewpoint that admitted the possible correctness of several theories of learning, none of them well defined (Tolman, 1949).

Skinner (1950) has argued against physiological reductionism but has simultaneously resisted all theorizing, even of a nonphysiological variety. His early theory of *reflex reserve* was later abandoned. His book written with Ferster, *Schedules of Reinforcement* (Ferster and Skinner, 1957), presents no theory of schedules of reinforcement (except a vaguely articulated notion, developed more precisely by Anger, 1956, and Shimp, 1967, that reinforced interresponse times tend to be repeated). If it had contained a theory, *Schedules of Reinforcement* could have been a much shorter book. It would have enabled the reader, from a set of general principles, to predict the performance of a pigeon exposed to a given schedule of reinforcement. The repetition upon repetition of cumulative records for each schedule of reinforcement would not have been necessary.

The more recent pattern in theorizing about behavior is to con-

1. This research was supported by a grant from the National Science Foundation.

struct an explanation about a circumscribed set of facts and then extend it over a wider range of facts. Various theories of reinforcement (Premack, 1965), of activity (Killeen, this volume), of timing (Gibbon, 1977), and of association (Rescorla and Wagner, 1972) have been or can be extended in such a way. In extending a behavioral theory, no predictions need be made on a physiological (or cognitive) level. When properly used, such theories are used to predict behavior under one set of conditions from behavior under another set. They need say nothing about events inside the head, physiological or otherwise.

The theory presented here is another tentative step at such an extension. Besides having obvious connections with the approaches of Herrnstein, Staddon, and McFarland (see Staddon, 1980, for a recent collection of such theories), the present theory also borrows from the earlier work of Lewin (1938). As Lewin did, I consider an organism as a point in a special kind of space wherein various environmental forces act on it to propel it this way and that. Lewin called this a life-space; it has also been called a behavior space, a state space, and a commodity space, but here I use the term *consumption space*.[2]

Consumption Space

Every commodity an organism consumes can be considered as a direction defined by an axis in consumption space. As the commodity is consumed, the organism may be thought of as moving positively in that direction at a speed proportional to consumption. But commodities also may be depleted. As the commodity is withheld, a deficit accumulates, which is assumed to grow with time. Thus as time passes the animal moves negatively in consumption space at a speed that varies depending on the commodity and the organism. With respect to each commodity, the animal is seen as a "leaky" repository, continuously losing the commodity and periodically replenishing losses and stocking up for the future.[3] For simplicity I will henceforth illustrate points using two or three dimensions, but what is said may apply to spaces of more dimen-

2. Unlike Lewin, I do not suppose that there exists inside the organism a *personality space* in which various events take place unobservable from the outside.

3. This representation follows Silby and McFarland (1974). Their analysis (still more molecular than mine) attempts to account for individual bouts of the two consumption activities.

sions. Figure 1 shows a space of two dimensions corresponding to consumption of two commodities, A and B. At an instant of time the organism (at point P) may be consuming A and B at rates r_A and r_B. Simultaneously, commodities A and B are being depleted at rates s_A and s_B. The notion that a commodity is depleted implies that the motivation to consume the commodity changes with time. For instance, the passage of time tends to increase consumption of the commodity water. Drinking, of course, counteracts this tendency, but the tendency is always there and may vary with conditions (such as temperature).

Rates of consumption and depletion can be represented by vectors acting on the point. Movement of the point in consumption space is the resultant of the vectors. We will call the path taken by

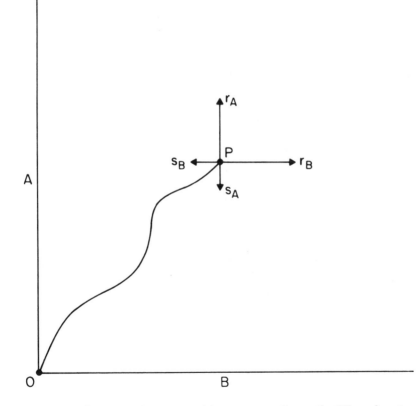

Figure 1. Consumption space with a consumption path, OP, and vectors representing consumption and depletion.

the point (*OP* in Figure 1) a *consumption path*. Of course the representation in Figure 1 is an abstraction and simplification. If A and B were food and water and the organism were a rat, consumption would occur alternately because a rat does not normally eat and drink simultaneously. Also, the rate at which a rat drinks water at any instant is relatively fixed at about 6 licks per second; a similar all-or-none pattern is frequently found with eating. So, a rat at any instant would be either eating or drinking (not both) and then would be eating or drinking at a fixed rate or not at all. Still further, eating and drinking tend to occur in bouts or "meals" (Collier, Hirsch, and Kanarek, 1977; Collier, this volume). The vectors r_A and r_B representing rates of eating or drinking are assumed to apply simultaneously and to be continuously variable. Thus conditions at an "instant" of time in the diagram of Figure 1 must actually be measured over a finite span of time during which consumption of commodities is integrated. The phenomenon of integration of consumption over time will be discussed again later, but even to construct the representation of Figure 1 some integration must be assumed.

The consumption space of Figure 1 is an *absolute consumption space*. Each point in that space represents an amount of A and an amount of B that has been consumed but not yet depleted. For instance, if a rat in an experimental chamber were drinking freely available water and eating freely available food, we can assume $r_A > s_A$ and $r_B > s_B$. The resultant of the four vectors, which determines the movement of the point, would be directed upward to the right—and the point would move upward to the right at a rate given by the length of the resultant. If the rat were then removed from the experimental chamber and put in its home cage without food or water, r_A and r_B would both be suddenly reduced to zero; the resultant of the vectors would point downward to the left, and the point representing the rat would move in that direction. The next day, when the rat was again put into the experimental chamber, with food and water, the point would move upward to the right again. Then, back in its home cage—downward to the left again, and so on. The space defined by the commodities is always there, and the point always has some position in that space—24 hours a day.

Standard experimental techniques with animals, keeping them at 80% of normal body weight or deprived of water for 23 hours, are designed (in terms of this representation) to begin each experimental session at the same point in absolute consumption space. The brevity of the typical experimental session relative to the time

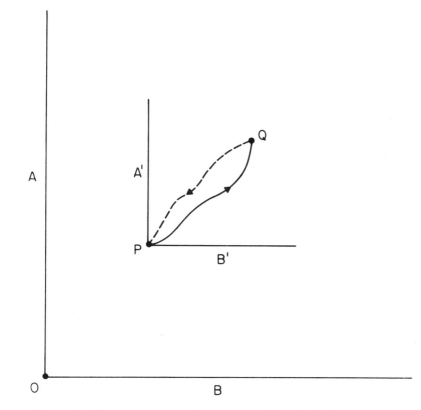

Figure 2. Absolute consumption space *A–B* and relative consumption space *A'–B'*. A consumption path *PQ* taken during an experimental session (*solid line*) and a return path *(QP)* assumed to occur between sessions are shown in relative consumption space.

in the home cage is designed to minimize the effects of s_A and s_B so that measured consumption (i.e., "amount of reinforcement") is the only significant variable. I will presently discuss whether such attempts have been successful.

Figure 2 shows an absolute consumption space *A–B* and the organism at point *P* in the space. Suppose *P* represents a rat at 80% of normal weight and 23 hours deprived of water. During the session, consumption of food (*A*) and water (*B*) brings the rat to point *Q*. The presumption behind daily brief experimental sessions is that s_A and s_B, acting over the 23 hours between sessions, bring the rat back to the conditions of deprivation that had obtained at the start so that next day it begins again at point *P*. Experimental sessions thus create a relative consumption space *A'–B'*, as Figure 2 shows. Henceforth I will indicate when I am discussing absolute consumption space and when I am discussing a relative consumption space within the absolute space. The distinction is important; Hursh (1980) has shown that experimental results can be quite different depending on whether they are obtained in absolute consumption space (sessions running 24 hours a day) or relative consumption space (brief daily sessions).

Figure 3a shows two consumption paths for a single rat in a relative consumption space. The curves show consumption under two conditions of deprivation in effect in the home cage at different times: water deprivation (23 hours) and food deprivation (80% of normal weight). The origin of the axes represents the start of the session. Sessions were run once a day for 45 minutes. During experimental sessions the rat pressed a lever for food pellets; each press was immediately followed by the delivery of three pellets (a continuous reinforcement schedule). A drinking tube was continu-

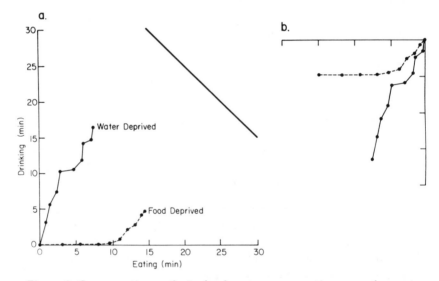

Figure 3. Consumption paths in food-water consumption space for a rat that was separately food- and water-deprived. The origin of graph 3a represents the beginning of a session. The points represent consumption during successive 5-minute periods. The diagonal line is part of graph 3a and represents the sum of eating and drinking times totaling 45 minutes, the session time. Graph 3b shows the same consumption paths as graph 3a but joined at their end points rather than their starting points. The end points, at satiation, are more likely than the starting points, at different deprivations, to represent a single state of the animal.

ously available. Each point on the consumption path represents cumulative eating (on the x axis) and drinking (on the y axis) for 5-minute periods. In drawing the consumption paths, depletion during the 45 minutes was assumed to be negligible ($s_A = s_B = 0$). Thus the abscissa and ordinate of the first point on a given path represent actual consumption of food and water during the first 5 minutes; the corresponding values of the second point represent actual consumption of food and water during the first 10 minutes, and so on, until the last point, which represents total consumption of food and water during the 45=minute session. Each point is the average consumption of five sessions. Thus the curves are smoother (less stepwise, or "mealwise") than they would be for individual sessions.

Both axes of Figure 3a were rescaled in temporal terms; that is, it was assumed that each lick at the water tube took .25 second and consumption of each pellet took 3.5 seconds. The temporal rescaling allows comparison of eating and drinking in the same units and also permits estimation of how much time was spent at activities other than eating and drinking. The diagonal line running downward to the right in Figure 3a is the locus of points where the sum of time spent eating and time spent drinking totals 45 minutes, the duration of the session. That the last point on the consumption path falls well below that line in both cases indicates that the rat spent considerable time at these other activities under both conditions of deprivation. Examination of the curves reveals that, well before the 45-minute session was over, the rat engaged in other activities. Even during the very first 5 minutes of the session the rat (deprived of food or water) did not consistently eat or drink and do nothing else; as the session progressed, other activities began to take up more and more time. This is shown by the fact that the points on each of the two curves are closer together toward the end of the session.

The appearance of other activities so early in the session indicates that it is not possible to study deprivation and consumption of a *single* commodity in isolation. We will see even more clearly later that an animal does not just make up for a deficit by consuming the deprived commodity only, even when it becomes freely available. Rather, it adjusts all its behavior at once. Deprivation of water affects eating—this is well known. But it may also affect all the rat's other activity (grooming, for instance). Thus it may not be possible to have a theory of eating or a theory of drinking in isolation. Any theory that purports to explain consumption (and this will be seen to include theories of reinforcement) would have to explain consumption in terms of all available commodities, not just the one the animal is deprived of outside an experimental chamber.

The consumption paths of Figure 3b are the same as those in Figure 3a, but they are joined at their terminal points rather than at their origins. Such a representation is more likely to reflect the relative positions of the two paths in absolute consumption space. The assumption behind this last statement is that the rat, in both cases of deprivation, is headed toward a single steady state of satiation. In such a state the vectors r_A and r_B would be constant and (still assuming $s_A = s_B = 0$) the consumption path would be a straight line. Skinner's (1938) early experiments with consumption of food by rats (deprived of food in their home cages) resulted in approximately linear consumption paths after 45 minutes of free access to food. Figure 4 shows the consumption path of the rat of Figure 3, deprived this time of both food and water (simultaneously) in its home cage and given free access to food and water in a 3-hour experimental session. The points in Figure 4 are averages of five sessions. Most of the curvature occurs before 45 minutes. Different conditions of deprivation in the home cage create different sets of vectors, hence different paths in absolute consumption space outside the experimental chamber. Thus, at the beginning of a session the rat would be at different points in absolute consumption space depending on the conditions of deprivation. During the 45-minute experimental session represented in Figure 3a, the rat

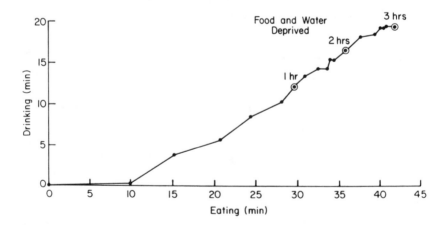

Figure 4. A consumption path for a rat deprived of both food and water at the same time. The experimental sessions lasted 3 hours.

was always treated identically (water and food both were freely available) regardless of its previous deprivation. Under such conditions consumption paths must tend to converge. The plot of Figure 3b is thus a more realistic picture of these paths in absolute consumption space than is that of Figure 3a.

I assumed that during the 45-minute sessions depletion (s_A and s_B) was effectively zero. I now reconsider that assumption, show that it is false in the present case, and see what can be done to correct for nonzero depletion during a brief session with constant conditions.

Figure 5 shows consumption paths for food deprivation and water deprivation of four rats plotted as in Figure 3b with terminal points together. A funnel-shaped pattern is evident in the functions.

At a certain more or less discrete point somewhere between 15 and 25 minutes after the beginning of the session, the two consumption paths become roughly collinear. Below that point they

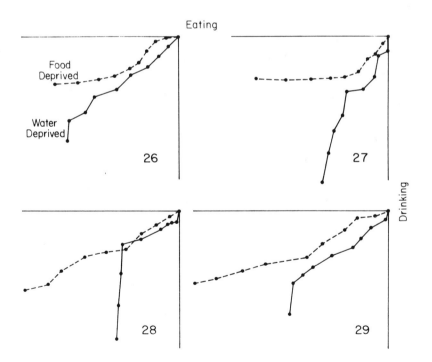

Figure 5. Consumption paths for four rats as in Figure 3b.

diverge: the water-deprivation curve bends downward rather sharply in two cases, less sharply in the other two cases; the food deprivation curve bends upward slightly in all cases. Above the bend the points representing 5-minute intervals in the session are closer together on the line. Below the bend the points representing 5-minute intervals are farther apart on the line. Figure 6a shows an average of the individual curves of Figure 5. (The end points and the points at which the lines bend are averages. The intermediate points, however, are assumed to lie on straight lines, equal distances apart.)

The rats with free access to both commodities during the 45-minute session first consumed the commodity of which they were relatively more deprived and then, when the deprivation was compensated for—after about 20 minutes of the session—settled down to normal consumption (with a secondary tendency to consume the *other* quantity a bit more during the latter part of the session—I will briefly discuss this slight but consistent tendency later). In the long run the rats must exactly balance depletion and consumption. Otherwise they would accumulate either infinite or zero amounts of the commodity. In absolute consumption space the consumption path should eventually reach a balance and then stop. The linearity of the consumption curves (45-minute and 3-hour) after the initial bend indicates that after this point balance was achieved. The reason the curve extends past the bend in the function in Figure 6a is that depletion has not been taken into account. If Figure 6a can be

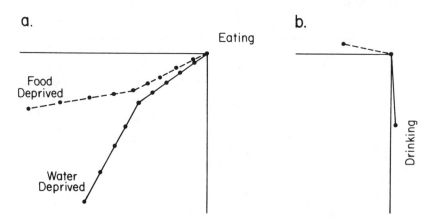

Figure 6. (a) Idealized set of consumption paths from Figure 5. (b) Consumption path with depletion subtracted.

considered a fair picture of an average rat's performance, it spent about 7 minutes eating and 4 minutes drinking during the last 25 minutes of the session compensating for depletion. This averages .28 minute eating and .16 minute drinking for each minute of the session. We assume that depletion occurred uniformly throughout the session. Subtracting appropriate fractions from each of the *first* 20 minutes of the session as well as each of the last 25 minutes, we get the net consumption curves of Figure 6b. This is as close as we can come to a representation in absolute consumption space. According to this representation, the hungry rat eats enough to compensate for depletion of food in the home cage, and the thirsty rat drinks enough to compensate for depletion of water in the home cage during the first 20 minutes of the session. Thereafter, the rat eats and drinks to compensate for ongoing depletion (standing still in absolute consumption space).

Figure 7 shows corresponding individual plots in absolute space for the four rats (assuming linearity and equal spacing of points on each branch of the consumption curve). Here, as in Sibly and McFarland (1974), depletion is subtracted from consumption. The deviation of the ends of the lines from the axes into the second and fourth quadrants was a consistent finding. The deviation of the food line indicates that as a hungry animal eats it loses ground with respect to drinking. The deviation of the water line indicates that as a thirsty animal drinks it loses ground in eating. This ground would presumably be made up later; my calculations of "normal" eating and drinking after the bend in the function of Figure 6a thus must be somewhat in error—animals deprived of food in their home cages would drink slightly more water, and animals deprived of water in their home cages would eat slightly more food during that period than would be required to balance depletion.

Values in Consumption Space

Consumption space and consumption curves in that space constitute a convenient method of representing behavior during an experimental session. This section presents the foundations of a theory by which behavior within that representation can be predicted.

The first and most critical assumption is that every point in absolute consumption space has a value and that these values, for a given organism at a given stage of development, are fixed. The point at which consumption and depletion are balanced is called a

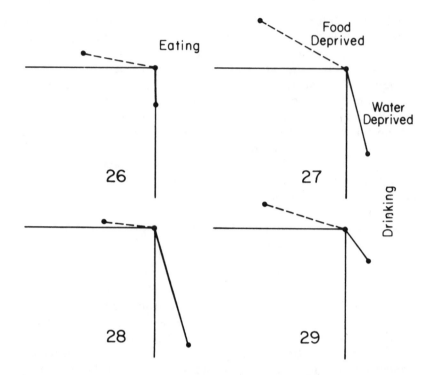

Figure 7. Consumption paths for four rats with depletion subtracted as in Figure 6b.

bliss point in absolute consumption space. If depletion is subtracted from consumption as in Figure 7, the bliss point is indeed a point. But if depletion is not subtracted the bliss point would actually be a *line* given by the resultant of the vectors r_A and r_B that just compensates for depletion. Let us call this line a *normal consumption path*.

Near the origin, there may be points that represent states at which life is impossible. With food and water, for instance, there must be a region of absolute consumption space that can truly be called a "life space," outside which the consumption path could not stray for long periods. Ultimately the values of the points in consumption space may correspond to physiological states, but no such correspondence is required by a behavioral theory.

Two tasks remain: to assign values to points in consumption space, and to describe how the consumption path moves from point to point.

Let us consider how values may be assigned to points. In both economics and psychology, a theory of the assignment of values to points in consumption space is a theory of utility. I consider two such theories here, one suggested in general form by Rachlin and Burkhard (1978) and more specifically formulated by Staddon (1979), and another also suggested by Rachlin and Burkhard (1978) and by Rachlin (1978). Staddon's suggestion is perhaps the simplest conceivable. According to it, there exists in consumption space a single point of highest value (the bliss point). All points at a given distance from the bliss point share the same value. Thus, as in Figure 8, a series of circular indifference contours of ever-de-

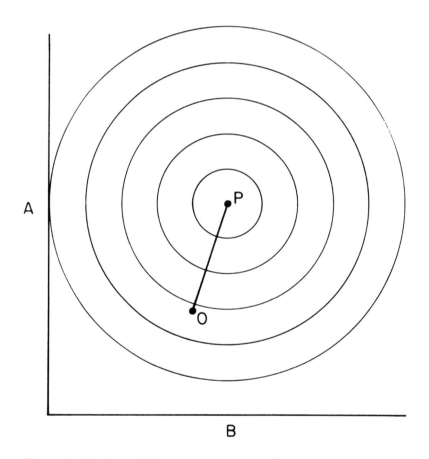

Figure 8. Circular indifference contours in absolute consumption space and consumption path *OP*, orthogonal to the contours.

creasing value can be drawn around the bliss point. All points on a single indifference contour have the same value. If one or both axes were rescaled, the circles would become ellipses. Since the scaling of the axes is to some extent arbitrary, Staddon's theory says that the indifference contours are ellipses of which circles are a special case. Along with this simple theory of value, let us consider a simple theory of consumption—that an organism consumes commodities A and B so as to move orthogonally across indifference contours. If we imagined the contours as altitude contours on a map, the bliss point would be the top of a hill. The consumption path in moving to the top perpendicular to the contours would always be taking the steepest (hence the shortest) available path up the hill. If the contours were indeed circles or ellipses, the consumption path would be a straight line, such as OP, leading to the bliss point from any other point in absolute consumption space. The straight-line paths drawn in Figure 7 are consistent with Staddon's theory. The utility equation (the equation of the contours) prescribed by this theory is the equation of an ellipse:

$$U = (y-pA)^2 + (x-qB)^2, \tag{1}$$

where A and B represent consumption of commodities in absolute consumption space, x and y are the coordinates of the bliss point, and p and q are conversion constants. It is important to bear in mind that by presuming the existence of a bliss point (rather than a normal consumption path) we also presume that depletion has been subtracted from consumption in drawing consumption paths.

SUBSTITUTABILITY

It is possible to consider indifference contours in such purely abstract terms as the circles, for instance, of Figure 8. A theory of behavior could be constructed with reference to nothing but such abstract figures. Yet it seems unlikely, to say the least, that the shape of indifference contours bears no relation to the nature of the commodities being consumed and the organism consuming them. We have evidence, in fact (Rachlin, Green, Kagel, and Battalio, 1976), that some quality of the commodities themselves determines the shape of the contours. This quality of commodities is their degree of substitutability for one another. Substitutability may, in turn, be due to similarity or sharing of common cognitive aspects (Tversky, 1972) or to ability to satisfy common drives. The underlying basis for substitutability does not concern us here. We are

concerned rather with how substitutability is represented by indifference contours—hence, how substitutability affects behavior.
At this point it is necessary to make a distinction between the
elasticity of substitution of two commodities and their marginal
rate of substitution. The former is reflected as the "sharpness" of
the contours. The latter refers to the slope of a contour at a particular
point. To illustrate the former, consider the following utility equation proposed by Rachlin, Kagel, and Battalio (1980):

$$U = pA^y + qB^y, \tag{2}$$

where A and B are the commodities consumed, p and q are constants
representing preference for A and B, and y is a constant that represents substitutability.

Figure 9 shows contours for values of y in Equation 2 of 1.0, .5,
−1.0, and −10.0 ($p = q = 1.0$).

As the parameter y varies downward from 1.0, the indifference

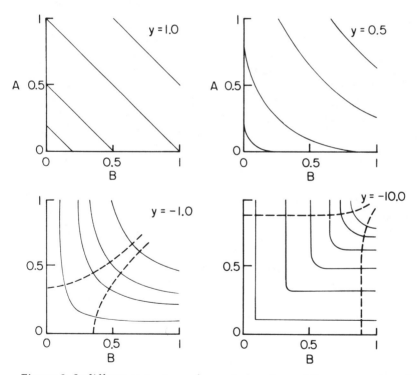

Figure 9. Indifference contours for various values of the exponent y of
Equation 2. The dotted lines are paths orthogonal to the contours.

contours change from straight lines to curved lines convex to the origin. The sharpness of the curve depends on the parameter y and the position of the indifference contour in consumption space. Consumption paths, orthogonal to the indifference contours, would be straight parallel lines at $y = 1.0$, curved lines pointing inward like the solid lines in the set of curves with $y = -1$, finally, at very low values of y, becoming straight again and near right-angled like the solid lines in the set of curves with $y = -10$.

These indifference contours contain no bliss point.[4] The consumption path increases indefinitely. Consumption is limited only by the time available. Thus Equation 2 is appropriate for data from sessions of limited duration from which depletion has *not* been subtracted. It is appropriate for the data of Figure 5 rather than those of Figure 7. Without actually attempting formal curve-fitting, it seems from Figures 5 and 9 that the constant n of Equation 2 would be negative, somewhere between -1 and -10. It is obvious that the kind of utility function that best fits the data will depend on whether those data represent absolute consumption or consumption minus depletion. If the data represent absolute consumption, the indifference contours *cannot* contain a bliss point (because once the bliss point was reached consumption would stop forever). If the data represent consumption minus depletion, the indifference contours *must* contain a bliss point (otherwise the organism would be continuously accumulating or continuously losing the commodity). Given a particular set of assumptions about depletion, it

4. Suppose depletion occurs in commodities A and B at rates s_A and s_B. We can define a new set of axes in consumption space, $\tilde{A}$ and $\tilde{B}$, such that:

$$\frac{d\tilde{A}}{dt} = \frac{dA}{dt} - s_A \; ; \; \frac{d\tilde{B}}{dt} = \frac{dB}{dt} - s_B \, .$$

In other words, the new axes (new variables) represent the old variables minus the rate of depletion. Integrating the above:

$$\tilde{A} = A - s_A T \; ; \; \tilde{B} = B - s_B T,$$

where T = the session time and A, $\tilde{A}$, B, $\tilde{B}$ are consumption over a session. Substituting into (utility) Equation 2:

$$U = p \, (\tilde{A} + s_A T)^y + q \, (\tilde{B} + s_B T)^y.$$

For a fixed session duration, $s_A T$ and $s_B T$ are constants. They define a point in absolute consumption space from which consumption curves would branch out. That is, they define a set of minima rather than a bliss point. If the constants p and q are replaced by z_A/y and z_B/y ($z > 0$, $y < 1$), economists will recognize the utility equation as a form of the constant elasticity of substitution (CES) function, where the elasticity of substitution is given by $1/(1-y)$. My colleagues and I (Rachlin, Battalio, Kagel, and Green, in press) are now studying the implications of this more complete equation for consumption. In this chapter I present the simplest form of the equation consistent with our purposes.

should be possible to convert from a utility equation based on absolute consumption to a utility equation based on consumption minus depletion. The mathematics of such conversions are beyond the scope of this paper and (at least for the present) of its author. I will avoid the mathematics henceforth by making no assumptions about depletion, presenting data in terms of absolute consumption and assuming indifference contours, such as those described by Equation 2 and illustrated in Figure 9, that contain no bliss points. With such contours, an animal beginning an experimental session at a given point in relative consumption space will approach a *normal consumption path* rather than a single bliss point. Although this procedure has the advantage of making no assumptions about depletion during an experimental session, hence no assumptions about the organism's internal state, it has the disadvantage of treating consumption during an experimental session differently from deprivation outside the session. Constant deprivation outside an experimental session is assumed to bring the animal back, between any two sessions, to the same point in absolute consumption space (as illustrated in Figure 2). A theory that included depletion (such as that of Silby and McFarland, 1974) would not need to make such a separation between intra- and intersession conditions.

LEISURE

The fact that in Figure 3a the consumption curve did not reach the diagonal line (which represents the locus of times summing to 45 minutes, the duration of the session) means that the rat represented spent a significant fraction of the session neither eating nor drinking. During the time it is not eating or drinking the rat obviously engages in many different activities. We have shown (Rachlin and Burkhard, 1978) that these other (unaccounted for) activities may be meaningfully represented by adding an additional dimension to the commodity space and treating all conceivable other activities as members of a single class—a sort of garbage-can commodity in itself. Here we call this commodity *leisure*.[5] Rachlin, Battalio, Kagel, and Green (in press) summarize some of the evidence that leisure behaves like other commodities. It is substitutable for such commodities as food and water, and as its price relative to those commodities is raised and lowered it is purchased in lesser and greater amounts. This evidence supports the notion that consumption of an

5. Herrnstein (1970) introduced the idea of such a garbage-can commodity. He called it r_e, the reinforcement for behavior other than the instrumental response. The variable r_e in the matching law analysis of behavior serves a function parallel to the function of leisure in the present analysis.

object in the environment (such as food or water) is an activity like any other. Eating and drinking thus are, like other operants (Skinner, 1938), *classes* of activities, delimited by their objects (the food or water).

The concept of *leisure* as an activity comes into use when we consider consumption of a single specific commodity such as food in a situation where other specific commodities are unavailable. If leisure is considered to be a commodity, we can think of food consumption as a choice between food and leisure and analyze such a choice just as we analyze the choice between food and water. This procedure provides a resolution for the traditional problem of the neo-Hullians, which was to relate single-alternative behavior (such as that exhibited by a rat in a straight alley) to choice behavior (such as that exhibited in a T-maze). A schedule of reinforcement of a single operant may be considered as another kind of choice behavior. Thus the laws and principles discovered in choice experiments may be extended to single-alternative experiments (or vice-versa).

How it is possible to relate choice with two commodities to choice with one commodity and leisure will become clearer after I show how all contingencies of reinforcement may be represented as constraints on movement of the consumption curve in consumption space.

Constraints

A consumption curve as it moves in consumption space is not normally free to move indefinitely. It is subject to constraints of various kinds on its movement. A major contention provided by theories of behavior now being developed in time allocation (Staddon, 1980) is that an instrumental contingency, or a schedule of reinforcement however complex, is essentially a delimiting of the area of consumption space (leisure considered as a commodity) within which the consumption path may move. There are many ways of applying constraints on behavior, of course, but there is only one way the constraints act—by limiting consumption.

TIME CONSTRAINTS

A fixed session time or a fixed time of observation constrains the consumption curve. Figure 10 shows a session-defined consumption space with commodities A and B. When a subject spends the entire session consuming A and B, the consumption curve will terminate on line ab, which represents the equation $A + B = T$, where T is the session duration. Figure 10b shows the constraint imposed in addition to the session constraint by simply limiting the availability of one commodity (A) and allowing the other (B) to be freely consumed. If A were food and B were leisure, Figure 10b represents the constraint imposed if a fixed amount of food were simply thrown into the experimental chamber. If the food were provided in small amounts at varying intervals during the session, the constraint would look like that of Figure 10c.

Where one of the commodities is leisure, which by definition exhausts the session, the constraint of Figure 10c can be determined in advance. But if the commodities are food and water, the consumption of which may not exhaust the session, the position of each step in consumption of commodity A will depend on consumption of commodity B, and the position of the steps (in two-dimensional space) will not be determinable in advance.

RATIO CONSTRAINTS

Figure 11a shows another kind of constraint demanding that A and B be consumed in a fixed ratio. For instance, if commodity A were food and commodity B were water and food and water were mixed together into an inseparable mush containing equal amounts of each, the consumption curve would be confined to the 45-degree line OP in Figure 11a. A less rigid constraint limits access to commodity A so that its consumption is no greater than a certain ratio to consumption of commodity B but allows less consumption of A than the ratio demands. This constraint is illustrated in Figure 11b.

If commodities A and B are like food and leisure in the sense that they exhaust the session, the ratio constraint of Figure 11b would be nothing but a continuous version of the time constraint of Figure

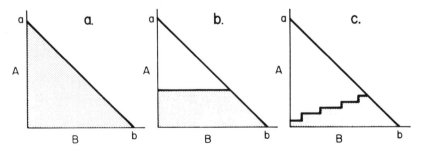

Figure 10. Various constraints (*shaded areas*) on available combinations of commodities A and B.

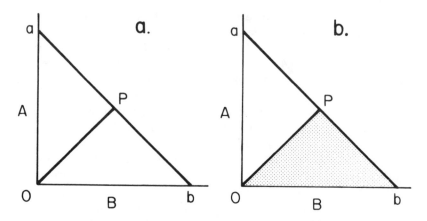

Figure 11. (a) Constraint imposed by fixing the ratio of commodity *A* to comodity *B*. (b) Constraint imposed by setting an upper limit on the ratio of cmmodity *A* to commodity *B*.

10c. If the ratio constraint were arranged so that a certain amount of *B* had to be consumed before a certain amount of *A* was provided (consumption of *A* and *B* exhausting the session), then a ratio constraint and a time constraint would be identical.

THE VALUE OF WORK ITSELF

In a Skinner box with a lever and a food magazine there are typically three responses to consider: consumption of the reinforcer; leisure; and operation of the manipulandum. Properly, one should consider these three responses in a three-dimensional space (see Rachlin and Burkhard, 1978), because all three responses have values relative to each other. It has nevertheless been possible to explain much behavior with concurrent and single-manipulandum schedules of reinforcement while ignoring the value of the instrumental response (work) itself and considering choice among various packages of eating and leisure (Rachlin, 1978). From this point of view the instrumental response is important in a positive sense only because food is contingent upon it and important in a negative sense only because while it is occurring leisure cannot be obtained. This ignores the value (negative with respect to food and leisure) of responding itself. With low rates of responding such a simplification may suffice (although low rates of work may be valued positively), but as rate of responding increases failure to consider the value of responding becomes more and more questionable (Rachlin, 1978).

DISCRETE TRIALS

The representational system I have been describing is designed to represent continuous behavior. Yet it is a general system and can, with the aid of certain assumptions, also apply to discrete trials. Consider a rat choosing between food and water at the ends of two arms in a T-maze. The rat's behavior may be divided into several responses: eating, drinking, leisure, and running. If running and leisure can be assumed to be the same on each trial, they may be ignored (not because they have no value but because, being the same on each trial, for each alternative, they cancel out), and the rat on a given trial may be considered to be choosing between two packages of so much eating versus so much drinking. Each trial then advances the rat a step on the eating or drinking dimension. Figure 12a shows the hypothetical results of eight trials with choices in the order E-D-E-D-D-D-D-E. What happens in the maze itself is ignored; only events in the goal box are considered to take up time. If each goal box contained both food and water but one contained a little more food and the other a little more water, the steps would lose their rectilinear character and become diagonal as in Figure 12b.[6]

The constraints in discrete trial experiments can be expressed in terms of the total number of trials and the size of the steps. Figure 12 ignores depletion between trials, but it would be possible to account for depletion with discrete trials, just as it could be accounted for with continuous consumption by moving the consumption curve downward and to the left as a function of time. It will be necessary to reconsider the sorts of choice diagramed in Figure 12 when we discuss self-control. Meanwhile let us turn to an application of the present model to the well-known experiment of Staddon and Simmelhag (1971).

The Staddon-Simmelhag Experiment

In 1971 Staddon and Simmelhag published a paper entitled "The Superstition Experiment: A Reexamination of Its Implications for

---

6. Of course the steps would still be rectilinear on a more molecular level as the rat ate and drank in a goal box.

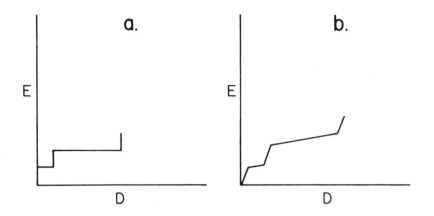

Figure 12. Constraints imposed by a T-maze on eating and drinking with (a) food in one goal box and water in another and (b) mixtures of food and water in both goal boxes.

the Principles of Adaptive Behavior." This paper was significant because its object was to incorporate "anomalous" findings, which at that time had been appearing frequently in the literature on animal behavior and animal learning (Seligman, 1970), into a general theory of behavior. Staddon and Simmelhag suggested revising general theories of behavior along more biologically oriented lines and abandoning the concept of reinforcement as the strengthening of a reflex. The theory presented here is in a large sense an outgrowth of their original suggestions. In this section I make no attempt to describe all the experiments, discuss all the data or trace all the theoretical lines of Staddon and Simmelhag's original paper. Rather, I will discuss one particular result, the result of the "superstition" experiment itself, and in a far from rigorous way try to explain it in terms of the present model. My object is not to provide evidence for any particular theory of utility but just to show how the model may be applied to this sort of data.

Staddon and Simmelhag repeated Skinner's (1948) original superstition experiment in which food was provided periodically to hungry pigeons. In one of their procedures food came at fixed intervals of 12 seconds; the food delivery consisted of 2-second access to a hopper. Thus a cycle lasted 14 seconds and consisted of 12 seconds without food and 2 seconds of eating; each daily session consisted of 64 cycles.

The pigeons were closely observed during the experiment, and 16 different activities were isolated that pigeons were capable of doing in the empty cage during the 12-second intervals between food deliveries. Each pigeon was monitored during each interval, and activities occurring at each second of the interval were observed. The experimenters found that the pigeons seemed to have two kinds of activity—interim activities, which began just after the food delivery ended, increased in frequency for a few seconds, reached their peak at about the middle of the interval, and then decreased in frequency, and terminal activities, which began late in the interval and reached their peak just when food was delivered. The character of the two kinds of activities was different. Interim activities seemed to be to some degree satisfying in themselves—preening, hunting for food on the floor, flapping wings, turning in circles. Terminal activities seemed to be preparatory for or to resemble eating—orienting to the wall where the food magazine was, and pecking the air or the wall of the cage. The experimenters felt that they could define two periods, an interim period just after food delivery and a shorter terminal period just before food delivery. Figure 13 shows the three activities in a typical cycle. The point of division between interim and terminal periods is not clearly defined, but one result was clear: when the intervals between food deliveries were not fixed at 12 seconds but varied from cycle to cycle, the terminal periods occupied a much greater proportion of each interval.

ANALYSIS OF STADDON AND SIMMELHAG'S FINDING

Let me first make a few casual observations. Because the pigeons were deprived of food we can assume that, were food freely available, the pigeons would have eaten for more than the permitted 2 seconds of the interval. Eating was the thing the pigeons in this experiment most preferred to do. But they did not just prefer to

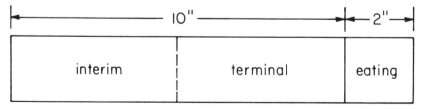

Figure 13. A cycle of the Staddon and Simmelhag (1971) experiment divided into interim, terminal, and eating periods.

eat—they preferred to first make a terminal response and then eat. It seems that the terminal response and eating are somehow better, more valuable, more preferred, if they occur together than if either occurs alone. I say this, first, because terminal responding did not occur when food was omitted. Thus terminal responding did not seem to be valuable in itself. Second, however, the pigeons seemed to go to great lengths to make terminal responses whenever food was expected. When food came at variable intervals, terminal responses were made throughout the session, at the expense of interim responses (which seem to have some slight value in themselves). Clearly, a critical factor is the timing of the terminal response. In terms of a consumption space I would say that a stepwise consumption curve consisting of a brief bout of terminal responding followed by eating is more valuable than the same amount of eating alone. I do not know the mechanism by which the terminal response enhances the value of eating. It may be that a brief period of terminal responding is always made willy-nilly before eating so that if food is presented during a period when interim responses are occurring, the time taken to make the terminal response would subtract from the food actually obtained or, at least, delay the food.

A hierarchy of values may be inferred:
1. Eating preceded by terminal responses.
2. Eating not preceded by terminal responses.
3. Interim responses.
4. Terminal responses by themselves.

According to Premack's (1965) theory of reinforcement, a response higher on such a hierarchy can reinforce a response lower on the hierarchy if the higher response is contingent on the lower. Thus, eating should reinforce terminal responses. Staddon and Simmelhag assert that terminal responses are equivalent to conditioned responses—that classical conditioning itself is nothing but the observation of terminal responses.

An economic analysis provides still another way of looking at this pattern of responses. According to an economic analysis, terminal responses and eating would have a low substitutability for each other. In other words, terminal responses and eating make each other more valuable—they are like two ingredients in an essential compound, relatively useless apart, relatively useful together. An example from everyday life would be the engine and the body of a car. A person with ten engines and no bodies would benefit by trading nine of the engines for one body (vice-versa for the person with ten bodies and no engines). The terminal response and eating, in other words, are much more valuable together than either is alone. In a utility equation such as Equation 2, y might be positive, but it would be small. We will consider eating and the terminal response as constituting a package. The interim response must then be considered as more or less substitutable for this package.

To be specific, let us symbolize the duration of the three responses (eating, interim, terminal) as E, I, and T. Let us suppose a unit cycle so that E, I and T represent fractions of the cycle summing to unity:

$$E + I + T = 1. \tag{3}$$

Now let us construct a set of utility equations like Equation 2 that would represent the above observations:

$$U = \left[E^y + qT^y\right]^v + rI^v. \tag{4}$$

Here E and T are considered to come together in a package with a mutual substitutability given by the exponent y. The interim response, I, is considered more or less substitutable for the package $E + T$ according to the exponent v. The form of the utility equation (4) represents a hierarchical model of choice like that of Tversky and Sattath (1979). (As more alternatives were taken into consideration, they would have to be placed in the hierarchy—grouped according to a tree-structure diagram. Ad hoc rules for such grouping are lacking at present.)

Let us now assign values for the constants roughly in accordance with these observations. To make the above rank ordering more specific, let us suppose that eating alone is 100 times as valuable as the terminal response alone (judging by their relative frequency when each is separately made available) and that the package of eating plus terminal responding is 4/3 as valuable as interim response alone ($p = 100\,q$; $r = .75$). Suppose that substitutability of interim responding for the package of terminal responding and eating is eight times the substitutability of terminal responding for eating ($v = 8\,y$). Then, we arbitrarily assign $q = 1$, $y = .1$. Thus:

$$U = \left[100\,E^{.1} + T^{.1}\right]^{.8} + .75I^{.8}. \tag{5}$$

Substituting $I = 1 - E - T$ from Equation 3 and setting $E = 2/14$ (2 seconds of the 14-second cycle), we can plot U (utility) as a function of T (the fraction of the cycle devoted to the terminal response). Figure 14 shows this plot. Of course the values of the constants we chose were arbitrary. But the shape of Figure 14 would be the same

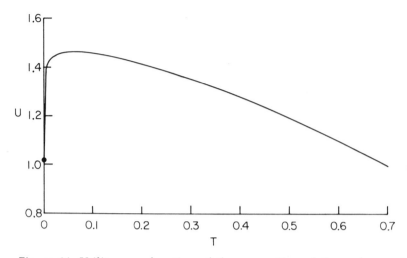

Figure 14. Utility as a function of the proportion of the cycle spent performing the terminal response, according to Equation 5.

over fairly wide ranges of constants as long as the relation between the two substitutabilities was about the same.

Maximum utility can be obtained at very low values of T. The maximum of this function is near $T = .1$ of the cycle. Note the sharp fall-off of utility below $T = .05$ as contrasted to the gradual fall-off above that point. Where there is uncertainty about food delivery, it is clearly less disastrous to increase terminal responding than to decrease it. With a completely random delivery of food, terminal responding could increase to completely displace interim responding (86% of the cycle, the rest spent eating), and utility would still not have decreased to its value with no terminal responding at all.

It follows from the above relation that the overall value of signaled food deliveries should be higher than the overall value of unsignaled food deliveries. With signaled food deliveries, terminal responding could be confined to the period of the signal and utility could remain high, as Figure 14 indicates. With unsignaled food deliveries, terminal responding would have to increase, with a concomitant decrease in utility. The signal in this sense is not valuable in itself or only because it allows an animal to prepare for the food (perform terminal responses); it is also valuable because it allows the animal time to perform interim responses. There is a fair amount of evidence that signaled reinforcers are indeed preferred to unsignaled ones (Bower, McLean, and Meacham, 1966; Badia, Ryan, and Harsh, 1981) and also, consistent with a symmetrical analysis that applies to aversive stimulation, that signaled shock is preferred to unsignaled shock (Badia, Culbertson, and Harsh, 1973). In the negative case, a shock delivered during a period of terminal responding would be less aversive than one delivered during a period of interim responding; the signaled shock would be more valuable both because of this fact and because interim responses could be performed (instead of the less valuable terminal responses) during the "safety" period.[7]

In this manner the economic model presented here forces one (as Collier, this volume, suggests) to focus on the organization of behavior as a whole rather than on the appearance or disappearance of a single response or the strengthening or weakening of a single reflex. With an economic model, context of reinforcement is not just tacked on but is an essential part of the allocation of behavior. Information provided by a signal is not just preparatory but allows for a total organization of all behavior (during an intermittent signal and in its absence) that is more valuable than the best organization possible without the signal.

Hill Climbing

I have assumed, generally, that in relative consumption space an organism starts out as a point at the origin and climbs a hill taking the steepest path possible. But at the very start I indicated that this was an abstraction and that even to assume a smooth consumption curve already involved some integration, some jumps over "rough spots."

A strict hill-climbing mechanism, whatever it might consist of, would be disastrous from the standpoint of survival of the organism that possessed it. Even a plant does not strictly follow movements of the sun in its orientation, nor do its roots respond to every tempo-

---

7. A pervasive finding apparently contradictory to this analysis is that delivery of food at variable intervals is preferred to delivery of food at equal rates but fixed intervals (Killeen, 1970). It would seem from the above analysis that fixed intervals allow more time for interim responding and should be preferred. The preference for variable intervals may be due to the occasional very short intervals and may be a problem of self-control at high levels of deprivation. (I will discuss self-control in the next section.) If so, exposure to fixed versus variable intervals of food over a long term, at high levels of satiation (by running sessions 24 hours a day) should reverse this preference.

rary increase in moisture. Rather, a degree of integration characterizes the behavior of all organisms, and, like an ocean liner that averages out small waves (as opposed to a rowboat that responds to each wave it encounters), organisms steer a steady course over a bumpy environment.

The necessity for integration of value is illustrated in the relative (session-defined) consumption space of Figure 15. Suppose consumption of commodities A and B exhausts all available time. As time progresses during a session we can imagine a line moving upward at a steady rate that indicates the locus of packages of A and B that can be obtained at that time. Say, for instance, that line 10–10 indicates the locus of packages that can be obtained at the end of 10 minutes (any combination of times of consumption of A and B that totals 10 minutes). At the end of 5 minutes, line 5–5 represents the locus of obtainable packages; at the end of 1 minute, line 1–1. These lines are time constraints. If the organism were maximizing utility at every moment, the point on the constraint line representing the package actually obtained would be at the tangent between the constraint line and an indifference contour. Suppose, as the principles of economic demand theory require (Newman, 1965), that there is only one such point of tangency for each constraint line. A conceivable set of such points is formed by the dots shown on each line of Figure 15. Now suppose the session is progressing and the organism consumes A and B so as to follow the dots from the origin to the circled point on line 5–5. To go farther, this hypothetical organism would have to give up some of commodity A. If the depletion rate of commodity A were low, this might take considerable time. Even if commodity B were consumed exclusively during that time, the depletion rate of commodity A might not be sufficient to bend the consumption curve downward to a sufficient degree. Even if a third activity were available, that activity might be of lower value than either A or B and thus reduce utility even more than would *any* combination of A and B, even submaximal combinations.

A fairly obvious solution to this dilemma is for the organism to consume commodities A and B in a constant ratio as indicated by the dotted line OP of Figure 15. To do this, the organism must ignore local maxima and head straight for the session maximum; point P. In other words, the organism must be able to integrate over the consumption space. A theory that postulates such integration need make no concession to mentalism. Plants and inanimate objects (even below the level of digital computers) can integrate in

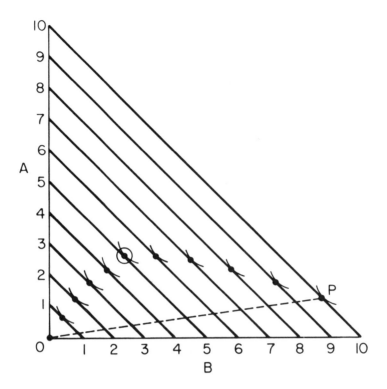

Figure 15. Constraints imposed by time within a session *(diagonal lines)* and combination of commodities A and B hypothesized to be of maximum utility for each constraint (points tangent to indifference contours). If the subject obtains the combination of A and B represented by the circled point, it conceivably could not obtain the combination labeled P at the end of the session. However, a subject that produced the consumption path represented by the dotted line OP would obtain the combination of A and B labeled P, higher in value than the circled point.

such a fashion. If variability of behavior is capable of occurring at the level of *paths* rather than discrete individual movements, integration can occur. With each exposure to the conditions defining a particular relative consumption space, a new path may be taken. With each new path a new level of utility is reached at the end. The organism may then be more likely to choose the highest utility.

The alert reader will have noticed that this is a form of reinforcement theory, a principle of learning; a high utility reinforces the path that leads to it. To avoid problems of reinforcement theory (Rachlin et al., in press), we may consider variability of behavior itself to vary inversely with utility. Where utility is high, variability is low and vice-versa. Thus behavior would vary widely in regions of low utility and tend to settle down in regions of high utility, producing the same effects that reinforcement would. What is reinforced, however, is not a reflex, a particular response, or an operant, but an entire mode of action, occurring over an extended time span. This mode of action is reinforced not by a discrete environmental event, but by the overall utility of all the actions and their consequences during the period in question. The reinforcer stamps nothing in; it merely tends to reduce variability of behavior much as Loeb's (1918) kineses tended to exert their effects on an animal's spatial path through variability. A wood louse, for instance, is not reinforced by the dark but is found in the dark because there its movements vary less. Similarly, an organism might take the dotted consumption path *OP* because *OP* was taken last time and its utility was high enough to reduce variability. Again, this follows the lines laid down by Staddon and Simmelhag (1971) who saw reinforcement not as a strengthening of behavior but as a failure to promote variation.

Having said this much, however, it would be foolish to conclude that any organism could integrate its behavior over any region of consumption space whatever. There must be limits. A way to characterize integration and its limits is to represent the organism not as a point in consumption space but as an irregular area (of unknown shape) with a point (representing a point in physical time) within it. The area extends around the point in all directions in consumption space. Figure 16 shows the implications of such a representation. An organism at point *P* that integrated utility would take the dotted consumption path *PR* without moving through point *Q*, higher in utility than point *P* but lower than point *R*.

SELF-CONTROL

With this way of representing behavior, self-control results from integration of utility over a relatively wide area of consumption space. Figure 17 shows a relative consumption space with eating and leisure as the commodities. A typical self-control experiment (Rachlin and Green, 1972) involves choice within a rigid set of constraints—the path *pqst* (involving a short period of delay, *pq*, and a relatively immediate reward, *qs*, then a long wait afterward,

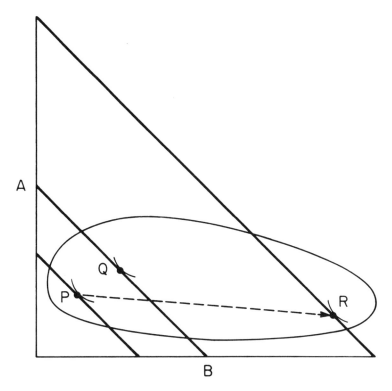

Figure 16. Area of integration that would allow consumption path *PR* to occur.

st) versus the path *pru* (involving a long delay, *pr* followed by a large reward, *ru*). By the end of a fixed period of time (represented by the diagonal line) the "self-control" alternative *pru* may well result in a higher utility than the alternative *pqst*. An organism at point *p* that integrates utility over an area encompassing point *u* would thus choose the self-control path. An organism with a smaller area of integration, which did not encompass point *u*, but only point *s*, would show lack of self-control.

The area of integration cannot be regarded as fixed, even for a given organism at a given time. It is tempting to regard the extent of such areas as a function of experience or of ontological or phylogenetic development (Rachlin, Battalio, Kagel, and Green, in press), or of normal as opposed to psychopathic behavior (as implied by Gorenstein and Newman, 1980). I hope some such extension of theory will be possible. But the integration of alternatives

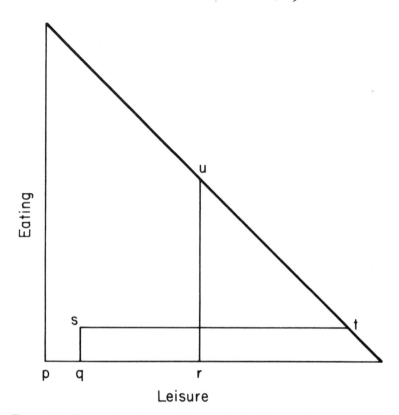

Figure 17. Constraints imposed by typical self-control experiment.

must also be a function of contingencies. Many organisms are capable of choosing between a pair of distant rewards that differ only in amount. Extending the segment *pq* of Figure 17 relative to *qr* can reverse the preference from *pqst* to *pru*. When both alternatives involve sudden shifts in utility at distant points, an organism that normally fails to integrate over that extent will consistently choose the larger of the two amounts. Thus an organism may be capable of integrating over large areas of consumption space and may do so under certain conditions but not others. It is not clear what causes such shifts. One possibility to consider is that integration itself involves a cost, a decrement in utility, that may be reduced with maturity or experience. Of course this is highly speculative, but it has the advantage over other speculative accounts of self-control (self-actualization, ego strength, private sidebets) of being descriptive rather than normative and of being easily related to experimental observation.

What the mechanism or mechanisms may be that actually accomplish these integrations is at present only a matter for speculation. A minimal requirement is a short-term memory for events that have just occurred. A longer-term memory is also necessary to integrate over areas of consumption space passed through previously (during previous experimental sessions) and now being traversed again. As when we travel on a familiar road, our long-term memory constitutes our expectancy of what is around the next bend, and our short-term memory is the signal (the "specious present") upon which this expectancy is based. Killeen's exponentially weighted moving average (Killeen, this volume) and Gibbon's (1977) scalar expectancy theory provide starting points for investigation of such mechanisms.

As an example of how they might work, let us consider how a much simplified short-term memory mechanism might apply to a familiar problem—behavioral contrast in multiple schedules of reinforcement. Suppose, for simplicity, that the power of an experience to affect current behavior does not decay exponentially as the experience recedes into the past (as Killeen suggests) but rather persists for a brief period (Δt) and then abruptly vanishes. The organism may be thought of not as a point in consumption space but as a window of width, Δt; all events in the window influence behavior. (It is evident that the notion of a window can replace the notion of depletion. As an event passes out of the window it is suddenly depleted to zero. Thus the supposedly cognitive mechanism of short-term memory has behavioral consequences similar to those of the supposedly motivational mechanism of depletion of a commodity. Both mechanisms define the active area of consumption space.)

Figure 18 illustrates the notion of the window. Suppose, as in the figure, that conditions have just changed (t_{VI} seconds ago) from extinction to variable-interval (VI) reinforcement. Suppose the rate of reinforcement programmed by the VI schedule is two per minute (VI 30 seconds) The subject behaves, now, so as to obtain a proportion of responding, eating, and leisure (that constitutes a package, within the window) that will maximize utility. Let us say that the package of maximum utility contains r seconds of responding, e seconds of eating, and l seconds of leisure, where $r+e+l = \Delta t$. We can use Equation 5 to calculate the proportions. Staddon and Simmelhag (1971), studying hungry pigeons pecking keys in a Skinner

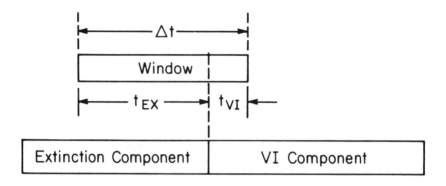

Figure 18. Subject as leading edge of window that has just passed from extinction to a variable-interval reinforcement in a multiple schedule.

box, found that the terminal response (emitted with no instrumental requirement) behaved similarly to the operant (instrumental response) when the operant was key-pecking and the reinforcers were brief presentations of grain. Thus, E, T, and I of Equation 5 may be replaced by e, r, and l of the present discussion. In my analysis of the Staddon and Simmelhag experiment, E (e) was fixed (at 2/14 of the cycle). In a VI schedule the relationship between e and r (the reward and the instrumental response) is fixed. This relationship is called a feedback function. There is some dispute about the form of this function for VI schedules, but the simple equation $e = ar^m$ will suffice for the present purposes. (The feedback function expresses a fixed value of e, as in Staddon and Simmelhag's experiment, by an exponent, $m = 0$. The coefficient a then equals the fixed reinforcement rate e.) For VI schedules $m = .1$ provides a fairly good approximation to data (Rachlin, 1978). The coefficient a is the fraction of the session that would be spent eating if the subject spent as much time as possible making the instrumental response. The coefficient (a) is proportional to the rate of reinforcement programmed by the variable-interval schedule. For a VI 30-second schedule of reinforcement with each reinforcement lasting 3 seconds, $a = 3/30 = .1$. Given the utility equation (Equation 5 with the same parameters used previously) and the feedback function, we can calculate the proportion of time on a VI 30-second schedule that would be spent eating (e), responding (r), and at leisure activities (l) for maximum utility. This proportion is $e = .09$; $r = .41$; $l = .50$. Thus, on a VI 30-second schedule, the subject can obtain 90% of the programmed reinforcement (obtained $e = .09$; programmed

$e = .10$) and still spend half its time on leisure activities (l max = .50).

During extinction, consumption of the reinforcer (e) is set at zero. According to Equation 5 (using the same parameters as before), the subject will maximize utility when $l = .9$ and $r = .1$. As I indicated before, during extinction r stands for terminal responses for which, during the VI 30-second schedule, the operant response is assumed to be substituted. Note that during extinction the proportion of time spent at r that maximizes utility is .1, whereas during the VI 30-second schedule that proportion rises to .41. If we assume that the signal marking the transition from extinction to VI-30 seconds is sufficiently salient to immediately generate the new proportion, an anomaly appears between long-term requirements and short-term contents at the moment of transition from extinction to VI. The long-term requirements demand a high proportion of r (.41), while the window actually contains a low proportion of r (.1). If the subject merely alters the rate of r (the operant response) from .1 to .41, the full increase in r will not be contained in the window until the entire window has passed out of the extinction component. But if the subject briefly accelerates beyond the new requirement, the proportion of r in the window can much more quickly be adjusted to its new value. To put it another way, during extinction the subject accumulates an excess of leisure (and a deficiency of r relative to the VI requirements). Upon switching to the VI, the subject "spends" the excess leisure. It gives up leisure so as to *quickly* obtain the new correct proportion of r, e, and l. A parallel situation is faced by a drive who wants to increase the speed of a car. If the driver just moves the accelerator from the old steady position to the new steady position, the car will accelerate slowly and eventually approach the new speed. But if the accelerator is depressed beyond its new position, the car will accelerate rapidly and quickly reach its new speed, whereupon the driver can ease up on the accelerator. The present model sees behavioral contrast as a similar process, a speeding up of responding so as to quickly reach a new steady balance between responding, leisure, and consumption of the food. With negative contrast the opposite is assumed to occur; the subject slows responding down below its asymptotic value so as to reach the new balance more quickly.

The above account of contrast sees the subject existing at the front edge of its window in physical time. That is, the contents of the window are entirely short-term memory. But, as I indicated previously, there is considerable evidence that, with training, subjects anticipate future conditions in current behavior. The area of integration in consumption space of Figure 16 extends into the future as well as into the past. With experience, the point representing the physical present must move backward from the front of the window; the subject behaves as if it had already obtained what it has yet to obtain. The subject is thus seen as sandwiched between immediate expectation and immediate memory. If this were so, by the same reasoning as above, behavioral contrast would appear at the end of the VI component—but it would not appear at the end as quickly as it would appear at the beginning—because immediate memory is assumed to form sooner than immediate expectation. But as expectation is formed, as the window advances in front of the subject in physical time, the leading edge of the window enters extinction before extinction has actually occurred, the subject experiences the reduction in r before such reduction is appropriate to current conditions, and the subject reacts by increasing r so as to restore the appropriate balance. Williams (1979) found such a late-developing positive contrast at the end of variable-interval components.[8] Again, the automobile analogy is relevant; the experienced driver speeds up or slows down *before* the conditions for doing so arrive.

Finally, it is worth saying again that the notion of a window (within which events remain at full strength) is a simplification. Events closer in time, in the past and in the future, are weighted more heavily than events further away. The moving window, if we can imagine such a thing, is clear only at its center—the point of the physical present—and must become progressively more smoky as the time from this point increases.

CONCLUSIONS

Behavior under free-consumption conditions, behavior under schedules of reinforcement, and behavior under complex contingencies involving periodic access to various commodities are all describable in terms of an underlying consumption space where points are assigned various values, a series of constraints on behavior in that space, and the assumption that behavior of organisms represents integration of areas within that space.

8. Collier (this volume) reports a similar effect with multiple-schedule "components" as long as a day. At the end of daily feeding periods birds store food in their crops and thus "tank up" in anticipation of a long extinction component to come.

Many of the speculations made here can be (and have been) expressed in quantitative terms as solutions to maximization problems. In this paper such mathematizations have been kept to a minimum partly for the sake of clarity and partly so the illusion of accuracy will not be conveyed where accuracy does not exist. Confirmation or disconfirmation of the statements made here will come only after more behavioral data are collected.

REFERENCES

Anger, D. The dependence of interresponse times upon the relative reinforcement of different interresponse times. *Journal of Experimental Psychology*, 1956, **52**, 145–161.

Badia, P., Culbertson, S., and Harsh, J. Choice of longer or stronger signalled shock over shorter or weaker unsignalled shock. *Journal of the Experimental Analysis of Behavior*, 1973, **19**, 25–32.

Badia, P., Ryan, K., and Harsh, J. Choosing schedules of signalled appetitive events over schedules of unsignalled ones. *Journal of the Experimental Analysis of Behavior*, 1981, **35**, 187–196.

Bower, G., McLean, J., and Meacham, J. Value of knowing when reinforcement is due. *Journal of Comparative and Physiological Psychology*, 1966, **62**, 184–192.

Collier, G., Hirsch, E., and Kanarek, R. The operant revisited. In W. K. Honig and J. E. R. Staddon (Eds.), *Handbook of operant behavior*. Englewood Cliffs, N.J.: Prentice-Hall, 1977.

Ferster, C. B., and Skinner, B. F. *Schedules of reinforcement*. New York: Appleton-Century-Crofts, 1957.

Gibbon, J. Scalar expectancy and Weber's law in animal timing. *Psychological Review*, 1977, **84**, 279–325.

Gorenstein, E. E., and Newman, J. P. Disinhibitory psychopathology: A new perspective and a model for research. *Psychological Review*, 1980, **87**, 301–315.

Herrnstein, R. J. On the law of effect. *Journal of the Experimental Analysis of Behavior*, 1970, **13**, 243–266.

Hursh, S. R. Economics and behavior analysis. *Journal of the Experimental Analysis of Behavior*, 1980, **2**, 219–238.

Killeen, P. Preference for fixed-interval schedules of reinforcement. *Journal of the Experimental Analysis of Behavior*, 1970, **14**, 127–133.

Lewin, K. *The conceptual representation and the measurement of psychological forces*. Durham, N.C.: Duke University Press, 1938.

Loeb, J. *Forced movements, tropisms and animal conduct*. Philadelphia: J. B. Lippincott, 1918.

Newman, P. *The theory of exchange*. Englewood Cliffs, N.J.: Prentice-Hall, 1965.

Premack, D. Reinforcement theory. In D. Levine (Ed.), *Nebraska Symposium on Motivation* (Vol. 13). Lincoln: University of Nebraska Press, 1965.

Rachlin, H. A molar theory of reinforcement schedules. *Journal of the Experimental Analysis of Behavior*, 1978, **30**, 345–360.

Rachlin, H., Battalio, R., Kagel, J., and Green, L. Maximization theory in behavioral psychology. *Behavioral and Brain Sciences*, in press.

Rachlin, H., and Burkhard, B. The temporal triangle: Response substitution in instrumental conditioning. *Psychological Review*, 1978, **85**, 22–48.

Rachlin, H., and Green, L. Commitment, choice and self-control. *Journal of the Experimental Analysis of Behavior*, 1969, **12**, 897–903.

Rachlin, H., Green, L., Kagel, J. H., and Battalio, R. C. Economic demand theory and psychological studies of choice. In G. Bower (Ed.), *The Psychology of learning and motivation* (Vol. 10). New York: Academic Press, 1976.

Rachlin, H., Kagel, J. H., and Battalio, R. C. Substitutability in time allocation. *Psychological Review*, 1980, **87**, 355–374.

Rescorla, R. A., and Wagner, A. R. A theory of Pavlovian conditioning: Variations in the effectiveness of reinforcement and non-reinforcement. In A. H. Black and W. F. Prokasy, *Classical conditioning* (2nd ed.). New York: Appleton-Century-Crofts, 1972.

Seligman, M. E. P. On the generality of the laws of learning. *Psychological Review*, 1970, **77**, 406–418.

Shimp, C. P. Reinforcement of short interresponse times. *Journal of the Experimental Analysis of Behavior*, 1967, **10**, 425–434.

Silby, R. M., and McFarland, D. J. A state-spence approach to motivation. In D. J. McFarland (Ed.), *Motivational control systems analysis*. London: Academic Press, 1974.

Skinner, B. F. *The behavior of organisms*. New York: Appleton-Century-Crofts, 1938.

Skinner, B. F. "Superstition" in the pigeon. *Journal of Experimental Psychology*, 1948, **38**, 168–172.

Skinner B. F. Are theories of learning necessary? *Psychological Review*, 1950, **57**, 193–216.

Staddon, J. E. R. Operant behavior as adaptation to constraint. *Journal of Experimental Psychology, General*, 1979, **108**, 48–67.

Staddon, J. E. R. *Adaptation to constraint: The biology, economics and psychology of individual behavior*. New York: Academic Press, 1980.

Staddon, J. E. R., and Simmelhag, V. L. The "superstition" experiment: A reexamination of its implications for the principles of adaptive behavior. *Psychological Review*, 1971, **78**, 16–43.

Tolman, E. C. There is more than one kind of learning. *Psychological Review*, 1949, **57**, 144–155.

Tversky, A. Elimination by aspects: A theory of choice. *Psychological Review,* 1972, **79,** 281–300.

Tversky, A., and Sattath, S. Preference trees. *Psychological Review,* 1979, **86,** 542–573.

Williams, B. A. Contrast, component duration, and the following schedule of reinforcement. *Journal of Experimental Psychology: Animal Behavior Processes,* 1979, **5,** 379–396.

Incentive Theory

Peter R. Killeen

Arizona State University

*L*et us define incentives as events that generate a heightened state of arousal and thereby increase the vigor of ongoing behaviors. While this does give us a handle on the constituent terms, it provides only a weak grip; our definition permits a very general effect for incentives, one that is much less specific than the role given to "reinforcers" by decades of connotation. But it does provide a context in which the notions of "arousal," "incentive," "vigor," and "ongoing behavior" may be related and may begin to exert mutual constraints on the way each is used. External constraints are provided both by data and by the nexus of other constructs that relate to the data set on which "incentive" impinges.

Whereas verbal models such as the definition above are indispensable for labeling and clarifying parts of the environment—for identifying the subjects and objects of our discipline—mathematics provides an unparalleled vocabulary of action. Because this is a chapter about the dynamics of behavior, it will employ numerous mathematical models; their role will be both to exemplify transitions of behavior and to translate the constraints placed by data on those transitions into constraints on boundary conditions—those stable end points that may in turn serve as the nouns of our theory.

Arousal

Every incentive an organism encounters increases its level of arousal. Over a period of time these inputs cumulate, carrying behavior through a phase of warm-up and eventually raising arousal to an asymptotic level. With the cessation of inputs, arousal decumulates and behavior undergoes extinction. In this section I develop a model for these dynamic processes, based on assumptions concerning the simplest and most effective ways that organisms might average inputs. When the model is elaborated by the addition of a correction for ceilings on response rate, we obtain a general theory of the dynamics of behavior. From this theory predictions of warm-up, asymptotic rates, extinction, and choice behavior can be derived and shown to provide reasonable descriptions of available data.

Precedents for generalized invigoration are ubiquitous:

> Tail pinch incites gnawing, eating, and licking (Antelmen and Szechtman, 1975; Koob, Fray, and Iverson, 1976; Rowland and Antelman, 1965); electric shock facilitates copulation (Barfield and Sachs, 1968; Caggiula and Eibergen, 1969), aggression (Caggiula, 1972; Ulrich and Azrin, 1962; Ulrich, Hutchinson, and Azrin, 1965), drinking (Amsel and Maltzman, 1950; Deaux and Kakolewski, 1970; Siegel and Siegel, 1949), eating (Siegel and Brantly, 1951; Ullman, 1951), key pecking (Bloomfield, 1971), and schedule-induced polydipsia (King, 1974a, 1975; Segal and Oden, 1969). To Myer (1971) "It seems possible that the effect of moderate pain is to potentiate any 'active' behavior which has a high probability of occurrence in the situation" (p. 505). Overmier and Schwartzkopf (1974) found that both food-motivated and shock-motivated responding were increased by a CS signalling the other event. (Killeen, 1979, p. 34)

The application of each incentive invigorates behavior slightly, and that invigoration decays slowly over time. If the effects of previous incentives have not completely dissipated, the effect of the most recent incentive will concatenate with the residues of the earlier ones. The nature of that concatenation—adding versus averaging—will be discussed below.

In addition to their invigorating effects, incentives have directive effects on behavior. The directive effects may be treated as incidents of sign-tracking (Hearst & Jenkins, 1974; LaJoie & Bindra, 1976), modulated by temporal control (Killeen, 1975), and by flexible delay gradients whose steepness is affected by the benefits and costs (incentives and disincentives) for that and competing behavior (Killeen, 1981b). But it is with the invigorating properties of incentives that we are now concerned.

To demonstrate the existence of generalized invigoration deriving from the application of a single incentive, Killeen, Hanson, and Osborne (1978) placed pigeons in a chamber with floor panels that would record movement, and, after a delay of up to half an hour, gave them brief access to grain; half an hour later they were removed from the chamber. Three diferent experiments of this kind were conducted, in different chambers, with different subjects, and with slightly different experimental parameters. The data, averaged over many such episodes and the several pigeons in each experi-

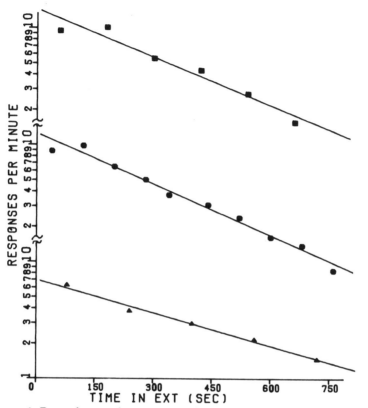

Figure 1. Rate of general activity as a function of the time since eating. The data are from three experiments employing food-deprived pigeons, and in these semilogarithmic coordinates indicate an exponential decay of arousal with a rate constant (beta) equal to .15 per minute. (From Killeen, Hanson, & Osborne, 1978; copyright 1978 by the American Psychological Association; reprinted by permission.)

ment, are shown in Figure 1. The effect is small: rates of panel activation are raised to approximately 10 per minute. But the effect is replicable, and the subsequent decay in movement is extremely regular. In these semilogarithmic coordinates a straight line indicates an exponential relation between the variables and suggests that arousal decays exponentially over time.

A similar experiment was conducted by Allen (1980), who deprived pigeons of water, then gave them one period of access to water in each session. The invigoration from the water was even smaller than in the above experiments, but again it decayed exponentially (see Figure 2). In another part of the experiment he also

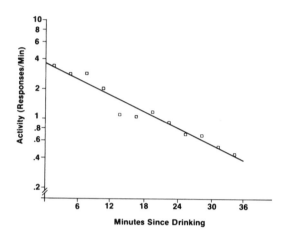

Figure 2. Rate of general activity as a function of the time since drinking. The data are from four water-deprived pigeons given 50 seconds access to water. Note that both the intercept (3.5 responses per minute) and the slope (.06 per minute) of this function are substantially less than those obtained with food incentives (Figure 1). Whereas the former might be due to differences in apparatus, the latter is probably due to the nature of the incentive; when Allen corrected for operant-level responding, he found that the slopes increased but were still less than .15. (From Allen, 1980.)

gave the pigeons, who were not food-deprived, access to food in the experimental chamber while replicating the water regimen. Again he found exponential decreases in both activity and food consumption. Furthermore, the presence of food seems to have added to the animals' activation, since the intercept for the activity function increased by 50% when food was available.

If subsequent feedings are delayed not 24 hours, but only one or two minutes, what would activity records look like? Figure 3 gives one picture. In constructing it, we assume that decay occurs at the same rate as shown in Figure 1, but that every 120 seconds (bottom curve) or every 30 seconds (top curve), another feeding occurs. If arousal cumulates, and if it is directly measurable as activity (an assumption that will be modified later to accommodate ceilings on response rate and competing behavior), the envelopes should approximately predict the increasing levels of activation. In a number of experiments we have found this to be the case. Figure 4 gives one example. A simple mathematical model captures the process shown in Figures 3 and 4 and provides explicit predictions for warm-up

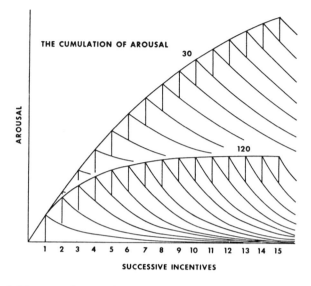

THE CUMULATION OF AROUSAL

AROUSAL

SUCCESSIVE INCENTIVES

Figure 3. The cumulation of arousal for interincentive intervals of 30 and 120 seconds, assuming a rate constant of .15 per minute. (From Killeen, Hanson, & Osborne, 1978; copyright 1978 by the American Psychological Association; reprinted by permission.)

and for the asymptotic levels reached by such regimens. In the following section I digress to show that that model is approximately isomorphic with one based on an answer to the question of how animals average.

AVERAGING THEORY

Many theories of behavior employ rate of reinforcement (or rate of punishment), as the prime independent variable. This tactic indicates that their authors take rates to be the variables controlling behavior—otherwise a simpler representation might be developed by employing more fundamental variables. But rates are complex constructs—they require that the occurrence of events be averaged over a period of time—and the most obvious ways to do this are too complicated to be acceptable as models of how animals themselves might average. The arithmetic mean, for example, requires that a number of events be counted and divided by the units of time that have elapsed. But animals are not good at counting. Furthermore, this algorithm has a fatal flaw: it becomes increasingly invariant as

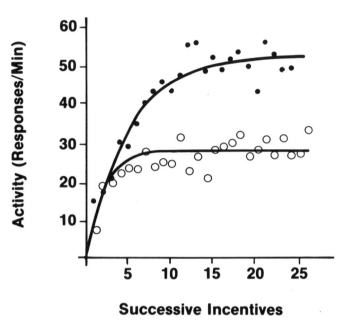

Successive Incentives

Figure 4. Rate of general activity when pigeons are first exposed to periodic feedings at intervals of 30 seconds (top curve) and 50 seconds (bottom curve). The lines are from Equation 3; they are not noticeably different from the curves generated by Equation 10, which takes into account ceilings on response rate. (The data are from Killeen, Hanson, &Osborne, 1978; copyright 1978 by the American Psychological Association; reprinted by permission.)

the data base keeps expanding with new input. What is needed is some type of moving average. But the most obvious moving average requires that a number of events be held in memory and that the earliest one be discarded as the newest is entered. This is too complicated for nonverbal animals. Furthermore, this algorithm generates a rectangular window, giving zero weight to all events outside it and equal weight to all events inside it. A continuous weighting scheme would be preferable, one that gives the greatest weight to the most recent event and smoothly decreasing weights to older and older events.

Fortunately, there exists an averaging algorithm that is simple, makes minimal demand on memory, provides continuous weighting, and permits the weights to be easily adjusted. It is the exponentially weighted moving average, or EWMA (pronounced "Yuma"), a first-order autoregressive process:

$$A_n = \beta v_n + (1-\beta)A_{n-1} \qquad (1)$$

Upon the occurrence of an event (v_n), the new value for the average (A_n) is calculated as the fraction beta of the new event plus the complement of beta times the old average: v_n is the value of the incentive occurring at the nth instant; when there is no incentive occurring it takes a value of zero.

Instead of updating the average with each new event, we may update it after each instant of time. This is a "clock-driven" averaging system, and, though we do not stipulate how often the calculation is effected, we may assume that it is at a high rate, and Equation 1 might easily be taken in the limit to be a continuous process.

To demonstrate how this averaging process works, consider Figure 5, which represents the brief presentation of an incentive at $t = 5$. Taking the currency parameter, β, $= .4$ and $v = 1.0$, A_6 would equal $.4$, $A_7 = .64$, $A_8 = .78$, and $A_9 = .87$. At this point the incentive ceases and the average decreases in a smooth geometric progression equal to $.87(1-\beta)^{t'}$, where t' is each successive period of nonreinforcement. This extinction process plots as a straight line in semilogarithmic coordinates; Figure 5 thus provides a model for the processes demonstrated in Figures 1 and 2.

In the case of repeated incentives, EWMA predicts an effect very similar to that shown in Figure 3 and first derived for a theory of arousal. An important difference is that, in Figure 3, the incentive impulses are represented as lines, with no internal processes being hypothesized. Averaging theory posits two internal processes: a concave increase in the average as a function of the current incentive, and a continuing exponential decrease in the old average with which it is concatenated. These dual processes are obvious in the explicit equation for a EWMA, derived from Equation 1:

$$A_T = \beta \sum_{j=0}^{T-1}(1-\beta)^j\, v_{T-j} + (1-\beta)^T A_0 \qquad (2)$$

It is important to note that these covert processes constitute the only differences between the adding (arousal) and averaging models. We may therefore use much of the mathematical development of Killeen, Hanson, and Osborne (1978; see also Killeen 1979, 1981a) to arrive at the following quantitative conclusions: the average arousal after N incentives of duration D, spaced T seconds apart is:

$$A_{N,D,T} = A_1\,(1-e^{-\lambda(T+D)N})/(1-e^{-\lambda(T+D)}) \qquad (3)$$

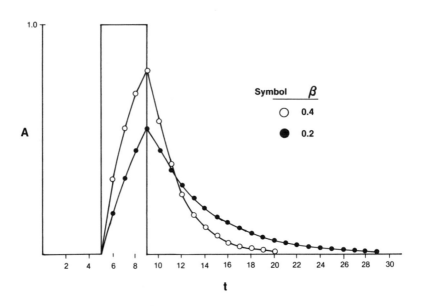

Figure 5. The response of an exponentially weighted moving average to an impulse starting at $t = 5$, for two values of the currency parameter. (From Killeen, 1981a; copyright 1981 by Elsevier North Holland, Inc.)

where

$$A_1 = v(1-e^{-\lambda D}), \tag{4}$$

that is, A_1 is the amount contributed by a single incentive, and

$$\lambda = -ln\,(1-\beta) \cong \beta. \tag{5}$$

The boundary conditions for Equation 3 are shown in Table 1. Whereas the first four lines merely corroborate the logic of the development, the last line leads to predictions for asymptotic arousal. Because lambda is usually very small, we may simplify that line by substituting the first terms of a power series for the exponential term; this will be valid except at very low rates of incitement. Letting $R = 1/T$ and including Equation 4 in the substitution yields:

$$A_{\infty,D,T} \cong vR/(R+ 1/D). \tag{6}$$

This equation predicts a hyperbolic relation between the rate of incitement, R, and the resulting arousal at asymptote.

Up to this point the parameter D has signified the duration of the incentive; it could have been incorporated into T with the under-

Table 1
Boundary Conditions for Equation 3

N	D	T	$A_{N,D,T}$
0	D	T	0
N	0	T	0
1	D	0	A_1
N	D	0	$v(1-e^{-\lambda DN})$
∞	D	T	$A_1/(1-e^{-\lambda(T+D)})$

standing that T then refer to real time and not to the interval between incentives. It has been kept explicit, however, because it will later become useful to treat it as a free parameter. Such a liberation of D is justified because an incentive may disrupt an animal's memory for previous events more than it is disrupted by an equivalent period of quiescence (Catania, 1973; Harzem & Harzem, 1981; Michael, 1979; Shimp, 1976; Staddon, 1974), and such disruption is captured by letting D measure the amount of quiet time that would age memory to the same extent as does the period containing an incentive. D sets a limit to the extent that arousal can cumulate; we now turn to another type of limit.

RESPONSE CEILINGS

We assume that the rate of emission of any behavior is proportional to the level of arousal:

$$B = kA. \tag{7}$$

But at very high rates of incitement arousal can approach extreme levels; few response systems can keep pace. In this section I develop a model for the bias introduced by physical limits on response rates. It is then straightforward to generalize that to the bias introduced by other responses that compete for the animal's time.

Responses require a minimal amount of time for their completion, which we signify by delta. The time available for responding is proportional to $(1-\delta B)$, where B is the number of responses of duration delta that occur in the unit interval of time. Equation 7 predicts the *theoretical* rate of responding, which we take to be the rate based on the time available for responding; it is related to measured rates of responding *(B)* by the equation

$$B = B/(1-\delta B). \tag{8}$$

Solving for B yields

$$B = \mathbf{B}/(1+\delta B). \tag{9}$$

As delta approaches zero, B approaches **B,** and, as delta gets larger, B approaches $1/\delta$, its ceiling rate. This treatment is similar to that of Staddon (1977) and Heyman and Bouzas (1980). It does not include demands on an animal's time that are independent of B, such as travel time from key to hopper, or the distraction of other activities such as interim behaviors and concurrently reinforced operants. But, unless these factors are of explicit interest, the above simpler model can accommodate them to a first approximation by inflating delta above its true minimum value.

By embedding Equation 3 in Equation 9 we may predict the time course of the "warm-up" that occurs when animals are exposed to a series of incentives:

$$B_n = (k'(1-e^{-\lambda(T+D)n})^{-1} + \delta)^{-1} \tag{10}$$

Where B_n is the response rate after the nth incentive, and

$$k' = (1-e^{-\lambda(T+D)})/kA_1. \tag{11}$$

As delta approaches zero, the warm-up function approaches the simple exponential-integral form that generated the curves in Figures 3 and 4; for larger values of delta they are of similar form, but with lowered asymptote and lowered rate of approach to asymptote.

There are not many data against which to test Equation 10; it is not a learning curve that accounts for the establishment of new associations, but rather a motivation curve that accounts for the increase in vigor of already learned or instinctive responses. Yet such motivational changes may be an important part of most conditioning. Hoffman, Fleshler, and Chorny (1961), Nakamura and Anderson (1962), and Olson (1971) all found that unsignaled presentation of a shock not only would reactivate extinguished behavior, but would also increase levels of ongoing performance. When such activation by the unconditioned stimulus is found in Pavlovian conditioning, the effect is labeled pseudoconditioning (see, e.g., Hall, 1976). Similar effects have also been demonstrated using positive reinforcers (Deluty, 1976; Downing & Neuringer, 1976; Eiserer, 1978; Steinhauer, Davol, & Lee, 1976; Terry, 1980). Whole ensembles of behavior have been demonstrated to be activated by periodic feeding (Staddon & Simmelhag, 1971); whether or not any of these contribute to the responses the experimenter is trying to shape will determine not only the extent of pseudoconditioning in that situation, but also the experimenter's success in obtaining the desired behavior (Bolles, 1976; Seligman & Hager, 1972; Shettleworth, 1975; Shettleworth & Juergensen, 1980).

Note that Equation 10 makes the somewhat counterintuitive prediction that rate of warm-up should increase as the interval between incentives increases (although asymptote will be lower for infrequent incentives, rate of approach to it will be faster). Hineline (1978b) and others, e.g., Galvani & Twitty, 1978) found such an effect and noted that it "appears to be inconsistent with all interpretations of the warmup that have been offered to date" (p. 281).

ASYMPTOTIC RATE

The substitution of Equations 6 and 7 into Equation 9 permits us to predict the asymptotic rate of responding as a function of the rate of incitement:

$$B = kvcR/(R+c/D), \tag{12}$$

where

$$c = 1/(1+\delta kv). \tag{13}$$

Equation 12 is identical to Herrnstein's (1970) hyperbolic equation for rate of responding as a function of rate of reinforcement, but with a different interpretation for the parameters. The composite parameter kv tells us the theoretical maximum number of responses that will be emitted for an incentive of value v of prolonged duration ($D \rightarrow \infty$), while the parameter c limits the expression of those responses as a function of the time required to make each response (δ). The composite parameter in the denominator, c/D, corresponds to Herrnstein's R_e, but in the present model it reflects the effects of two independent ceilings, one on response rates and one on the cumulation of arousal. Of course, only two composite parameters need to be estimated to fit this equation to data: *(kvc)* in the numerator and *(c/D)* in the denominator.

Equation 12 predicts a correlation between the parameters in the numerator and those in the denominator, since both contain the factor c. Such a correlation has been noted by Staddon (1977), who developed a similar model of response ceilings. Equation 12 also predicts that the parameter c/D will get smaller, and the function therefore more concave, as the duration of the incentive (or of its disruptiveness to memory) increases. Curvature will also be increased as the minimal duration of a response is increased. All these predictions, which differentiate this model from Herrnstein's, are subject to empirical test.

The equations above may be rearranged to yield further predictions of response rate as a function of incentive value:

$$B = \delta^{-1}v/(v+(1+1/DR)/k\delta), \qquad (14)$$

and as a function of incentive duration:

$$B = kvcD/(D+1/(R(1+\delta v))), \qquad (15)$$

where c is defined in Equation 13.

Note that in both cases the hyperbolic form of the relation between independent and dependent variables is retained. deVilliers (1977) and deVilliers and Herrnstein (1976) reviewed the literature and concluded that the hyperbola *was* the proper form of the function for those variables. Note also that when duration of incentive is varied (Equation 15) the coefficients of D in the numerator include v; if the value of the incentive is then varied parametrically, it should affect the height to which the function rises. This was the case in the two studies they reported employing duration as the variable and value as the parameter (Keesey, 1964; Dinsmoor & Hughes, 1956); this is an important prediction because it contrasts with deVilliers and Herrnstein's prediction of an invariant coefficient. In the great majority of cases employing value as the variable, the coefficient did remain invariant over parametric changes in the duration, as predicted by Equation 14.

Concurrent Schedules

Alternate activities, including those elicited by concurrent schedules of reinforcement, reduce the time available for the primary behavior. Equation 8 may be expanded to take into account such temporal constraints:

$$\mathbf{B}_1 = B_1/(1-(\delta_1 B_1+\delta_2 B_2)). \qquad (16)$$

This equation states that the corrected rate for response B_1 equals the number of B_1 responses over one minus the proportion of the unit time interval occupied by B_1 responses ($\delta_1 B_1$) and B_2 responses ($\delta_2 B_2$).

Since the two behaviors will reciprocally constrain or inhibit one another, it is necessary to write a similar equation for $\mathbf{B}_2$ and solve them simultaneously for B_1. The result is

$$B_1 = \mathbf{B}_1/(1+\delta_1 B_1+\delta_2 \mathbf{B}_2). \tag{17}$$

As either δ_2 or $\mathbf{B}_2$ approaches zero, this equation approaches Equation 9. Note that the denominator is symmetric in $\mathbf{B}_1$ and $\mathbf{B}_2$; this entails that a relative measure of the observed response rates is simply:

$$B_1/B_2 = \mathbf{B}_1/\mathbf{B}_2. \tag{18}$$

Substituting from Equations 6 and 7 yields the important conclusion:

$$\frac{B_1}{B_2} = \frac{k_1 v_1 R_1(R_2+1/D_2)}{k_2 v_2 R_2(R_1+1/D_1)}. \tag{19}$$

When $v_1 = v_2$ and $D_1 = D_2 = D$, we may let $k = k_1/k_2$ and more simply state:

$$\frac{B_1}{B_2} = k \frac{R_1}{R_2} \frac{(DR_2+1)}{(DR_1+1)}. \tag{20}$$

Although this equation applies to concurrent schedules of reinforcement, it is not the familiar matching equation (Herrnstein, 1961, 1970) that is usually held to account for such data. Nor is it the generalized version of the matching law proposed by Baum (1974; also by Staddon 1968):

$$B_1/B_2 = k (R_1/R_2)^a. \tag{21}$$

Only when D is zero does Equation 20 equal Equation 21, in which case the exponent in Equation 21 must take the value of 1.0. But, just as we assume that D is usually finite, the value of a is usually found to be less than 1.0 (Myers & Myers, 1977); this is referred to as "undermatching." Although Baum (1979) suggests a number of plausible sources of undermatching, the generalized matching law has remained an empirical correction rather than a law. Recently Allen (1981) has argued that certain very general types of biases will lead to power functions such as Equation 21. Equation 20 provides a different type of explanation, one subject to empirical test: undermatching derives from the disruption of the memory of earlier reinforcers by the current reinforcer. Events that make reinforcement more disruptive, such as increasing its duration or enhancing concomitant stimulus change, should increase undermatching.

Although Equation 20 predicts a relationship of a form different from that of Equation 21, the differences are not obvious to visual inspection. In Table 2 I list the results of fitting the data from several experiments with both models (I thank Bill Baum for summary

Table 2

Investigator, Species, and Incentive	Subject	Averaging Theory		Power Function	
		D	ω^2	a	ω^2
Bradshaw, Szabadi, & Bevan (1976)	AM	0	.96	1.15	.98
Humans, 150 msec light & counter	SM	10	.97	.84	.98
Davison & Ferguson (1978)	161	0	.79	1.15	.80
Pigeons, 3 sec wheat	163	0	.81	1.15	.82
	164	35	.89	.62	.89
	165	8	.87	.86	.87
	166	30	.95	.64	.96
Logue (1978)	R1	200	.48	.32	.39
Rats, 40 sec escape from noise	R5	140	.94	.60	.93
	R6	100	.69	.42	.75
	R7	60	.91	.49	.92
Matthews & Temple (1979) Cows, 5 sec hay, meal	Group	49	.93	.64	.95
McSweeney (1975)	842	22	.97	.75	.94
Pigeons, 4 sec grain	877	11	.88	.90	.86
	884	0	.95	1.0	.95
	889	17	.86	.78	.85
Schroeder & Holland (1969) Humans, illuminate pointer deflection	Group	0	.97	1.04	.98
Trevett, Davison, & Williams (1972) Pigeons, 3 sec wheat	Group	29	.99	.73	.99
Wheatley & Engberg (1978)	KT1	18	.94	.86	.93
Pigeons, 3 sec grain	KT2	15	.56	.74	.62
	KT3	110	.70	.50	.76
	TT1	220	.73	.28	.74
	TT2	5	.82	.95	.81
Average			.85		.86

tables of these and other data). Both account for the same proportion of data variance. But incentive theory provides an explicit interpretation for its parameters, and this makes additional predictions possible: when the reinforcing event is extended in time or is exceptionally disruptive, the values of D should be larger. Note that the values of D are exceptionally large for Logue's data; the reinforcer she employed was 40 seconds of time out from an aversive noise. Similarly, the value of D for Matthews and Temple's data is larger than the nominal 5-second duration of the feeding. They reinforced cows with access to hay or meal, and it would not be surprising if the cows continued to chew for 45 seconds after each feeding. Conversely, in experiments employing humans, the reinforcer is often a brief flash of light or an increment on a counter (e.g., Baum, 1975; Bradshaw, Szabadi, and Bevan, 1976; Bradshaw, Ruddle, and Szabadi, 1981; Schroeder & Holland, 1969), and the values for D are usually close to zero.

There may be causes for undermatching other than deterioration of memory for previous reinforcements (Baum, 1979), but Equation 20 is forced to accommodate them by inflating the value of D. Thus, we note that one of Wheatley and Engberg's pigeons required a D of almost 4 minutes, even though the reinforcer was a standard 3-second dollop of grain. Only when other sources of undermatching, such as failure to adequately discriminate the schedules, are minimized can the absolute values of D be taken as an unbiased measure of the disruptiveness of reinforcement.

Baum has recently (1981) described a situation in which overmatching was routinely obtained; pigeons were impeded from alternating between schedules by a physical barrier. The only way the current formulation can accommodate overmatching is by letting D take on negative values. Although this maneuver might be justified if the reinforcer acted as a reminder of the previous reinforcers, such an interpretation is not particularly suitable for the paradigm employed by Baum. In general, overmatching falls outside the boundaries of the current model; it is therefore fortunate that it is so rare.

The two models are functionally quite similar; values for k, bias for one alternative, are always almost identical. Visually, the predictions are almost identical. Even the values of D and the exponent are closely related: the correlation between the logarithm of D and beta is $-.92$. One can therefore estimate the value of D from the value of a, which is easier to obtain.

Another type of prediction is possible based on the averaging model. As the absolute values of concurrent schedules are increased, while keeping their ratio constant, preference should regress toward indifference. Fantino, Squires, Delbruck, and Peterson (1972) performed the relevant experiment and found the predicted shift (from 66% to 61% when pigeons were shifted from variable interval [VI] 1 versus VI 2 to VI 10 versus VI 20; the predicted preferences are 65% and 57%), although it was of only marginal statistical significance ($t = 1.72$; $df = 12$; $p < .06$).

In an important paper, McDowell and Kessel (1979; see also McDowell & Sulzen, 1981) treated organisms as simple linear filters of the input reinforcement schedules and employed the Laplace method to generate a transfer function that predicts output. They also invoked the notions of ceilings on response rate and disruption by reinforcement ("response width" and "reinforcement width") and derived predictions equivalent to many of those outlined above. Subsequently, McDowell (1980) further simplified the predictions and derived an expression for concurrent schedules (his Equation 10) that may be reduced to Equation 20 by a simple power-series expansion.

DURATION OF INCENTIVES

Both McDowell and Kessel (1979) and the current version of the averaging model predict an identical concave relation between the duration of an incentive and its effect on behavior. In single-operandum studies, that concavity is easily confounded with ceilings on response rate, but in concurrent studies it should be demonstrable: long durations of incentives should be slightly less than proportionately as effective as short durations. This would be manifested as a preference for constant- over variable-duration incentives when they have the same mean durations—a finding noted by Menlove, Inden, and Madden (1979), and Walker and Hurwitz (1971), but not by Essock and Reese (1974), Staddon and Innis (1966), or Young (1981).

When a researcher attempts to capture the effects of variable-duration incentives using a power function of the ratios of durations, the decreasing marginal utility of longer durations should be manifested as fractional exponents for the functions. This has been found to be the case (Schneider, 1973; Todorov, 1973). But, unlike the power function models, the present theory does not predict that equal ratios of durations will have equal effects: the greater the absolute durations of the incentives, the more that preference should regress toward indifference, and the smaller should be the exponent.

The predictions above require a currency parameter on the order of .1 per second, much larger than that typically found for our EWMAs; for smaller and more typical values of beta, the effects of incentives would be approximately linear with their duration (as was found in many of the cited studies). The possibility that animals may in some cases effectively "speed up their clock" during incentives is discussed in a subsequent section.

Concurrent-Chain Schedules

Animals may be given a choice not between different amounts of reward, but between different schedules under which they may work for reward. In the typical procedure, the animal repeatedly responds to either of two concurrently available operanda; when one of the schedules operative for those alternatives sets up, the next response results not in a reward, but in a change of the stimuli to signal that one operandum is now enabled to provide food according to some reinforcement schedule and the other operandum is inoperative. Since the schedules in the concurrent initial links (choice portion) are usually equivalent variable-interval schedules, differences in response rates during them may be taken as an indication of the differential reinforcing effectiveness of the terminal link schedules (work portions), as signaled by the terminal link stimuli.

There is a large literature on concurrent-chain research, which was initiated by Autor (1960/1969), popularized by Herrnstein (1964a), and recently reviewed by Fantino (1977). The most important variable controlling the relative rate of responding in the initial links (which is interpreted as a measure of choice between the alternatives) is the immediacy of the ensuing reward. Herrnstein (1964a) showed that choice was proportional to the rates of reinforcement provided by variable-interval (VI) and variable-ratio schedules in the terminal links. But when one terminal link is a fixed-interval (FI) schedule, with reinforcement scheduled for the first response after a fixed time period (not after a time period chosen from a distribution, as is the case for variable-interval schedules), the proportionality rule breaks down: subjects prefer variable-interval schedules over fixed-interval schedules with equal means (Herrnstein, 1964b). Killeen (1968) took this as evidence that the pigeons were using some way of averaging the delays until forthcoming incentives other than arithmetic mean; he explored alternative averages that are described by the general mean theorem (Hardy, Littlewood, & Polya, 1959) and found that the harmonic mean of the VI intervals predicted the FI schedule that was equally reinforcing. Pigeons seemed to calculate the rate of forthcoming incentives not as the reciprocal of the average of the intervals, but as the average of the reciprocal of the intervals.

Although this formulation predicted *indifference* points quite well, it did not accurately predict *preference* at other points. In the simple case of preference between two FI schedules, where all types of mean must give the same measure, preference for the shorter schedule routinely exceeds the relative immediacy of reinforcement provided by it (Herrnstein, 1964b; Killeen, 1970). These results provide an intriguing problem. In many ways concurrent schedules are simpler than schedules programmed singly, because vicissitudes of motivation level, distractions, and satiation will, to a first order of approximation, cancel out of relative measures of behavior, making them more orderly and amenable to analysis. At the same time, various constants of proportionality may cancel out of the predicting models, thereby reducing the number of free parameters and permitting tighter prediction. The important question is not whether animals "match" but whether, in this close to ideal situation, models of response strength may be found whose ratios predict the ratios of the concurrent behaviors. The problem has proved attractive to a number of researchers (e.g., the laboratories of Davison and Fantino), who have made contributions both to the data base and to the theory of these schedules. Incentive theory may be extended to address this paradigm, and that is essayed here.

Three factors are important in predicting response rates in concurrent-chain schedules. The first is the estimate of the relative rate of primary reinforcement, for which Equation 19 can be generalized by replacing R_1 with R'_1, which equals $1/(I_1 + T_1)$, I_1 being the duration of the initial link for alternative i and T_1 the duration of the terminal link for that alternative.

The second factor is the value (v_i) of the delayed incentive, which will be debased as some function of the duration of the terminal links. There have been numerous speculations about the form of that function—the "delay of reinforcement gradient" (e.g., Hull, 1943; Chung, 1965; Chung & Herrnstein, 1967), and I propose here a simple model that converges on the exponential decay function favored by Hull and by Chung. Assume that a reinforcer immediately following a response will be associated with that response with probability p. If the reinforcement is delayed for a second, the probability that a more salient response will occur and become associated with the reinforcer (cf. Williams, 1978), we take to be q, so the probability that the original connection was made and still holds is $p(1-q)$. After 2 seconds the probability is $p(1-q)^2$, and after T seconds, $p(1-q)^T$. This geometric expression may, of course, be approximated by the exponential pe^{-qT}. This model requires the decay of effect to depend on the original salience of the response (p, which in concurrent situations we may presume is equal for both responses) and on the opportunity for intervening responses (q, which will be affected by the illumination of the chamber, and by the presence of stimuli eliciting other responses).

Like many of the important expressions in averaging theory, this "forward-looking" model involves an exponential function but it is not otherwise related to the averaging model. In particular, we expect its rate constant, q, to be a function of different variables than is the currency parameter, beta. The assumptions of this model are quite testable, by manipulation of the values of both p and q. During this symposium Collier noted that rats' preference for moderately weighted levers (Jennings & Collier, 1970; Kanarek & Collier, 1973), may be due to the increase in salience that the weight confers on the instrumental response. This type of explanation contrasts with optimal foraging models, which must either predict a preference for the lightest levers or else assume a "psychological effort" that is nonmonotonic with physical effort.

So far our model is appropriate for unsignaled delay of reinforcement paradigms, but the concurrent-chain schedule introduces a third factor, the terminal link stimuli that immediately reinforce the last initial link response by signaling the onset of the terminal link delay. The strength of this conditioned reinforcer is a function of the rate of reinforcement it signals, and employing a power-series approximation for the EWMA, as we did for the first factor, we may take it as proportional to the reciprocal of the terminal link duration. Expanding Equation 20, the complete model is

$$\frac{B_1}{B_2} = k \; \frac{R'_1(DR'_2+1)\,(pe^{-qT_1}+c/T_1)}{R'_2(DR'_1+1)\,(pe^{-qT_1}+c/T_2)} \tag{22}$$

This may be simplified for the present discussion by presuming negligible key bias $(k = 1)$, minimal disruption of memory $(D=0)$, and equal weight for primary and conditioned reinforcement $(p=c)$:

$$\frac{B_1}{B_2} = \frac{R'_1(e^{-qT_1}+c/T_1)}{R'_1\,(e^{-qT_2}+c/T_2)}. \tag{23}$$

Equation 23 is similar to the model of Davison and Temple (1973), except for the inclusion of the exponential terms to account for the direct, delayed effects of the primary reinforcer. Also, this model presumes an equal exposure to each of the alternatives; when that varies, as it does in many scheduling arrangements when preference becomes extreme, an additional correction factor, such as that employed by Davison and Temple, would improve accuracy. Figure 6 shows the performance of Equation 23 in predicting the results of a number of concurrent-chain schedule performances. The value of q was fixed at .12 for all of these studies; the fit to predictions would have been made somewhat better by tailoring its value to

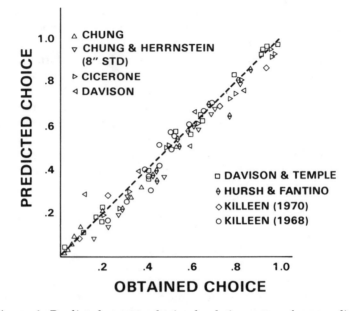

Figure 6. Predicted versus obtained relative rates of responding on various concurrent-chain schedules of reinforcement. The model is Equation 23 with $q = .12$.

each experiment, but optimal values for q tended in any case to cluster between .09 and .14. One can see the predictions are quite good, surpassing those of any other treatment of this paradigm. The average deviation between obtained and predicted rates is less than 4%.

Not included in Figure 6 are the data of MacEwen (1972) and those of Gentry and Marr (1980). MacEwen's data were uniformly more extreme than predicted, and Gentry and Marr's were more moderate than predicted, with a curious reversion of preference toward indifference at the most extreme delays (Equation 23 does predict a reversion of preference toward matching with very long delays, as the conditioned reinforcement factor progressively outweighs the direct reinforcement factor, but not past matching toward indifference). A problem with these studies is their sequencing of conditions, with MacEwen keeping the longest of each pair of delays always on the same key and Gentry and Marr systematically alternating the longest delay from one side to the other for all subjects. The concurrent-chains paradigm suffers from hysteresis effects, especially when fixed delays are scheduled in the terminal links (Williams & Fantino, 1978), and the scheduling techniques employed by the above investigators biased their data away from their predicted locations exactly as one might expect.

An advantage of the present formulation is that it reconciles the paradox of approximate "matching" when variable-interval schedules are employed in at least one of the terminal links with the more extreme preference ("overmatching") found when fixed delays are employed in both links. The circles in Figure 6 are from an experiment in which VI schedules were used in one of the terminal links and FI in the other; Cicerone (1976), and Davison and Temple (1973) and Hursh and Fantino (1973), used an FI as one alternative and either an FI or a VI with only two components as the other; Davison (1969) and Killeen (1970) used FI schedules in both terminal links; and Chung (1965) and Chung and Herrnstein (1967) used fixed delays in both terminal links. It is clear that Equation 23 can easily accommodate a range of different conditions, and thus it provides a general account of preference for work schedules.

Just as Equation 23 predicts the relative strength of incentives, it also predicts the relative (punitive) strength of disincentives. Badia, Harsh, and Coker (1975) found that shocks presented on a variable schedule were more aversive than shocks presented on a fixed schedule with an equal mean interval. When the investigators presented a brief signal before the variable shock, it became less aversive. The signal weakened the conditioned reinforcer (actually, conditioned punisher) associated with entry into the variable shock schedule by overshadowing it with one delayed from the choice response and much more contiguous with the shock. A complementary effect, a decrease in preference for a terminal link ending in positive reinforcement when it is segmented by a series of stimuli, has been reported by Duncan and Fantino (1972). The magnitude of the preference is sufficiently large that one suspects not just a failure of effective conditioned reinforcement for the segmented links, but an actual punishment of the choice behavior that leads to a stimulus correlated with nonreinforcement.

Some of the studies whose data are depicted in Figure 6 involved delayed reinforcement in which no explicit signal was given to the animals telling them which terminal link they were in; yet we maintained a fixed value for c, the weight given to the conditioned reinforcement factor in Equation 22. This is because there probably was no ambiguity about the length of the delay as long as the animals maintained some orientation to the key or lever last operated. If steps are taken to disrupt such bootleg conditioned reinforcers, we would expect preference to become less extreme. This has been found. Williams and Fantino (1978) alternately flashed the terminal link cues in one condition and found that the pigeons were much less extreme in their preference. Similarly, Nevin and Mandell (1978) required rats to move to a common operandum for the terminal link, and they found preference to be more extreme when unambiguous cues were associated with each of the terminal links than when no differential cues were presented. Equation 23 predicts these results if we replace the differential values of T_1 and T_2 with their average (it is not conditioned reinforcement that is lacking, just *differential* conditioned reinforcement; the separate occurrence of T_1 and T_2 in the primary reinforcement exponents are left unaltered).

The present model provides a static picture of choice behavior occurring at some point before entry into the terminal links. But behavior early in the initial choice link differs from that late in that link. One report (Killeen, 1970) showed a large negative recency effect, with pigeons' choice ratios biased away from the key on which they last received reinforcement. The longer the initial link schedules are, the more we might expect this and other such regressive factors to weaken control by the terminal link schedules and move preference toward indifference. Fantino (1969), and Squires and Fantino (1971) have demonstrated that this does happen and have provided models that predict the extent of such changes in preference.

There may be other ways of arranging the factors in Equation 22 or eliminating some, such as R', that will provide a better account of the concurrent-chains literature and at the same time address the closely related phenomena of observing behavior (Fantino, 1977; Green & Rachlin, 1977) and commitment (Ainslie, 1975; Rachlin & Green, 1972; Deluty, 1981). But any such extensions or modifications are likely to retain the separate accounting of direct and conditioned effects of the reinforcers that was developed here.

EXTINCTION

Just as much of the change in behavior that is recorded in a learning curve may reflect changes in motivation rather than changes in learning, extinction may be viewed as primarily a demotivational process. Decay in arousal is exponential, corresponding to the right addend of Equation 2, and the level from which it declines is given by Equation 6. The theoretical decay in response rate is then:

$$B = vRe^{-\lambda/R}/(R+1/D). \tag{24}$$

If this is combined with the model for response constraint (Equation 9), the predicted extinction function is a logistic:

$$B = (\delta + k'e^{\lambda t})^{-1} \qquad (25)$$

with

$$k' = (DR+1)/kvDR. \qquad (26)$$

Note also that if delta is small relative to k'—that is, if response rates are not close to their ceiling—the process is essentially exponential. These effects are shown in Figures 7 and 8. The first figure shows the decrease in pecking of a single pigeon exposed to various interval schedules, as a function of time into extinction; there is a marked ogival form to the functions. The second figure (from Powell, 1972) shows, in semilogarithmic coordinates, the extinction curves for two groups of rats previously trained on free-operant avoidance and then switched to a no-shock extinction session. The top curve is for rats given 60 minutes of avoidance conditioning at the beginning of the extinction session, and the bottom curve is for rats given only 1 minute of avoidance conditioning. Only the exponential portion of the curve is apparent. Note that, although the

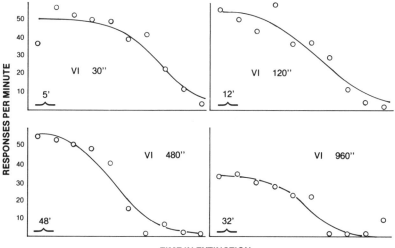

Figure 7. The response rate in extinction for one pigeon after training on various VI schedules; the theoretical curves are from Equation 25. (The data are from an unpublished study by Lasiter, 1980, the figure from Killeen 1981a; copyright 1981 by Elsevier North Holland, Inc.)

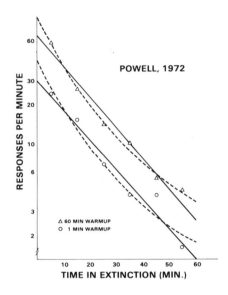

Figure 8. The response rate in extinction for two groups of rats after training on a shock-avoidance schedule, each group having different amounts of exposure to the training conditions at the start of the extinction session. The straight lines are from Equation 25 with delta set to zero; the dashed lines are from an adaptive averaging model discussed below. (The data are from Powell, 1972.)

different amounts of warm-up given to the animals affected the intercept (k'), they had no effect on the slope of the extinction curves, as predicted by the model.

Rates of extinction are usually not invariant over training conditions, and the nature of this change in rate will be examined below. Note, however, that operations that increase response rates toward their ceiling (or lower the ceiling, by response constraint or other means) will flatten the top of the extinction curve and may give the appearance of increased persistence—even though intrinsic rates of extinction (as measured by lambda) are the same or even increased.

ADAPTIVE AVERAGING

Animals trained on intermittent schedules take longer to extinguish than animals trained on continuous schedules, a phenomenon known as the partial reinforcement extinction effect (PREE). Up until this point is has been assumed that the currency parameter was constant. Such constancy would require that the slopes of extinction curves be invariant. Figure 9 shows that this is not the case: the time constants (the inverse of the currency parameter) for extinction curves from a variety of studies using fixed- and variable-interval schedules are seen to increase in a regular fashion with the interreinforcement interval during training.

Variability in the currency parameter has no effect on the predictions of asymptotic behavior (Killeen, 1981a) but does affect predictions of warm-up and extinction, a domain where the data are, in any case, fragmentary. In the remaining part of this section I outline a model of adaptive averaging and indicate how it might address not only extinction data but a range of other motivational phenomena.

Adaptive control processes are ones in which some parameter of the system changes in response to input (Milsum, 1966; McFarland, 1971). Let us assume that in an environment where not much is happening, it is best for an animal to be guided by events that have happened over some relatively long period of time. Conversely, if

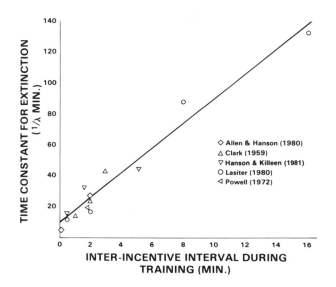

Figure 9. The time constants (1/λ) found in several studies of experimental extinction, plotted against the interincentive interval experienced during training. The positive relation exemplifies the partial reinforcement extinction effect—the decrease in the rate of extinction with decreases in the rate of incentives during training.

the environment is rapidly changing, the animal should pay most attention to recent events (i.e., have a large currency parameter). For simplicity, we might assume that the currency parameter changes in the same manner (a EWMA) as the average itself changes. Then

$$\beta_t = \gamma v_t + (1-\gamma)\beta_{t-1} , \tag{27}$$

and, as before,

$$A_t = \beta_t v_t + (1-\beta_t)A_{t-1} , \tag{28}$$

with v_t the value of the incentive (if any) at instant t. Note that if gamma is zero, beta remains fixed at its original value of β_0, and Equation 28 becomes equivalent to Equation 1. For nonzero values of gamma, this model states that the clock speeds up during an incentive and slows down during extinction. On intermittent reinforcement schedules, an equilibrium between these processes will be struck that will leave the clock at slower speeds for greater interincentive intervals, thus capturing the PREE.

We must immediately ask whether this biological "relativity theory" will accommodate other basic phenomena of extinction. We have heretofore treated the extinction curves as basically exponential in form (with temporal constraints causing a rounding of the top into a logistic ogive when response rates are high). The present model requires that they be curvilinear, even in semilogarithmic coordinates. Such curvilinearity would be masked by the ogival form and so must be sought in extinction curves where response rates are well below their ceiling. We can see in Figure 8 that adaptive averaging with values of .02 per minute for gamma and .09 per minute for β_0 at the start of extinction generates curves that fit Powell's data as well as the regression lines with a rate constant of .05 per minute.

The first and major effect of increased numbers of training trials is to increase the level of arousal, which will in turn increase the response rate at the start of extinction and the total number of responses in extinction. But note in Figure 3 that arousal level can approach asymptote rather quickly, especially when the interincentive interval is moderate or large. After a score of trials, additional training may have little incremental effect on arousal level but will continue to increase the speed of the clock. (This latter effect is also an equilibrium process, with the increases becoming smaller and smaller with each additional trial.) We expect *rate* of extinction to increase monotonically with the number of training trials, but the total *number* of responses in extinction will be determined by the arousal level and the rate of the clock at the start of extinction. The trade-off between these processes will be optimized with a moderate number of training trials, and additional training beyond that point will decrease the number of responses in extinction. This "overtraining extinction effect" has been found (see, e.g., Ison, 1962), although the diversity of results is "confusing" (Mackintosh, 1974; Valle, 1975). The equations above provide a novel basis for interpreting the results in terms of the diversity of training conditions. They also permit the prediction that continuous reinforcement interpolated between intermittent reinforcement and extinction will decrease resistance to extinction (Stalling, Moreland, Merrill, & Scotti, 1981).

Another type of prediction is possible, one that is similar in logic: reinforcers of long duration should speed up the clock more and lead to faster rates of extinction than reinforcers of short duration. The literature concurs: "the conclusion that large rewards in acquisition can increase the subsequent rate of extinction is securely established" (Mackintosh, 1974, p. 427), under conditions of continuous reinforcement. My model predicts the same effect, diminished in magnitude, for variations in amount of reward on partial reinforcement schedules, but here the literature seems to show the reverse to be true: large rewards appear to retard extinction in that case. But these reports are often confounded by differences in response rates and in proximity to ceiling response rates. Explicit analyses of these archival data are difficult, because the logistic form in conjunction with the adaptive averaging process provides a model too flexible to be adequately constrained by the fairly undistinguished extinction curves. New experiments are called for.

Equations 27 and 28 provide a minimal model of adaptive control; it is unlikely that the clock speed ever closely approaches zero, though these equations would permit that. An additional parameter is easily added to accommodate such boundary conditions, but again the data are not yet rich enough to justify such a refinement. Other specifications also need to be fixed: Equation 27 has the speed of the clock depending on the value of the incentive; it could easily be modified to depend only on its presence or absence, thereby reconciling other phenomena, such as data that show that varying the concentration of sucrose does not have the same effects on overtraining as varying the amount of sucrose. Much work needs to be done on these issues, starting with a modeling of acquisition and extinction phases using consistent parameters to derive nonarbitrary values for A and beta at the start of extinction.

DISCRIMINATION

Arousal level is conditionable (Killeen, 1979); animals placed in an environment where they have in the past been fed become excited. Both response rate in the presence of such stimuli and differential approach to such stimuli may thereby be facilitated. Equation 1 is the basic dynamic model that underlies the Rescorla and Wagner (1972) treatment of discrimination learning; their difference equation may be rewritten:

$$Vax = \beta v + (1-\beta)V'ax, \tag{29}$$

where Vax is the associative strength of the compound stimulus ax, $V'ax$ is its strength on the previous trial, beta is the learning rate parameter, and v is the asymptote of learning; the stimulus salience (α in their equation) is assumed unitary, and v is assumed 0 on extinction trials. The critical conceptual difference, and the essence of their original model, is the attention they paid to apportioning the associative strength (arousal) to elements of a compound stimulus ($Vax = Va + Vx$). Because of this close affinity, the elaborations noted on the basic averaging model may be transported to the area of discrimination learning, for whatever insights they may yield. The current models may, for instance, be applied to the overtraining reversal effect, a discrimination analogue of the overtraining extinction effect; they may furthermore shed some light on the relation between motivational variables (e.g., amount, probability, and spacing of rewards) and associative processes. These possibilities are mentioned only as avenues for future research—nothing fundamental has yet been accomplished in relating the two areas of inquiry.

CONSTRAINTS ON RESPONDING

Equation 16 is a "time-allocation constraint"; it may be rearranged to reveal B_1 as a linear function of B_2. This is a form often taken by the data (Staddon & Motheral, 1978), and, as Staddon (1979a) points out, it is a simple interpretation of the linear functions predicted by conservation theory (Allison, Miller, & Wozny, 1979; Timberlake & Allison, 1974; Timberlake, in press). It thus forms an important part not only of the present theory of behavior dynamics, but of Rachlin's and Staddon's economic analyses. Reinforcement schedules are a second type of constraint, generating a specified relation between two or more behaviors. In the case where one of the behaviors is the consummatory response, this constraint is called the "schedule feedback function" and takes the form of a

mathematical statement of the contingencies exerted by the reinforcement schedule.

Constraints also play an important, if often implicit, role in
theories of optimal foraging (see, e.g., Kamil & Sargent, 1980;
Staddon, 1980; Horn, Mitchell, & Stairs, 1979; Krebs, 1978). In field
observations and empirical studies (e.g., Killeen, 1974; Kramer &
Nowell, 1980; Smith, Maybee, & Maybee, 1979), animals must
traverse greater distances to obtain more abundant food, or, as they
continue to forage in a particular patch, their depletion of the food
increases the search time for additional food. In a few experimental
studies, such as Collier's (e.g., Collier, this volume; Collier, Hirsch,
& Hamlin, 1972; Hirsch & Collier, 1974; Collier & Rovee-Collier,
1980; Killeen, Smith, & Hanson, 1981), the constraints are manipulated to provide more powerful tests of the models.

Although these varied approaches concur on the importance of
response constraints and on their explicit expression within their
models, there is divergence concerning the level at which behavior
should be analyzed. Incentive theory is mechanistic and molecular,
whereas optimality approaches are functional and molar. This important distinction is examined in the last section of this paper.

Maximization Models: Economic, Ecological, and Stochastic

The vulgar characterization of the operative factor in evolution as
the "survival of the fittest" has recently been replaced with the
notion of "maximizing one's genetic contribution to ensuing generations" (see, e.g., Clutton-Brock & Harvey, 1978). Although such
maximization is accomplished through the interaction of organis-
mic variability and environmental selection, neither of which is
purposeful, the teleonomic presumption that most adaptations
serve the purpose of maximization permits many useful and powerful predictions.

OPTIMIZATION

In similar fashion, behavior theorists have recently explored the
utility of presuming that behaviors of individual organisms
maximize some good (e.g., Rachlin, this volume; Rachlin, Green,
Kagel, & Battalio, 1976; Staddon, 1979b, 1980), such as acquiring an
optimal combination of inputs given the costs involved in obtaining them. In models of optimal foraging, the presumption may be
made that animals strive to achieve the maximum input of calories

per unit time, or the maximum input for a given output of calories, or an adequate input while minimizing exposure to predators, and so on. The various presumptions are realized as different models and may be tested against the data. It is possible that the use of the formalism provided by the economic analysis (both the new behavioral type and the more traditional literature, such as that on the optimal location of factories; see, e.g., Dean, Leahy, & McKee, 1970; Faden, 1977) will greatly aid the analysis of foraging behavior, just as the notion of optimal foraging has itself given a fresh perspective and rationale to the study of reinforcement schedules.

Economic behavior theories also assume that animals respond so as to optimize a weighted combination of the available goods, perhaps first converting the measure of those goods to an equal-interval scale of utility that is then maximized (Rachlin & Burkhard, 1978), or, alternatively, that they respond to minimize the discrepancy between where they are and some ideal combination of the goods (Staddon, 1979b; Rachlin, Battalio, Kagel, & Green, 1981). Is it possible to presume the contrary, that animals do not optimize, and still account for behavior that seems well adapted to the animal's niche? I believe it is, and I will even take the position that more powerful predictions may follow from the presumption that it is not utility that is maximized, but randomness.

To argue against optimality theories is not to argue against adaptedness; we might even infer that a well-adapted organism is making optimal use of its resources and still reject theories that attempt to account for its behavior by setting some derivative equal to zero. A way of thinking about optimization is by reference to "hill-climbing" techniques used in computers to maximize some variable. The most elegant techniques use information about the slope of the hill in all directions before moving off in a direction closer to the maximum. This information is found in the derivatives of the functions that describe the contour of the hill at that point. It is this technique that economic behavior theories emulate, with the height of a point corresponding either to the sum of the utilities of the commodities controlling the behavior or the proximity of the combination of commodities to the ideal, or "bliss" point.

Proponents of these theories do not argue that an organism actually has available all of the necessary analytic information about the slopes; they would argue that simpler mechanisms requiring less information will suffice. Another hill-climbing technique is the random search, with the computer experimenting with small steps in random directions; each time one of these steps leads to an improvement, the origin of the search is relocated to that point, and the random exploration begins again. This process is much slower and less elegant, but more robust, and is applicable to functions that are highly discontinuous. Perhaps the animal makes this sort of speed/simplicity trade-off and simply sniffs out the best direction in which to move. In fact, Tolman (1939) suggested this in his analysis of vicarious trial-and-error learning for the behavior of rats at a choice point (as did Feynman in his analysis (Feynman, Leighton, & Sands, 1963) of Fermat's principle of least time for the behavior of light at a choice point!). Nonetheless, analytic models might accurately characterize the results of such random search processes.

A few simple, low-level mechanisms would help improve the efficiency of the search. We may, for instance, add momentum (Rachlin, this volume): the computer's first exploration after a success might be in the same direction as the previous step. Staddon (1973, 1975, in press) has also argued that higher-order laws, such as the law of effect, are composed of simpler mechanisms, just as the apparently purposeful behavior of some bugs may be analyzed into a few simple taxis. Economic models offer a relatively elegant way to summarize the effects of a few simple, though currently only poorly understood, mechanisms that have evolved to provide animals with behaviors that suit them to their environment. In fact, we could even account for deviations from what our a priori notions might take to be optimal behavior by arguing that the cost of the additional calculations might make anything other than first-order approximations to bliss become cost ineffective! Once we retrench from a continuum to a finite number of mechanisms, such creative accounting becomes not only attractive but inevitable. The animals' limitations of information and mechanism become a set of implicit constraints; it is not just expensive to exceed them, it is impossible. Witness the poor pigeon tantalized by a schedule of negative automaintenance! But if the economic analyses are summaries of the effects of simple mechanisms, a theory of simple mechanisms is preferable (Lewontin, 1979). That is offered here.

I first note that the "optimality" account of interval-schedule performance suffers a problem of face validity: a 100% increase in response rate on a VI 1-minute schedule, from 40 to 80 responses per minute, will provide an increase in reinforcement rate of at most 1%, calculated using the schedule feedback function of Staddon and Motheral (1978). The functions of Baum (1973) and Prelec and Herrnstein (1978) provide even less leverage on response rates. (See Nevin & Baum, 1980, and Rachlin, 1978, for still other feedback functions.) I submit that animals are not sensitive to the difference between a VI 1.025 and a VI 1.013, as they would have to be for it to control their behavior with a minimal error of 100%. Optimality explanations of responding on interval schedules that are based on improvements in average rate of reinforcement are incredible and ought to be abandoned.

It is difficult to improve upon Herrnstein's hyperbola (Equation 12) as an account of behavior under variable-interval schedules; that model is derivable without reference to optimization. But, whereas the rate of reinforcement on interval schedules does not change very much over wide changes in response rate, ratio schedules program a direct proportionality between response and reinforcement rate. Here at least there is an opportunity for a plausible process of maximization. Again, however, I argue that maximization of utility plays no part in the control of response rates. On the one hand, small changes in the contingencies of reinforcement on interval schedules that make performance more ratiolike (e.g., tandem ratio requirements; Killeen, 1969) can greatly increase rate of responding even though rate of reinforcement remains relatively constant. On the other hand, contingencies that permit animals to greatly increase their rate of reinforcement by emitting a single response (e.g., timing of the interval is initiated by the first postreinforcement response; Shull, 1970) are singularly ineffective in motivating response. Other mechanisms are controlling behavior here (see, e.g. Herrnstein and Vaughan, 1980), and, though they are good enough to have helped our subjects survive outside the laboratory, they are easily revealed by laboratory analysis to be evidence against maximization.

In the case of ratio schedules, one such mechanism is the differential reinforcement of fast responding (or, more correctly, the reinforcement of responding, whereas on interval schedules responses following a pause are differentially reinforced). Another important factor is the dependence of reinforcement rate, and therefore arousal, on response rate. If we write the schedule feedback function for ratio schedules as $R = B/FR$, where B is the rate of responding, FR the value of the ratio, and R the resulting rate of reinforcement, we may substitute into Equation 12 to get the following prediction:

$$B = (k' - FR/D)/(1 + k'D/FR), \qquad 30$$

with $k' = kvc$.

Because this equation leaves out the important contribution that ratio contingencies make in defining the response unit, it should be

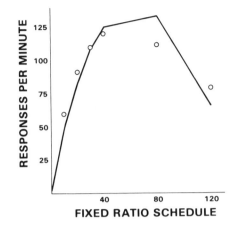

Figure 10. The response rate of rats on various fixed-ratio schedules. The solid line is the prediction of Equation 30 with $D = 11$ seconds. (The data are from Barofsky & Hurwitz, 1968.)

viewed only as a part of a proper model. Figure 10 shows it applied to the data of Barofsky and Hurwitz (1968). It errs systematically in that it predicts too slow a rise and then too fast a drop in response rate. It shows the same bias when applied to other sets of ratio data. But it does about as well by ratio data as do the economic models, and it does so with one less parameter.

These paragraphs underline the importance of schedule feedback functions but demonstrate that they may be used independently of the assumptions of economic behavior theories to specify the value of one of the variables (rate of incitement) that is crucial in controlling animals' behavior. When the amount of feedback (variance in the environment attributable to variance in behavior) is minimal, as it is on interval schedules, such covariation may be ignored with impunity, and behavior may be accurately predicted from rates of incitement directly. On ratio schedules, the loop must be closed by use of a schedule feedback function. In no case is the assertion of optimality a necessary axiom. (The question of optimization as a fact is not at issue: natural selection favors those organisms that are better at the basics, but being better suffices—there is no "best," there is only a "best possible" or a "best given. . . ." The "givens" are constraints. In simple situations they can be specified beforehand, and this permits the strongest analysis; in complicated situations they must be inferred. Optimality analysis is a technique of inference: its validation is to be found not in the face of its assumptions, but in the utility of its inferences.)

The areas in which incentive theory is mute and optimality approaches hold the greatest promise involve more complicated situations, involving factors such as tradeoffs between various commodities, depletion-repletion mechanisms, and the ecological analysis of foraging behavior. The contributions to this volume therefore provide complementary approaches to the analysis of animal behavior.

THE MAXIMIZATION OF RANDOMNESS

I close with an intriguing demonstration, due to Stephen Hanson (1980), of the utility of assuming not that animals maximize benefit, but rather that they maximize randomness. No instrumental or evolutionary function is assumed for such maximization, and so in this case the passive voice is actually more appropriate—we presume that entropy is maximized, subject to constraints on the animal's time and arousal. We merely ask: What is the most likely distribution of behavior after all the constraints we can name have been satisfied?

Hanson employed the maximum entropy formalism (Levine & Tribus, 1979), and specifically the Boltzmann distribution (see, e.g., Fast, 1962), to predict the distribution of time an animal will spend in various behaviors when subject to two explicit constraints. These constraints are that the amount of time spent in each of the activities must sum to the total session time,

$$T = \Sigma t_i, \tag{31}$$

and that the arousal required to activate a particular activity, multiplied by the amount of time spent in that activity and summed over all of the activities, must equal the arousal level of the animal (as defined in earlier sections of this paper):

$$A = \Sigma a_i t_i. \tag{32}$$

Unfortunately, the level of arousal required to activate any particular behavior is unknown. Here Hanson made a bold conjecture: he assumed that each category of behavior differed in activation level (a_i) from the others by an equal number of units, so that by rank-ordering the activities in terms of their probabilities we obtain a scale that is proportional to one based on an independent measure of activation level.

The number of ways any particular stable distribution of activities can occur is given by the multinomial coefficient:

$$W = \frac{T!}{\pi t_i!}, \qquad (33)$$

where t_i is the time spent engaged in activity i and T is the total session time. When this coefficient is maximum, randomness is maximum—behaviors are allocated in the most likely (and therefore least informative) way: Brillouin (1962) explicitly adopted log $(W)/T$ as an index of entropy, or randomness. The use of Equation 33 engages two additional constraints: first, we must presume that the distribution is stationary, thus ruling out the use of this model for behavior in transition. If we redraw the coordinates of Rachlin's graphs as *rates* of consumption, after the animal's state has returned to equilibrium the consumption vectors will describe a type of random walk around the point of average ad libitum consumption (see Collier's comments on path independence, this volume). It is only in this area that the entropy model may be applied (although Jaynes, 1981, has speculated about the nature of the paths a system might take in its approach to maximum entropy). The second constraint is that there be no important sequential dependencies in the behavior from one moment to the next; this rules the model out for situations in which there are strong schedule effects (see, e.g., Annable & Wearden, 1979, where the imposition of reinforcement contingencies ruins the prediction of a Boltzmann distribution).

Noting these many boundary conditions, let us proceed with the formal development: transforming Equation 33 and employing the method of Lagrange multipliers yields

$$L = \log (W) + \phi T + \psi A. \qquad (34)$$

Next we substitute from Equations 31 and 32 and set the partials to zero. This yields the Boltzmann distribution

$$t_i = ke^{-\psi a_i}, \qquad (35)$$

(where $k = e^{-(1+\phi)}$), which predicts an exponential function relating the time spent in an activity and the activation necessary for its emission.

Since we do not know the characteristic activation level of each behavior, we rely on Hanson's conjecture and simply rank order them in terms of their frequency of occurrence (measured as the time spent engaged in them), and predict that the actual frequency of a behavior will be a negative exponential function of its rank.

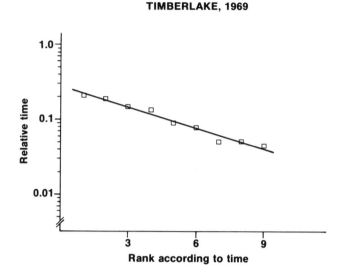

Figure 11. A Boltzmann curve for grooming and exploratory behavior for six rats exposed to constant conditions (habituation). (The data are from Timberlake, 1969; the figure is from Hanson, 1980.)

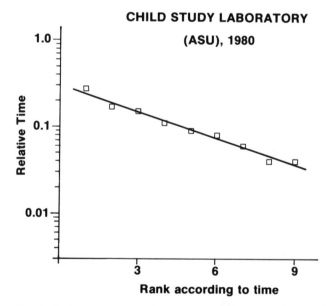

Figure 12. A Boltzmann curve for nine activities in a play setting, collected from seven children over a 20-minute period. (From Hanson, 1980.)

Hanson (1980) presents data that seem to vindicate this chain of assumptions. Examples are given in Figures 11 and 12, where the activities of rats in an unchanging environment are plotted in semilogarithmic coordinates, and the activities of children in a play environment are plotted in a like manner. The predicted relationship is found. These results have been noted in numerous contexts, but there are notable exceptions: Zipf (1949) found that the relationship between the frequency of use of a word and its rank is hyperbolic, not exponential. Hanson suggests that this difference is due to the sequential dependencies found in all textual material: simulations of random distributions with sequential dependencies added biased the data from an exponential toward a hyperbolic form.

Little is known about an error theory for this type of representation; reranking the order of activities after an intervention "uses up" many degrees of freedom, and we may find that common distributions of data, such as the Gaussian, conform reasonably well to the Boltzmann when plotted appropriately. During this symposium, Don Jensen demonstrated that a large error component added to a nonexponential distribution can generate a good fit to the Boltzmann when the data are reranked. Even if these statistical problems are overcome, we may wonder whether the data tell us more about a priori categories of behavior or about human categorization of behavior. Preliminary results by Craig Allen using automatic recording and cluster analysis suggest the former. Hanson's work is provocative in that it calls forth many questions and at the same time justifies their consideration by the promise of a new approach to the description of behavior—one that has already demonstrated impressive regularities.

Summary

Several diverse models have been presented here, all explorations of the postulate that incentives excite animals. This arousal is presumed to be not a simple physiological response to ingested food, but rather a functional property of behavior, one that guides learning and performance. If our research involved predators, rather than omnivores and granivores, or if it involved noxious stimulation, we might find that incentives generated quiescence—stalking or freezing—even though the dynamic properties of that response followed similar laws.

Such excitement cannot last forever—and must not if it is to be functional. In earlier work I posited a simple exponential decay of arousal. In this article I show that a consideration of the ways an animal might integrate events over time leads to the choice of an exponentially weighted moving average as the preferred mechanism. This mechanism makes the same predictions as arousal theory, predictions that were verified by examination of warm-up and extinction curves.

As behavior increases in rate and vigor, it approaches physical limitations on its expression. A simple "refractory-period" model was used to permit predictions of behavior at moderate to high rates. This correction for response ceilings does not greatly affect the predicted shape of the warm-up functions, but it does transform the extinction functions from exponential to logistic form. It predicts a hyperbolic relation between rate of responding and rate of reinforcement, a relation first demonstrated by Herrnstein (1970). The current development makes different statements about the nature of the parameters, ones subject to experimental test. One of the parameters is the amount of decay in arousal (or in memory for the previous incentives) that occurs during the delivery of an incentive. This parameter, D, plays an important role in the extension of the model to concurrent schedules of reinforcement. That extension predicts a nonlinear relation between behavior ratios and reinforcement ratios—a prediction that conflicts both with the "matching law" and with its generalization as a power function. The basic model for concurrent schedules may be further extended to concurrent-chain schedules, and by distinguishing between the separate but additive effects of the primary reinforcer and the conditioned reinforcers (terminal link cues) it is able to account for most of the data from this paradigm.

An adaptive averaging algorithm was introduced to accommodate the partial-reinforcement extinction effect. It provides a treatment of extinction phenomena that is consistent with many of the data, and, as a new theory of the extinction process, it provides a perspective that can help make sense of the large diversity of results in this area.

Incentive theory was contrasted with optimization theories, such as economic behaviorism and optimal foraging. It was demonstrated that incentive theory can predict schedule effects at least as well as optimization theories and can do so without assuming that animals maximize anything. The assumption of optimization is a potentially useful technique of inference that is simply unnecessary for the analysis of schedule effects.

An alternate technique of inference is to assume that, once we have taken into account all explicit constraints, the behavior of animals is allocated among the available activities in the most likely way. Hanson (1980) proceeded on this assumption and, invoking the constraint that the total amount of arousal is conserved in that allocation, arrived at the powerful prediction that the frequency of any activity will be an exponential function of its rank. The prediction was validated.

Conclusion

This paper presents a series of models that together form a theory of behavior. It is called incentive theory, and it is primarily concerned with the invigoration of behavior, not with its direction. All the models are simple, both in form and in the assumptions they make. Most of them could be replaced with similar forms without greatly altering the nature of the theory. What I have attempted is a coherent approach to some of the phenomena of behavior; much work still is necessary in applying it to other phenomena and modifying it where needed. I beg forgiveness of the cautious reader for presenting this theory in its current provisional state and doing so in a manner that seems to breeze past difficulties. Difficulties have been much on the mind of learning theorists lately and have distracted some to a study of exceptions and constraints, others to a search for analogues to constructs that have been employed in an attempt to understand human cognition. I think behavior is simpler than that, and susceptible to some general theories. The current theory is grounded in universal processes—averaging, response constraints, entropy. Insofar as these have been captured correctly in our models, the current theory will provide secure footing for a broader exploration of motivational processes.

REFERENCES

Ainslie, G. Specious reward: A behavioral theory of impulsiveness and impulse control. *Psychological Bulletin*, 1975, **82**, 463–496.

Allen, C. M. Patterns of activity and food oriented behavior induced by schedules of water reinforcement. Master's thesis, Arizona State University, 1980.

Allen, C. M. On the exponent in the "generalized" matching equation. *Journal of the Experimental Analysis of Behavior*, 1981, **35**, 125–127.

Allen, C. M., & Hanson, S. J. Studies of extinction in the pigeon. Unpublished manuscript, Arizona State University, 1980.

Allison, J., Miller, M., & Wozny, M. Conservation in behavior. *Journal of Experimental Psychology: General*, 1979, **108,** 4–34.

Annable, A., & Wearden, J. H. Grooming movements as operants in the rat. *Journal of the Experimental Analysis of Behavior*, 1979, **32,** 297–304.

Autor, S. M. The strength of conditioned reinforcers as a function of the frequency and probability of reinforcement. Originally published 1960. Reprinted in D. P. Hendry (Ed.), *Conditioned reinforcement.* Homewood, Ill.: Dorsey Press, 1969.

Badia, P., Harsh, J., & Coker, C. C. Choosing between fixed time and variable time shock. *Learning and Motivation,* 1975, **6,** 264–278.

Barofsky, I., & Hurwitz, D. Within ratio responding during fixed ratio performance. *Psychonomic Science*, 1968, **11,** 263–264.

Baum, W. M. The correlation-based law of effect. *Journal of the Experimental Analysis of Behavior*, 1973, **20,** 137–153.

Baum, W. M. On two types of deviation from the matching law: Bias and undermatching. *Journal of the Experimental Analysis of Behavior*, 1974, **22,** 231–242.

Baum, W. M. Time allocation in human vigilance. *Journal of the Experimental Analysis of Behavior*, 1975, **23,** 45–53.

Baum, W. M. Matching, undermatching, and overmatching in studies of choice. *Journal of the Experimental Analysis of Behavior*, 1979, **32,** 269–281.

Baum, W. M. Changing over and choice. In C. M. Bradshaw, E. Szabadi, and C. F. Lowe (Eds.), *Quantification of steady-state operant behavior.* New York: Elsevier, 1981.

Bolles, R. C. Learning, motivation and cognition. In W. K. Estes (Ed.), *Handbook of cognition and learning* (vol. 1). New York: Academic Press, 1976.

Bradshaw, C. M., Ruddle, H. V., & Szabadi, E. Studies of concurrent performances in humans. In C. M. Bradshaw, E. Szabadi, & C. F. Lowe (Eds.), *Quantification of steady-state operant behavior.* New York: Elsevier, 1981.

Bradshaw, C. M., Szabadi, E., and Bevan, P. Behavior of humans in variable-interval schedules of reinforcement. *Journal of the Experimental Analysis of Behavior*, 1976, **26,** 135–141.

Brillouin, L. *Science and information theory* (2nd ed.). New York: Academic Press, 1962.

Catania, A. C. Self-inhibiting effects of reinforcement. *Journal of the Experimental Analysis of Behavior*, 1973, **19,** 517–526.

Chung, S.-H. Effects of delayed reinforcement in a concurrent situation. *Journal of the Experimental Analysis of Behavior*, 1965, **8,** 439–444.

Chung, S.-H., & Herrnstein, R. J. Choice and delay of reinforcement. *Journal of the Experimental Analysis of Behavior*, 1967, **10,** 67–74.

Cicerone, R. A. Preference for mixed versus constant delay of reinforcement. *Journal of the Experimental Analysis of Behavior*, 1976, **25,** 257–261.

Clark, F. C. Some quantitative properties of operant extinction data. *Psychological Reports*, 1959, **5,** 131–139.

Clutton-Brock, T. H., & Harvey, P. H. (Eds.). *Readings in Sociobiology*. San Francisco: Freeman, 1978.

Collier, G., Hirsch, E., & Hamlin, P. H. The ecological determinants of reinforcement in the rat. *Physiology and Behavior*, 1972, **9**, 705–716.

Collier, G. H., & Rovee-Collier, C. K. A comparative analysis of optimal foraging behavior: Laboratory simulation. In A. C. Kamil & T. Sargent (Eds.), *Foraging behavior: Ecological, ethological and psychological approaches*. New York: Garland Press, 1980.

Davison, M. C. Preference for mixed-interval versus fixed-interval schedules. *Journal of the Experimental Analysis of Behavior*, 1969, **12**, 247–252.

Davison, M., & Ferguson, A. The effects of different component response requirements in multiple and concurrent schedules. *Journal of the Experimental Analysis of Behavior*, 1978, **29**, 283–295.

Davison, M. C., & Temple, W. Preference for fixed-interval schedules: An alternative model. *Journal of the Experimental Analysis of Behavior*, 1973, **20**, 393–403.

Dean, R. D., Leahy, W. H., & McKee, D. L. (Eds.). *Spatial economic theory*. New York: Free Press, 1970.

Deluty, M. F. Excitatory and inhibitory effects of free reinforcers. *Animal Learning and Behavior*, 1976, **4**, 436–440.

Deluty, M. F. Self-control and impulsiveness involving short-term and long-term punishing events. In C. M. Bradshaw, E. Szabadi, & C. F. Lowe (Eds.), *Quantification of steady-state operant behavior*. New York: Elsevier, 1981.

deVilliers, P. A. Choice in concurrent schedules and a quantitative formulation of the law of effect. In W. K. Honig & J. E. R. Staddon (Eds.), *Handbook of operant behavior*. Englewood Cliffs, N.J.: Prentice-Hall, 1977.

deVilliers, P. A., & Herrnstein, R. J. Toward a law of response strength. *Psychological Bulletin*, 1976, **83**, 1131–1153.

Dinsmoor, J. A., & Hughes, L. H. Training rats to press a bar to turn off shock. *Journal of Comparative and Physiological Psychology*, 1956, **49**, 235–238.

Downing, K., & Neuringer, A. Autoshaping as a function of prior food presentations. *Journal of the Experimental Analysis of Behavior*, 1976, **26**, 463–469.

Duncan, B. & Fantino, E. The psychological distance to reward. *Journal of the Experimental Analysis of Behavior*, 1972, **18**, 23–34.

Eiserer, L. A. Effects of food primes on the operant behavior of nondeprived rats. *Animal Learning and Behavior*, 1978, **6**, 308–312.

Essock, S. M., & Reese, E. P. Preference for and effects of variable- as opposed to fixed-reinforcer duration. *Journal of the Experimental Analysis of Behavior*, 1974, **21**, 89–97.

Faden, A. M. *Economics of space and time*. Ames: Iowa State University Press, 1977.

Fantino, E. Choice and rate of reinforcement. *Journal of the Experimental Analysis of Behavior,* 1969, **12,** 723–730.

Fantino, E. Conditioned reinforcement: Choice and information. In W. K. Honig and J. E. R. Staddon (Eds.), *Handbook of operant behavior.* Englewood Cliffs, N.J.: Prentice-Hall, 1977.

Fantino, E. Contiguity, response strength, and the delay reduction hypothesis. In P. Harzem & M. D. Zeiler (Eds.), *Advances in the analyses of behavior.* Vol. **2.** *Predictability, correlation and contiguity.* Chichester: John Wiley, 1981.

Fantino, E., Squires, N., Delbruck, N., & Peterson, C. Choice behavior and the acessibility of the reinforcer. *Journal of the Experimental Analysis of Behavior,* 1972, **18,** 35–43.

Farley, J., & Fantino, E. The symmetrical law of effect and the matching relation in choice behavior. *Journal of the Experimental Analysis of Behavior,* 1978, **29,** 37–60.

Fast, J. D. *Entropy.* Eindhoven, Holland: Philips Technical Library, 1962.

Feynman, R. P., Leighton, R. B., & Sands, M. *Lectures on physics.* Menlo Park: Addison-Wesley, 1963.

Galvani, P. F., & Twitty, M. T. Effects of intertrial interval and exteroceptive feedback duration on discriminative avoidance acquisition in the gerbil. *Animal Learning and Behavior,* 1978, **6,** 166–173.

Gentry, G. D., & Marr, M. J. Choice and reinforcement delay. *Journal of the Experimental Analysis of Behavior,* 1980, **33,** 27–37.

Green, L., & Rachlin, H. Pigeons' preferences for stimulus information: Effects of amount of information. *Journal of the Experimental Analysis of Behavior,* 1977, **27,** 255–263.

Hall, J. F. *Classical conditioning and instrumental learning.* Philadelphia: J. B. Lippincott, 1976.

Hanson, S. J. Studies of diversity in the pigeon. Ph.D. diss., Arizona State University, 1980.

Hanson, S. J., & Killeen, P. R. Measurement and modelling of behavior under fixed-interval schedules of reinforcement. *Journal of Experimental Psychology: Animal Behavior Processes,* 1981, **7,** 129–131.

Hardy, G. H., Littlewood, J. E., & Polya, G. *Inequalities.* Cambridge: Cambridge University Press, 1959.

Harzem, P., & Harzem, A. L. Discrimination, inhibition, and simultaneous association of stimulus properties: A theoretical analysis of reinforcement. In P. Harzem & M. D. Zeiler (Eds.), *Advances in the analysis of behavior.* Vol. 2: *Prediction, correlation and contiguity.* Chichester: John Wiley, 1981.

Hearst, E., & Jenkins, H. M. *Sign-tracking: The stimulus-reinforcer relation and directed action.* Austin: Psychonomic Society, 1974.

Herrnstein, R. J. Relative and absolute strength of response as a function of frequency of reinforcement. *Journal of the Experimental Analysis of Behavior,* 1961, **4,** 267–272.

Herrnstein, R. J. Secondary reinforcement and rate of primary reinforcement. *Journal of the Experimental Analysis of Behavior,* 1964, **7,** 27–36. (a)

Herrnstein, R. J. Aperiodicity as a factor in choice. *Journal of the Experimental Analysis of Behavior*, 1964, **7**, 179–182. (b)

Herrnstein, R. J. On the law of effect. *Journal of the Experimental Analysis of Behavior*, 1970, **13**, 243–266.

Herrnstein, R. J., & Vaughn, W. Jr. Melioration and behavioral allocation. In J. E. R. Staddon (Ed.), *Limits to action*. New York: Academic Press, 1980.

Heyman, G. M., & Bouzas, A. Context dependent changes in the reinforcing strength of schedule-induced drinking. *Journal of the Experimental Analysis of Behavior*, 1980, **33**, 327–335.

Hineline, P. N. Warmup in avoidance as a function of time since prior training. *Journal of the Experimental Analysis of Behavior*, 1978, **29**, 87–103.

Hineline, P. N. Warmup in free-operant avoidance as a function of the response-shock = shock-shock interval. *Journal of the Experimental Analysis of Behavior*, 1978, **30**, 281–291. (b)

Hirsch, E., & Collier, G. Effort as a determinant of intake and patterns of drinking in the guinea pig. *Physiology and Behavior*, 1974, **12**, 647–655.

Hoffman, H. F., Fleshler, M., & Chorny, H. Discriminated bar-press avoidance. *Journal of the Experimental Analysis of Behavior*, 1961, **4**, 309–316.

Horn, D. H., Mitchell, R., & Stairs, G. R. (Eds.). *Analysis of ecological systems*. Columbus: Ohio State University Press, 1979.

Hull, C. L. *Principles of behavior*. New York: Appleton-Century, 1943.

Hursh, S. R., & Fantino, E. Relative delay of reinforcement and choice. *Journl of the Experimental Analysis of Behavior*, 1973, **19**, 437–450.

Ison, J. R. Experimental extinction as a function of number of reinforcements. *Journal of Experimental Psychology*, 1962, **64**, 314–317.

Jaynes, E. T. Entropy as a prediction-generating functional. Invited address, American Physical Society, Phoenix, Ariz., 1981.

Jennings, W., & Collier, G. Response effort as a determinant of instrumental performance in the rat. *Journal of Comparative and Physiological Psychology*, 1970, **72**, 263–266.

Kamil, A. C., & Sargent, T. *Foraging behavior: Ecological, ethological, and psychological approaches*. New York: Garland Press, 1980.

Kanarek, R. B., & Collier, G. Effort as a determinant of choice in rats. *Journal of Comparative and Physiological Psychology*, 1973, **84**, 332–338.

Keesey, R. E. Duration of stimulation and the reward properties of hypothalamic stimulation. *Journal of Comparative and Physiological Psychology*, 1964, **58**, 201–207.

Keller, J. V., & Gollub, L. R. Duration and rate of reinforcement as determinants of concurrent responding. *Journal of the Experimental Analysis of Behavior*, 1977, **28**, 145–153.

Killeen, P. R. On the measurement of reinforcement frequency in the study of preference. *Journal of the Experimental Analysis of Behavior*, 1968, **11**, 263–269.

Killeen, P. R. Reinforcement frequency and contingency as factors in fixed-ratio behavior. *Journal of the Experimental Analysis of Behavior*, 1969, **12**, 391–395.

Killeen, P. R. Preference for fixed-interval schedules of reinforcement. *Journal of the Experimental Analysis of Behavior*, 1970, **14**, 127–131.

Killeen, P. R. Psychophysical distance functions for hooded rats. *Psychological Record*, 1974, **24**, 229–235.

Killeen, P. R. On the temporal control of behavior. *Psychological Review*, 1975, **82**, 89–115.

Killeen, P. R. Arousal: Its genesis, modulation and extinction. In M. D. Zeiler & P. Harzem (Eds.), *Reinforcement and the organization of behavior*. New York: John Wiley, 1979.

Killeen, P. R. Averaging theory. In C. M. Bradshaw, E. Szabadi, & C. F. Lowe (Eds.), *Quantification of steady-state operant behavior*. New York: Elsevier, 1981. (a)

Killeen, P. R. Learning as causal inference. In M. L. Commons & J. A. Nevin (Eds.), *Quantitative analyses of behavior: Discriminative properties of* rein- *forcement schedules*. New York: Pergamon Press, 1981. (b)

Killeen, P. R., Hanson, S. J., & Osborne, S. R. Arousal: Its genesis and manifestation as response rate. *Psychological Review*, 1978, **85**, 571–581.

Killeen, P. R., Smith, J. Phillip, & Hanson, S. J. Central place foraging in *Rattus norvegicus. Animal Behaviour*, 1981, **29**, 64–70.

Kramer, D. L., & Nowell, W. Central place foraging in the eastern chipmunk, *Tamias striatus. Animal Behaviour*, 1980, **28**, 772–778.

Krebs, J. R. Optimal foraging: Decision rules for predators. In J. R. Krebs & N. B. Davis (Eds.), *Behavioral ecology: An evolutionary approach*. London: Blackwell, 1978.

LaJoie, J., & Bindra, D. An interpretation of autoshaping and related phenomena in terms of stimulus contingencies alone. *Canadian Journal of Psychology*, 1976, **30**, 157–173.

Lasiter, P. Models of response strength. Unpublished manuscript, Arizona State University, 1980.

Levine, R. D., & Tribus, M. (Eds.). *The maximum entropy formalism*. Cambridge: Massachusetts Institute of Technology Press, 1979.

Lewontin, R. C. Fitness, survival and optimality. In D. H. Horn, R. Mitchell, & G. R. Stairs (Eds.), *Analysis of ecological systems*. Columbus: Ohio State University Press, 1979.

Logue, A. W. Escape from noise by rats and undermatching. *Psychological Record*, 1978, **28**, 273–280.

MacEwen, D. The effects of terminal-link fixed-interval and variable-interval schedules on responding under concurrent chained schedules. *Journal of the Experimental Analysis of Behavior*, 1972, **18**, 253–262.

Mackintosh, N. J. *The psychology of animal learning*. New York: Academic Press, 1974.

Matthews, L. R., & Temple, W. Concurrent schedules assessment of food preference in cows. *Journal of the Experimental Analysis of Behavior*, 1979, **32**, 245–254.

McDowell, J. J. An analytic comparison of Herrnstein's equations and a multivariate rate equation. *Journal of the Experimental Analysis of Behavior*, 1980, **33,** 397–408.

McDowell, J. J., & Kessel, R. A multivariate rate equation for variable-interval performance. *Journal of the Experimental Analysis of Behavior*, 1979, **31,** 267–283.

McDowell, J. J., & Sulzen, H. M. Dynamic equilibrium on a cyclic-interval schedule with a ramp. *Journal of the Experimental Analysis of Behavior*, 1981, **36,** 9–19.

McFarland, D. J. *Feedback mechanisms in animal behaviour*. New York: Academic Press, 1971.

McSweeney, F. K. Matching and contrast on several concurrent treadle press schedules. *Journal of the Experimental Analysis of Behavior*, 1975, **23,** 193–198.

Menlove, R. L., Inden, H. M., & Madden, E. G. Preference for fixed over variable access to food. *Animal Learning and Behavior*, 1979, **7,** 499–503.

Michael, J. L. Reinforcement magnitude and the inhibiting effect of reinforcement. *Journal of the Experimental Analysis of Behavior*, 1979, **32,** 265–268.

Milsum, J. H. *Biological control systems analysis*. New York: McGraw-Hill, 1966.

Myers, D. L., & Myers, L. E. Undermatching: A reappraisal of performance on concurrent variable-interval schedules of reinforcement. *Journal of the Experimental Analysis of Behavior*, 1977, **25,** 203–214.

Nakamura, C. Y., & Anderson, N. H. Avoidance behavior differences within and between strains of rats. *Journal of Comparative and Physiological Psychology*, 1962, **55,** 740–747.

Nevin, J. A., & Baum, W. M. Feedback functions for variable-interval reinforcement. *Journal of the Experimental Analysis of Behavior*, 1980, **34,** 207–217.

Nevin, J. A., & Mandell, C. Conditioned reinforcement and choice. *Journal of the Experimental Analysis of Behavior*, 1978, **29,** 135–148.

Olson, R. D. The effect of warm-up on the PRE in the discriminated avoidance paradigm. *Psychonomic Science*, 1971, **23,** 253–254.

Powell, R. W. Analysis of warm-up effects during avoidance in wild and domesticated rodents. *Journal of Comparative and Physiological Psychology*, 1972, **2,** 311–316.

Prelec, D., & Herrnstein, R. J. Feedback functions for reinforcement: A paradigmatic experiment. *Animal Learning and Behavior*, 1978, **6,** 181–186.

Rachlin, H. A molar theory of reinforcement schedules. *Journal of the Experimental Analysis of Behavior*, 1978, **30,** 345–360.

Rachlin, H., & Burkhard, B. The temporal triangle: Response substitution in instrumental conditioning. *Psychological Review*, 1978, **85,** 22–47.

Rachlin, H., & Green, L. Commitment, choice, and self-control. *Journal of the Experimental Analysis of Behavior*, 1972, **17,** 15–22.

Rachlin, H., Battalio, R., Kagel, J., & Green, L. Maximization theory in behavioral psychology. *Behavioral and Brain Sciences,* 1981, **4,** 371–417.

Rachlin, H., Green, L., Kagel, J. H., & Battalio, R. C. Economic demand theory and psychological studies of choice. In G. H. Bower (Ed.), *The psychology of learning and motivation* (Vol. 10). New York: Academic Press, 1976.

Rescorla, R. A., and Wagner, A. R. A theory of Pavlovian conditioning: Variations in the effectiveness of reinforcement and nonreinforcement. In A. H. Black & W. F. Prokasy (Eds.), *Classical conditioning.* Vol. 2. *Current research and theory.* New York: Appleton-Century-Crofts, 1972.

Schneider, J. W. Reinforcer effectiveness as a function of reinforcer rate and magnitude: A comparison of concurrent performances. *Journal of the Experimental Analysis of Behavior,* 1973, **20,** 461–471.

Schroeder, S. R., & Holland, J. G. Reinforcement of eye movement with concurrent schedules. *Journal of the Experimental Analysis of Behavior,* 1969, **12,** 897–903.

Seligman, M. E. P., & Hager, J. L. (Eds.). *Biological boundaries of learning.* New York: Appleton-Century-Crofts, 1972.

Shettleworth, S. J. Reinforcement and the organization of behavior in golden hamsters: Hunger, environment, and food reinforcement. *Journal of Experimental Psychology: Animal Behavior Processes,* 1975, **1,** 56–87.

Shettleworth, S. J., & Juergensen, M. R. Reinforcement and the organization of behavior in golden hamsters: Brain stimulation reinforcement for seven action patterns. *Journal of Experimental Psychology: Animal Behavior Processes,* 1980, **6,** 352–375.

Shimp, C. P. Optimal behavior in free-operant experiments. *Psychological Review,* 1969, **76,** 97–112.

Shimp, C. P. Short-term memory in the pigeon: The previously reinforced response. *Journal of the Experimental Analysis of Behavior,* 1976, **26,** 487–493.

Shull, R. L. The response-reinforcement dependency in fixed interval schedules of reinforcement. *Journal of the Experimental Analysis of Behavior,* 1970, **14,** 55–60.

Smith, J. Phillip, Maybee, J. G., & Maybee, F. M. Effects of increasing distance to food and deprivation level on food hoarding in *Rattus norvegicus. Behavioral and Neural Biology,* 1979, **27,** 302–318.

Squires, N., & Fantino, E. A model for choice in simple concurrent and concurrent-chains schedules. *Journal of the Experimental Analysis of Behavior,* 1971, **15,** 27–38.

Staddon, J. E. R. Spaced responding and choice: A preliminary analysis. *Journal of the Experimental Analysis of Behavior,* 1968, **11,** 669–682.

Staddon, J. E. R. On the notion of cause, with applications to behaviorism. *Behaviorism,* 1973, **1,** 25–63.

Staddon, J. E. R. Temporal control, attention, and memory. *Psychological Review,* 1974, **81,** 375–391.

Staddon, J. E. R. Learning as adaptation. In W. K. Estes (Ed.), *Handbook of learning and cognitive processes* (Vol. 2). Hillsdale, N.J.: Erlbaum, 1975.

Staddon, J. E. R. On Herrnstein's equation and related forms. *Journal of the*

Experimental Analysis of Behavior, 1977, **28,** 163–170.

Staddon, J. E. R. Regulation and time allocation: Comment on "Conservation in behavior." *Journal of Experimental Psychology: General,* 1979, **108,** 35–40. (a)

Staddon, J. E. R. Operant behavior as adaptation to constraint. *Journal of Experimental Psychology: General,* 1979, **108,** 48–67. (b)

Staddon, J. E. R. (Ed.). *Limits to action: The allocation of individual behavior.* New York: Academic Press, 1980.

Staddon, J. E. R. Behavioral competition, contrast and matching. In M. Commons and J. A. Nevin (Eds.), *Quantitative analyses of operant behavior: The second Harvard symposium.* Cambridge, in press.

Staddon, J. E. R., & Innis, N. K. Preference for fixed vs. variable amounts of reward. *Psychonomic Science,* 1966, **4,** 193–194.

Staddon, J. E. R., & Motheral, S. On matching and maximizing in operant choice experiments. *Psychological Review,* 1978, **85,** 436–444.

Staddon, J. E. R., & Simmelhag, V. L. The "superstition" experiment: A re-examination of its implications for the principles of adaptive behavior. *Psychological Review,* 1971, **78,** 3–43.

Stalling, R. B., Moreland, J. W., Merrill, K. H., & Scotti, J. Continuous reinforcement interpolated between intermittent reinforcement and extinction decreases resistance to extinction. *Behaviour Analysis Letters,* 1981, **1,** 89–95.

Steinhauer, G. D., Davol, G. H., & Lee, A. Acquisition of the autoshaped key peck as a function of amount of preliminary magazine training. *Journal of the Experimental Analysis of Behavior,* 1976, **25,** 355–359.

Terry, W. S. Effects of food-reinforcer primes during acquisition of an instrumental running response in rats. *Journal of General Psychology,* 1980, **102,** 265–274.

Timberlake, W. Continuous coding of general activity in the rat during repeated exposure to a constant environment and to stimulus change. Ph.D. diss., University of Michigan, 1969.

Timberlake, W. A molar equilibrium theory of learned performance. In G. Bower (Ed.), *The psychology of learning and motivation* (Vol. 14), in press.

Timberlake, W., & Allison, J. Response deprivation: An empirical approach to instrumental performance. *Psychological Review,* 1974, **81,** 146–164.

Todorov, J. C. Interaction of frequency and magnitude of reinforcement on concurrent performances. *Journal of the Experimental Analysis of Behavior,* 1973, **19,** 451–458.

Tolman, E. C. Prediction of vicarious trial and error by means of the schematic sowbug. *Psychological Review,* 1939, **46,** 318–336.

Trevett, A. J. Davison, M. C., & Williams, R. J. Performance in concurrent interval schedules. *Journal of the Experimental Analysis of Behavior,* 1972, **17,** 369–374.

Valle, F. P. *Motivation: Theories and issues.* Monterey, Calif.: Brooks/Cole, 1975.

Walker, S. F., & Hurwitz, H. M. B. Effects of relative reinforcer duration on concurrent response rates. *Psychonomic Science*, 1971, **22**, 45–47.

Walker, S. F., Wheatley, K. J., & Engberg, L. A. Choice performance in several concurrent key-peck treadle-press reinforcement schedules. *Journal of the Experimental Analysis of Behavior*, 1978, **29**, 181–190.

Wheatley, K. L., & Engberg, L. A. Choice performance in several concurrent key-peck treadle-press reinforcement schedules. *Journal of the Experimental Analysis of Behavior*, 1978, **29**, 198–190.

Williams, B. A. Information effects on the response-reinforcer association. *Animal Learning and Behavior*, 1978, **6**, 371–379.

Williams, B. A., & Fantino, E. Effects on choice of reinforcement delay and conditioned reinforcement. *Journal of the Experimental Analysis of Behavior*, 1978, **29**, 77–86.

Young, J. S. Discrete-trial choice in pigeons: Effects of reinforcer magnitude. *Journal of the Experimental Analysis of Behavior*, 1981, **35**, 23–29.

Zipf, G. K. *Human behavior and the principle of least effort.* Cambridge: Addison-Wesley, 1949.

The Imposition of Structure on Behavior and the Demolition of Behavioral Structures

Donald M. Baer

University of Kansas

THE ABUNDANCE OF BEHAVIORAL STRUCTURES

*I*n the descriptive study of behavior, we inevitably find structures. These structures take the forms of stimulus-response dependencies and response-response dependencies. The stimulus-response dependencies have only a few forms: some behavior seems to occur only in response to a certain stimulus; some behavior occurs in response to certain stimuli and at other times as well; some behavior seems never to occur in the presence of certain stimuli; and some behavior, at first responsive to certain stimuli, becomes unresponsive to them (sometimes temporarily, sometimes permanently) if these stimuli occur too quickly or too often. The response-response dependencies appear in somewhat greater variety: some behaviors seem to be chained together in an invariable sequence; some behaviors co-occur loosely on appropriate occasions, as if each were substitutable for any other; some behaviors co-occur on appropriate occasions but in an invariant hierarchy, as if one were most appropriate to the occasion, another appropriate only in case the first cannot occur, a third appropriate only in case neither of the first two can occur, and so forth; some behaviors seem to depend on the prior existence of certain other behaviors in the organism's repertoire; some behaviors will occur because they provide the opportunity for certain other behaviors to occur; and some behaviors will not occur if they reduce the opportunities for certain other behaviors to occur.

In the descriptive study of behavior, these structures are encountered often enough to provoke labels: reflexes, instincts, traits, preferences, schemata, prepotencies, prerequisites, and so on. Labels, it seems, help to ensconce whatever they label as actual, fundamental, and natural. Thus, in the descriptive study of behavior, if it is inevitable to find such structures, and if they are found often enough to be labeled as such, then it will be inevitable to ask whether these structures may not be necessary—whether they are the essential characteristics of at least some behaviors and must be as they are.

In the analytic study of behavior, we inevitably find ways to make structures, remake them, and unmake them. Indeed, that is in large part the goal of the analytic study of behavior: to discover those variables that bring behavior under experimental control and that make it into any shape or organization imaginable. In pursuing that goal, behavior analysts have achieved great success; they have found a relatively small body of environmental variables, mainly in the form of stimulus-response-stimulus contingencies (usually called operant conditioning) that yield very thorough control over a considerable variety of behaviors. (For a chronological view of this achievement see Skinner, 1938; Keller & Schoenfeld, 1950; Skinner, 1953; Honig, 1966; Millenson, 1967; Honig & Staddon, 1977). That control did indeed allow the making of behavioral structures, so comprehensively that Skinner (1953, p. 91) summed it up in metaphor:

> Operant conditioning shapes behavior as a sculptor shapes a lump of clay. Although at some point the sculptor seems to have produced an entirely novel object, we can always follow the process back to the original undifferentiated lump, and we can make the successive stages by which we return to this condition as small as we wish. At no point does anything emerge which is very different from what preceded it. The final product seems to have a special unity or integrity of design, but we cannot find a point at which this suddenly appears. In the same sense, an operant is not something which appears full grown in the behavior of the organism. It is the result of a continuous shaping process.

In justification of this metaphor, Skinner could display a body of experimental results in which each of the behavioral structures just outlined had been constructed at least a few times, and sometimes in very many examples; and in which some already existing structures had been encountered, deliberately demolished, and remade according to experimental specifications. At the time he wrote, this had been done with a few examples in a small number of species; by the time of Honig and Staddon anthology (1977) it had been done much more diversely in a wider range of species, and in particular had been extended to many of the important, real-life behaviors of humans (especially those considered problems) (cf. Leitenberg, 1976; Kazdin, 1978).

The Null Hypothesis

If, in the analytic study of behavior, structures are made, demolished, and remade easily, frequently, and with increasing generality across behaviors, species, and settings, it will be inevitable to ask whether all behavioral structures might be alike in this respect. Experimental structures represent strong cases for this question: we know how they are made and unmade. Already existing structures represent weak cases for this question: we knew nothing about how they were made, if they were made; we know only that they are there now. Thus the strong case is likely to push us toward a null hypothesis: *Behavior has no necessary structure other than trivial.*

It is important to remember what a null hypothesis is. In experimental science, a null hypothesis is stated simply to make explicit what experimental question is being asked and answered, and to make clear where the burden of proof lies. This null hypothesis follows from strong knowledge that some structures are unnecessary, in that we made them or remade them experimentally, and the weak knowledge that other structures exist now but for unknown reasons. Thus the burden of proof is given to any assertion that some structures are necessary structures (because what we know about the ones that we know about is that they are unnecessary).

In other words, this null hypothesis is stated because it is inductively obvious. Our experimental experience with behavior, when positive, is that behavior is always available to be shaped into any reasonable form and brought under the control of any reasonable stimulus, and that this can be done with more than one behavior at a time, so that behaviors acquire interdependencies. Implicit in this inductive generalization is an absence of a formal definition of the unit of behavior. Skinner made that point central (1953, pp. 94–95), arguing that what *we* call "responses" are more usefully thought of as aggregates of "elements": In reinforcement,

> the *elements* are strengthened wherever they occur. This leads us to identify the element rather than the response as the unit of behavior. It is a sort of behavioral atom, which may never appear by itself upon any single occasion but is the essential ingredient or component of all ob-

served instances. The reinforcement of a response increases the probability of all responses containing the same elements. . . .

We lack adequate tools to deal with the continuity of behavior or with the interaction among operants attributable to common atomic units. The operant represents a valid level of analysis, however, because the properties which define a response are observable data. A given set of properties may be given a functional unity. Although methods must eventually be developed which will not emphasize units at this level, they are not necessary to our understanding of the principal dynamic properties of behavior.

Thus, for this null hypothesis, the definition of operant behavior can always be functional: it is simply that event of the organism that best brings about the environmental consequence specified in the shaping contingency. To the extent that we can arrange the necessary events contingent on just that aspect or form of the behavior that we desire, to that extent we can produce just that aspect or form of behavior for performance by the organism. Furthermore, we can do this with a number of behaviors at more or less the same time, concurrently attach them to common or diverse stimuli, and chain them together into sequences we have chosen, as arbitrarily as we like. Thus the structure of operant behavior is limited primarily by the structure of our ability to arrange the environment into contingencies with that behavior; to the extent that we can wield the environment more and more completely, to that extent behavior has less and less necessary structure. This is tantamount to saying that it is mainly our current relatively low level of technological control over the environment that seems to leave behavior with apparently necessary structure, and that such a limitation is trivial, in the sense of not intrinsic to the nature of the behavior in question, and to some extent is temporary, anyway.

The other trivial limiting case is the physical limitation of the behaving organism. Pigs don't fly. But such physical limitations can be considered trivial because they leave a great deal of room for behavior to have any structure we choose, within them; and because we know some of them, and see that they are trivial to what we want to analyze; and because we are ignorant of some of them, and so can do nothing about them; and because they are often temporary. Pigs don't fly. Neither do humans, except anyplace in their environment that they want to. Humans *didn't* fly, until they made tools that brought flying within their physical attainments; hang gliders, pedal-driven propellor-impelled gliders, Piper Cubs, jumbo jets, and rockets represent an extraordinary range of such tools, but they are all essentially environmental devices that allow humans to fly. Most of the behavior we study in other organisms requires a piece of the environment for its definition (rats press bars, pigeons peck keys, humans write words on paper with pens). The distinction between pieces of the environment exogenous to the organism (bars, keys, pens) and endogenous to the organism (feathers, fingers, vocal apparatus), while real, need not be fundamental, if the principles of behavior with exogenous tools are the same as the principles of behavior with endogenous ones. (Pigs are not likely to invent flying tools, granted. But is there any doubt that if we presented them with a pig-sized airplane, we could teach them to fly it? Or that if they grew wings aerodynamically capable of lifting them, they would learn to use them? As humans learn to swim?)

The preceding array of inductive generalization and logic predisposes us to a null hypothesis that behavior has no necessary structure other than trivial. But the predisposition is not overwhelming, for the logic is partial, and the inductive generalization is only inductive, and selective besides. Nevertheless, it is there. However, a better case lies in the classic nature of null hypotheses: they state the simplest case, the already known case, the case that new knowledge is to confirm or contradict, if found valid. The null hypothesis is the most conservative statement available at the moment; it is posed to show that the burden of proof lies with any more radical thesis. In the present case, the simpler and more conservative hypothesis is that behavior has no necessary structure. A science of behavior based on that premise is a less complex science than one based on its opposite—compare modern functional theories with either modern or traditional structural ones for exemplification of this argument.

Six Possible Sources of Behavioral Structure

Null hypotheses have one other function: they invite contradiction; and, although it is an invitation to contradict only by hard proof, it is still an invitation, often tendered in the expectation that it will be successfully accepted. That is precisely its role in this chapter and in this volume. The arguments to be put forward now are offered not to settle these issues, but to invite contradiction by proof. This chapter is not meant to conclude that behavior has no necessary structure, but instead to hypothesize that it has none, and so invite a thorough exploration of what will be required to assert any case of necessary structure. Toward that end, the next order of business is to sketch six possible sources of such cases—six sources of assertions that behavior does have some necessary structure:

1. The operant-respondent distinction.
2. Species-specific stereotyped response chains (instincts).
3. Stimulus and response generalization gradients.
4. Response classes
   a. that covary positively.
   b. that covary negatively.
5. Programmed instruction: the ability to find and use sequences of successive instruction to produce a final that apparently could not be produced by its own differential reinforcement.
6. The limited amount of time within which to perform behaviors of various rate and duration characteristics.

THE OPERANT-RESPONDENT DISTINCTION

A distinction between operant and respondent behaviors appeared in Skinner's *Behavior of Organisms* (1938) and has been reiterated since. Respondents are those behaviors, control of which is found in preceding environmental stimulus events. These preceding stimuli elicit the subsequent respondent behavior; that is the essence of its control by the environment. Operants are those behaviors, control of which is found in the environmental consequences that they consistently produce (or that consistently follow them, whether mechanistically produced by them or not).[1] These environmental consequences are said to reinforce the operant; they increase its future probability of occurrence. That is the essence of its control by the environment.

Thus the structure of the environment is the structure of these behaviors. Respondents will occur when their particular eliciting stimuli occur; whatever the environmental structure of their elicitors (and conditioned elicitors), it will be reflected by them in a rather simple correspondence. Operants, by contrast, will reflect the environmental structure of their reinforcers much less stereotypically, probably because the environmental structure of their consequences is determined in great part by them: operants are responses that operate on the environment to change it, exactly in ways relevant to the occurrence of their reinforcers; respondents much less often rearrange the environmental structure of their elicitors. The occurrence of operants will be determined by their

---

1. Perhaps: cf. Staddon's discussion of adventitious reinforcement (1977, pp. 127–128).

contingency with reinforcers; but that contingency can take a great many forms, and many of those forms will confer a different pattern on their effective operants. In particular, the contingency between operant and reinforcer can be one of adding or increasing a stimulus event in the environment, or one of subtracting or lessening such a stimulus event. And in each of these cases, the schedule intervening between operant and reinforcer can take on a formidable variety of relations: according to the passage of time, and to the amount of behavior performed, and to the interaction of the two, and in still different patterns, and in patterns of patterns (cf. Ferster & Skinner, 1957; Staddon, 1977). Consequently it is not useful to discuss operants as having a structure reflecting the structure of their reinforcers in the environment;[2] but it can be simple and descriptive to discuss respondents as reflecting the structure of their elicitors in the environment. Indeed, the existence of a consistent stimulus-response (S-R) relationship is a statement of response structure, even without a discussion of stimulus structure.

The question for this argument is whether S-R dependencies are necessary dependencies. A common implication of many discussions of S-R respondent reflexes is that they are indeed necessary, in that they reflect the biological nature of the organism in its response to the environment. That implication was not part of Skinner's original statement of the operant-respondent distinction; it may have been encouraged slightly by Keller and Schoenfeld's remark that respondents were "commonly, if not always, mediated by the autonomic nervous system, involving smooth muscles and glands" (1950, p. 51).[3] Simply as a matter of observation, it appears that a number of respondents are elicited by a very restricted set of particular stimulus antecedents. If these observations are thorough, and general, then they may represent necessary S-R dependencies, perhaps not because of biological structure, but just because that is

2. Perhaps there are cases in which the structure of an operant is the very restricted choice of reinforcer necessary to control it in a particular way. Teitelbaum (1977) offers an example: rats consistently presented with a distinctive pattern of light, sound, and taste and then made nauseated learn to avoid the taste, not the light or the sound; but rats consistently presented with a distinctive pattern of light, sound, and taste and then shocked learn to avoid the light or the sound, not the taste (pp. 13–14). Yet, in that same chapter, Teitelbaum offers a strong argument against overinterpreting such apparent constraints as necessary structures and suggests that environmental factors may make them less necessary.

3. "If not always" is one of those unfortunate idioms that sometimes is used to mean "but not always" and sometimes is used to mean "and perhaps always." In this instance context does not conclusively determine which meaning was intended.

the way that this response works whenever we observe it. The trouble with this conclusion is that it is limited by the generality of our observation, and by the undoubtable fact that operants come under the control of preceding discriminative stimuli that definitely cannot be considered necessary S-R dependencies.

Operants, defined as such because of their control by their stimulus consequences, can be attached to stimulus antecedents as well, especially if the function of those antecedents is to mark the occasion for some schedule of those consequences. It is well known that the schedule of functional consequences can be made *very* intermittent, such that it will require correspondingly intensive and extensive observation to note its existence and functional operation (Ferster & Skinner, 1957; Staddon, 1977). Such operants then look like respondents, in that they seem to portray an invariant S-R dependency, apparently independent of functional consequences. In fact, of course, they are not independent of functional consequences; the antecedent stimulus—the discriminative stimulus— exerts its control over the operant only because it sets the occasion for the operant's (very occasional) reinforcement. If we know the total history of this response, we also know that this S-R dependency is arbitrary, not necessary: the stimulus can be almost anything to which the organism can respond, and the dependency can be demolished by either extinction or abolition (i.e., by ending all reinforcement or by reinforcing the operant equally well in the absence of the discriminative stimulus and in its presence). If we do not know, but can observe intensively for an extended period, we shall finally note the very occasional contingency with a stimulus consequence and suspect a case of discriminative (unnecessary) stimulus control, even if we are not certain. But if we do not know the history of the response and the discriminative stimulus; or do not observe the response intensively and extensively enough to note its contingencies; or are dealing with a reinforcement contingency of a sort previously unknown to us, such that we fail to attend to the functional consequent stimulus as a conceivably important one (even though it is there before our eyes)—then all we shall know is that this stimulus seems to enter into an invariant S-R dependency, and how will we diagnose it as necessary or unnecessary? Yet it is unnecessary: it is a dependency chosen by the conditioning agency—the experimenter, so to speak—and could have been chosen differently, or left alone as a nondependency; and it can always be unmade, and remade differently.

Thus, discriminated operants can be made to simulate respondents, except, of course, to the agency that made them that way. If we are not that agency, and observe what appears to be an invariant, general S-R dependency, we may be tempted to conclude that it is respondent or necessary or both, but the knowledge that unnecessarily discriminated operants can be made to masquerade in just that way will prevent this conclusion. The difficulty here is largely in the negative definition of respondent or of *necessary* that emerges from the knowledge that operants can be discriminated to arbitrary antecedent stimuli that mark very difficult to observe reinforcement schedules: A respondent is now seen to be essentially a behavior involved in a consistent S-R dependency that has not yet been shown to be fundamentally operant. Respondents are respondents only until shown to be operants (again, cf. Teitelbaum, 1977); thus, necessary is necessary only until shown to be arbitrary or modifiable. A concept of behavioral structure that will collapse as soon as a demonstration of modifiability is gained is a very fragile structure, hence the previous null hypothesis. Furthermore, if discriminated operants can be made to simulate respondents except to the agency that made them that way, then the most powerful research tactic is to attempt to be the agency that makes them that way. Success in that attempt cancels a conclusion of necessary. Failure never means anything more than failure so far, and the most powerful research tactic still is to attempt (differently and better) to be the agency that makes them that way, hence (again) the previous null hypothesis.

SPECIES-SPECIFIC STEREOTYPED RESPONSE CHAINS: FIXED ACTION PATTERNS OR INSTINCTS

Some observed S-R dependencies come in chains of S-R-S-R-S-R . . ., rather than in simple S-R relations. Some of them appear to be stereotypical, occurring always in extremely similar ways, both within a single organism and across organisms of the same species; many of them appear to be species-specific, taking one thoroughly stereotyped form within a given species but a different yet equally stereotyped form within another species; and they frequently serve some very general function, such as grooming, courtship, mating, rearing young, aggression, killing, and the like. One of their most important characteristics is the apparent dependence of each response in the chain on the preceding stimulus, not the consequent one: numerous studies show that experimental removal of some stimuli in the chain stops the chain by aborting the next response, not the preceding one (Tinbergen, 1951). In theoretical approaches such as ethology, they are said to be *fixed action patterns* and *instinctive:* In those approaches they are indeed a structure of behavior, and a necessary and invariant one.

Nevertheless, they look just like respondents, but in chains; they are chained respondents in that each response either contains in itself or automatically produces in the environment the stimulus for the next response. Thus a cat, in close proximity to a mouse, leaps at the mouse claws and head first, which brings its whiskers into contact with the mouse, which elicits a head-turning response in the cat that brings its lips into contact with the mouse, which elicits a mouth-opening response, which produces touch and taste stimulation to mouth and tongue that elicits biting.

If the operant-respondent distinction is not a satisfactory source for rejecting the null hypothesis that behavior can have a necessary structure, then the chained operant–chained respondent distinction will do no better. The crucial observation in faulting the operant-respondent distinction was the ability to construct unnecessary discriminated operants that could simulate respondents as apparently invariant S-R dependencies; again, the crucial observation in faulting fixed action patterns, or instincts, is the ability to construct unnecessary chains of discriminated operants that can simulate apparently invariant S-R-S-R-S-R dependencies, in which the final stimulus (the ultimate reinforcer) is scheduled to the point of near-invisibility to everyone except the scheduling agency. Again, as before, the best research tactic is to attempt to be that scheduling agency, because, as before, the implicit definition of fixed action pattern is a negative one: a fixed action pattern, again, is behavior that has not yet been shown to be unnecessary. Showing a pattern to be unnecessary is a positive act—it can succeed, and when it does its message of nonnecessity is clear. By contrast, trying to show a pattern to be necessary is a negative act: patterns are never shown to be necessary; at best they are shown to be stereotyped, species-specific S-R dependencies that have not yet been analyzed as something else and something unnecessary in its structure. The gradual removal of that "not yet shown to be something else" status was both exemplified and made logically inevitable by Beach many years ago (1955). Even at that time he could show that the essence of arguments about instincts was that they represented only cases in which we did not see the possibility of learning; his reproach was in the form of a survey of the literature of the day indicating that the variety of ways a behavior could be learned was too wide to be tried and exhausted (so that a surviving behavior could then be labeled *unlearned* with certainty). Even demonstrations that a behavior could be brought under close experimental control through selective breeding of an organism's ancestors sometimes were found to be cases in which it was not the behavior that was genetically controlled, but rather the uterine environment of an organism's mother: the behavior was "learned" or not "learned" in that uterine environment (probably by biochemical mechanisms rather than contingencies); the uterine environment might be a necessary structure of that mother, but the behavior the fetus "learned" there was not—it could be modified by transplanting the just-fertilized embryo into the uterus of a mother from another genetic strain. (And was that maternal uterine environment actually a necessary structure? Did it not also require an experimental transplanting of that potential mother, as a fetus, into the uterus of a mother from another strain, to see if she could be influenced by its uterine environment not to develop the critical uterine environment in herself?) Beach's point was that, as long as instinct was defined negatively, as an absence of environmental control, it would remain a fragile construct doing little more than waiting for disconfirmation, case by case. Teitelbaum (1977) exemplified the same logical argument 20 years later, described more of just those cases, and made some suggestions for yet further cases. And Baer (1981a) applied the same logic against the claim that some retarded persons could not profit by attempts at their habilitation (so to speak, that the current nonstructure of their behavior was a necessary nonstructure).

The positive accomplishments of operant conditioning show that chains can be made; that their membership, in terms of both stimuli and responses, can be quite arbitrary; that ordinary discrimination and differentiation techniques can be applied to those stimuli and responses to make them as specific, delimited, and hence stereotyped as desired; that their ultimately supportive reinforcer can be scheduled very intermittently; and that the stimulus controls operating within the chain will prove more crucial to the next response when they are removed experimentally than to the preceding response (of course: a response separated from its reinforcer will show some resistance to extinction, and thus still answer its discriminative stimulus, depending on its previous schedule; but a tightly discriminated operant will rarely be seen in the absence of its discriminative stimulus [or stimuli]). Furthermore, a widely uniform environment can produce uniform chains in all organisms living in that environment: Munn (1955), in an introductory-level developmental psychology text of quite some years ago, used the term *coenotrope* to label behaviors that were learned by virtually everyone in the same way. Humans eat with a tool, for example, despite their ability to eat their food directly by mouth, off the floor, like a dog; in doing so they present a stereotyped, species-specific response, yet one that we know we teach our children rather insistently as a mark of their socialization into humanness. These chains typically[4] represent unnecessary structures that need not have been brought into existence (even though some of them are highly probable, in the absence of a determined experimenter) or can be modified into other forms. Then how can we know that any observed chain is a necessary structure? A conventional answer is to subject these chains to a *deprivation* experiment: to rear or maintain an organism apart from some set of environmental influences that might represent its source of learning, to see if the organism develops that chain anyway. Again, Beach (1955) pointed out that such experiments are competent to prove that the chain is learned in the environment from which the organism was experimentally separated, if the chain fails to develop under those conditions, but are incompetent to prove that the chain, if not learned there (when it develops anyway, despite the deprivation of that environment from the organism), still was not learned somewhere else. Significantly, one of the most difficult environments from which to separate a learning organism is itself. Thus, for example, the very likely behavior of putting our fingers in our mouths can serve as a learning ground for the skillfully gentle use of teeth and jaws, as well as their forceful use (which is what eating teaches us). An organism that licks and mouths its genital area, for example (and such organisms are numerous), may learn there how later to carry its newborn young in its mouth without breaking skin and drawing blood, and such a (learned) skill may be crucial to the continuation of the distinctive, stereotyped chains that constitute mothering in those species. Then the discovery that an organism reared in deprivation of social contact with its mother and other mothers of its species does not display the stereotypic mothering behavior of that species indicates forcefully that such behavior was acquired somehow through that contact (and thus seems to be learned behavior). But the discovery that the distinctive mothering chains survive that

4. But recall the apparent partial exceptions noted by Teitelbaum (1977, under the heading Puzzling Operants [pp. 13–14]); however, at the same time, be sure to follow the totality of Teitelbaum's argument about their significance.

deprivation does not prove that they were not learned and thus are a necessary structure of the species' behavior; it proves only that, if the behavior was learned, it was not learned there.

The fundamental point of Beach's argument was that instinct, as a case in point of necessary behavioral structure, inevitably was negatively defined as unlearned behavior; it can maintain its status as unlearned behavior only as long as we fail to see how it could have been learned. Thus its nonnecessity is something that might be proved positively one day; its necessity is something that is never proved, but merely continues to survive a current absence of proof to the contrary. The force of that point for the special case of instinct is no less than its force for the general case of necessary behavioral structure. A better than negative definition of necessary behavioral structure will be needed if the null hypothesis is to be rejected.

RESPONSE AND STIMULUS GENERALIZATION GRADIENTS

When a response is changed directly (e.g., by environmental contingencies), then other responses are likely to change too, even though they were not touched directly by those change techniques (Catania, 1979, pp. 119–127). Frequently these indirectly changed responses physically resemble the directly changed response; indeed, the degree to which they are changed usually is about the degree to which they physically resemble the directly changed response. Then the physical structure of behavior is a functional structure as well, reminiscent of Skinner's (1953) guess about behavioral units quoted earlier ("a sort of behavioral atom, which may never appear by itself upon any single occasion but is the essential ingredient or component of all observed instances. The reinforcement of a response increases the probability of all responses containing the same elements" [p. 94]). This structure is referred to sometimes as *response generalization*, sometimes as *induction*.

But this structure is a very brief one: as the directly changed response is maintained in its new state, or pushed even further to some different state, the indirectly changed responses, if they never come in contact with any of those change techniques, or any comparably effective ones, promptly revert to their prior state: the generalized or induced change disappears, and the status quo ante is recovered. Indeed, if the behavior-change techniques are reinforcement or punishment contingencies or both, then these contingencies can be applied with little, moderate, or great force to modify the momentary gradient of generalized or induced response changes. Those responses that are desired can be reinforced strongly on rich and consistent schedules; those responses that are not desired can be subjected to perfectly consistent nonreinforcement, or even punishment, to hasten their disappearance; or to merely differential reinforcement, to retard their disappearance or to maintain them indefinitely but at different strengths than the more earnestly desired responses. Virtually any shape of response generalization or response induction can be maintained; and the change or maintenance of that shape over time can itself be shaped. If there is a core of necessary structure in this phenomenon, attributable to the physical similarity of some responses to others, it is short-lived and rather easily covered over by quite arbitrary structures. It is response differentiation that is robust, not response generalization or induction. But response differentiation is as non-necessary as the arbitrariness with which we care to arrange the differentiating contingencies; its structure is what we choose it to be. If there are limits on this range of choice, we have no positive knowledge of them; our positive knowledge is of the changes we can make. If there are apparent limitations, they probably have the same logical status as instincts.

A parallel argument can be made for stimulus-generalization gradients. When a response is changed directly (e.g., by contingencies) in a consistent stimulus situation, then it is likely to change in the same way without direct instigation in other stimulus situations as well; often the degree to which the response is likely to change in these other situations is about the degree to which they physically resemble the stimulus situation in which the response was changed directly. Then the physical structure of stimuli is a functional structure of behavior as well. This structure is sometimes referred to as *stimulus generalization* or *stimulus control*. Its brevity as a source of behavioral structure is comparable to that of response generalization or induction. Discrimination training—the differential application of behavior-changing contingencies to the behavior of operating in these various stimulus situations—will modify these structures quickly or slowly, as desired, and into a wide variety of stimulus controls (cf. Catania, 1979, pp. 139–165; Rilling, 1977). A concept of "stimulus atom," comparable to and interactive with Skinner's "behavioral atom," is easy to posit and is increasingly substantiated empirically as specific experimental cases in point (Rilling, 1977); in those cases they become observable and experimentable and need not be considered either atoms or metaphors. Rilling describes a number of such studies, then summarizes them in terms just short of atomic:

> the presentation of an intermediate test stimulus following discrimination training between two stimuli does not produce a constant, intermediate rate of responding. A significant component of the original behaviors which were conditioned during training remains during generalization testing. . . the microanalysis of stimulus control is to determine and isolate the variables responsible for the mixture of responses which result in the stimulus-generalization gradient. [p. 439]

Rilling's description of such research may be said to be quasi-structural, just as Skinner's positing of behavioral atoms might. But, just as Skinner immediately went on to assert that an analysis of behavioral function made an understanding of behavioral atoms unnecessary at present, Rilling described a set of functional analyses of stimulus control accomplishing the same outcome. Stimulus generalization gradients, like response generalization (or induction) gradients, still seem to be structures to be unmade and remade, rather than categorized, dignified, and institutionalized.

Thus, in summary, response- and stimulus-generalization gradients exist and are momentarily plausible instances of necessary behavioral structure. But they exist so briefly, and are so readily changed into unnecessary structures of so wide a variety open to our choosing, that they have little importance here other than their momentary flouting of the null hypothesis that behavior has no necessary structure.

RESPONSE CLASSES

Behavior can appear to have structure because behaviors co-occur systematically. In some instances this co-occurrence is positive, in others it is negative. These two cases will be discussed separately, for clarity.

Positive co-occurrence. It is a matter of common observation that normal children are capable of imitating almost any reasonable response topography demonstrated to them, especially if it is accompanied by an instruction to imitate. Each imitation is a different response from every other in terms of topography, yet each is clearly an "imitation" at the same time. "To imitate" is a response class in normal children; its members, virtually infinite in number,

all are controlled similarly by the same instruction (e.g., "Do this").
In profoundly retarded children, by contrast, imitation will often be
totally absent—that is, it is a class with no members at all. If, in an
unrealistically bizarre experiment, normal children were invited to
imitate a series of demonstrations, accompanied by the words "Do
this," only to encounter punishment for each successive correct
imitation, they would soon cease to imitate even once any further
demonstrations, despite the insistent "Do this" accompanying
each of them. If, in a benevolent, difficult, but realistic experiment,
profoundly retarded children have shaped in them responses imitative of demonstrations by their teacher, one after another, as
laboriously as will prove necessary, then eventually these children
will begin to display any reasonable untaught, unshaped imitations of new demonstrations by their teachers (Baer, Peterson, &
Sherman, 1967). (The process may require the shaping of 10 to 200
successive different imitations, the first several of which—perhaps
the first many of which—will not deserve the label.) Both experiments demonstrate that imitation is a response class: response-
changing contingencies applied to only some members of the class
produced a similar result in all members of the class (cf. also Baer &
Sherman, 1964). In the bizarre experiment imagined for the normal
children (and in the quite real Baer and Sherman study of 1964), the
origins of the imitative class as a class are unknown—that is simply
the way these behaviors work; why they work in that way is
unexplained. In the benevolent study of the profoundly retarded
children, the origin of their imitative class is clearly in a repetitive
training program applied to them. In the former example the structure revealed by the experiment is, for all we know, necessary; in
the latter example it is obviously unnecessary, in that it is the
experimenter's product.

Quite similar examples can be found, and can be made, in the
classes of behavior called compliance with instructions (Bucher,
1973; Doleys, Wells, Hobbs, Roberts, & Cartelli, 1976), grammar
(Guess, Sailor, Rutherford, & Baer, 1968; Schumaker & Sherman,
1970; Guess & Baer, 1973), syntax (Garcia, Guess, & Byrnes, 1973;
Lutzker & Sherman, 1974), matching to sample (Honig, 1965; Malott
& Malott, 1970), and others. Virtually all these examples are also
instances of concept formation, and thus of stimulus classes, as
much as of response classes; both kinds of classes typically operate
together (cf. Catania, 1979, pp. 159 ff.).

Clearly these are all instances of response structure. But of greatest significance for the present argument is that these instances

represent both natural cases, already in operation in the behavior of many organisms, and constructed instances created experimentally. They are best understood, of course, as constructed classes, especially when they are constructed apparently for the first time in subjects previously deficient in them: In those cases it is tempting to suppose that the experimental procedures found sufficient to accomplish the construction of the response class are relatively clear and relatively complete, and thus that relatively few if any of the events essential to the development of these classes remain unknown in the organism's history. (Certainly this argument is relative, not absolute. There still might be events in the organism's history that are prerequisite to the success of the currently applied experimental events yet produce no discernible part of the desired response class by themselves.)

In constructing these classes, the following characteristics of the process of construction and its results emerge:

1. Some classes must be taught one member at a time, or several at a time; some can be taught all at once. Virtually any teaching method can be useful, depending on the class (including simple instruction, for certain capable organisms). Thus, for example, the reader of this chapter could be asked to underline every word in the text that contains a *ui* digraph. Any reader could then exhibit the response class of underlining every *ui* that appears; readers who also know the definition of "digraph" would systematically underline only some of the *ui*'s, as in *guide* but not as in *tuition;* and readers given the definition of "digraph" then could behave like readers who already know it. These are examples of totally new response classes for all but the most unusual readers, yet they could be established in a moment. That they would depend on the prior existence of several more basic response classes is typical.

2. In those classes that must be taught one or a few members at a time, as more and more members of the class are taught, new members are found to be progressively easier to teach.

3. Eventually (especially in classes that can be generalized), new members begin to appear without direct teaching and will be maintained as class members without explicit maintenance procedures such as experimentally programmed reinforcement.

4. If the teaching was reinforcement-based, and if reinforcement is discontinued for all those members that had previously been reinforced, then all members of the class, previously reinforced and unreinforced alike, extinguish.

5. It is clear that subjects receiving this teaching often can dis-

criminate between reinforced and never-reinforced members of the class, yet they continue to perform both types similarly, unless asked or told not to do so (e.g., Steinman, 1970; Steinman & Boyce, 1971). There are a variety of ways to ask subjects to display this discrimination (e.g., Peterson, 1968; Peterson, Merwin, Moyer, & Whitehurst, 1971) and a variety of explanations of why, when they are not asked, they usually do not display it (e.g., Baer, Peterson, & Sherman, 1967; Bandura & Barab, 1971; Gewirtz, 1971).

6. The range of the final total response class apparently can be controlled by restricting the range of those members used to train the class directly. This is clearest (so far) in the case of imitation. If training is restricted to imitations performed by only finger-hand-arm responses, then untrained, unreinforced finger-hand-arm imitations will emerge and be maintained, yet whole-body imitations and vocal imitations will not; and if training is restricted to whole-body imitations, then untrained, unreinforced whole-body imitations will emerge and be maintained, yet finger-hand-arm imitations and vocal imitations will not. When training is extended from one subclass to another, untrained, unreinforced generalization becomes extended from that subclass to the other, whether it is from the finger-hand-arm subclass to the whole-body subclass, or vice-versa (Garcia, Baer, & Firestone, 1971).

7. Some response classes, such as imitation and compliance with instructions, are generalizable to new instances without direct training. But some other response classes are constructed of arbitrary members and thus cannot systematically be generalized to new members without direct training to establish the new members as members. Thus, if you are taught that $A, C, H, I,$ and R are members of one response class (in that they are established as responses to similar instructions and produce similar reinforcement), and also are taught that $F, G, L, P,$ and T are members of another response class, you have no way of categorizing, say, Q as a member of either the first or the second class. That need not stop you from doing so, but it is a problem that probably precludes seeing systematic response across subjects, or, within one subject, across time. Even so, these arbitrary response classes still behave like classes, in that behavior-change operations applied to only some of their members will produce similar effects in all their members.

Catania (1979, pp. 120–127) points out that there are two definitions of response class in use: (1) those responses that produce similar consequences in similar circumstances, and (2) all those responses systematically produced when a certain set of responses produces similar consequences in similar circumstances:

> For convenience, we will occasionally speak of an operant solely in terms of a class defined by consequences or solely in terms of the distribution generated by these consequences, but it is important to remember that the operant is more strictly defined in terms of the correspondence between these two classes (cf. Catania, 1973a). [p. 127]

In these terms, it is when the correspondence is not perfect (one-to-one) that we find that operations applied to some members of a class produce similar results in all members of the class, and it is this observation that most clearly shows a structure to behavior. Response classes typically look like "traits" of the organism, especially when they operate in a unified way. When we are dealing with an already-existing class we have no knowledge of whether this structure is necessary or nonnecessary; but when we are dealing with those classes that we make experimentally, then the seven characteristics just listed, and especially the sixth of them, show that we are dealing with a largely nonnecessary structure—one that we make in a variety of ways, and can remake in a variety of ways, and can unmake.

In the preceding sentence, *largely* is an important term. Its significance can be appreciated by first contrasting the characteristics of response classes to those of response generalization, which proceeds essentially on a basis of physical similarity. Response classes include responses that have virtually no physical similarity. When an untouched response is affected in the same way by some behavior-changing procedure as is a response to which that procedure is applied directly, and when the responses are physically similar, it is easy to suppose that Skinner's "behavioral atoms" constitute the explanation: it is they who were touched directly in one of those responses, and some of them are in both responses. But when the two responses seem to have no physical resemblance, no behavioral atoms in common, then how do we explain the fact that they are organized into the same response class, such that operations applied to only one of them affect the other in the same way? One tactic is not to explain it at all, and to settle instead for a statement of the procedures that establish and modify this phenomenon, as if they were its explanation. When these procedures can be stated fully enough to account for all the variance ever observed in the phenomenon, they may indeed represent a quite defensible form of explanation. However, some scientists will not remain content with this tactic; they will go on to ask whether some other behavior by the organism is responsible for the organization of these (physically dissimilar) responses into the same response class.[5] Asking this kind of question is tantamount to asserting that just because responses are established by similar consequences in similar circumstances is not enough to *explain* their organization into a response class. Instead, it supposes that these procedures, rather than accomplishing the organization of the class in themselves, prompt some other behavior of the organism into (so to speak) *noting* that these responses have similar consequences in similar circumstances, and (so to speak) doing something organizational about that observation. If so, then these procedures accomplish the creation of a response class only through the mediation of the process by some already-existing behaviors—call them skills—of the organism. If the existence of response classes is taken as evidence of necessary behavioral structure, and if this approach toward explanation is taken, then the significant place to look for necessary structure is in those posited mediating skills, rather than in the initiating environmental procedures, which so clearly have no necessary structure in *them*. In that case the question is whether

---

5. Going on to ask for explanation is clearly a behavior of the scientist, as is not going on to ask for explanation. An analysis of the events that control this behavior is thus an analysis of much of the structure of scientific theory. (When the theory is specifically behavioral theory, we have a case of using a behavioral theory to analyze the behavior of people who make the behavioral theory that is used to analyze the behavior of people who . . . In this sentence, it should be recognized that *using* and *used, analyze,* and *make* all are behaviors too. This apparent lifting by its own bootstraps is one of the explicitly accepted distinctive problems of radical behaviorism.) And what is the stimulus event that separates those scientists satisfied with it as an explanation of response classes from those scientists not yet satisfied with it as an explanation? In general, a scientist seems to behave as if a phenomenon has been explained when it has been related to those terms that the scientist does not attempt to explain; terms are not explained when it seems clear (or likely) that the explanation will have to be made in other terms outside the science as he or she knows it. Such terms are primitive terms of the science, as the scientist knows it. For most behaviorists, reinforcement is such a term—the explanation of why certain stimuli are capable of reinforcing at least some behaviors under at least some conditions is assumed to lie in the neurology, physiology, and biochemistry of the organism, none of which seems within the definitional realm of the behavioral science that the scientist knows or intends to construct. The term discrimination is another such term—the explanation of why the effects of reinforcement become specific to certain stimuli consistently discriminative for the reinforcement contingency again is assumed to lie elsewhere. Thus effort is given to discover *how* reinforcement can be scheduled into what variety of contingencies, and *how* discriminative stimuli can be associated with those scheduled contingencies, rather

those mediating behaviors are necessary or arbitrary. In calling the mediating behaviors *skills*, above (on the premise that something like them is to be considered at all), the possibility is at least suggested that they are acquired, *teachable* behaviors, and, if so, that they can be taught and learned in a variety of ways, in a variety of shapes and forms, and to various degrees of completeness and generality in each of those shapes and forms. If that were true, necessity of structure again would dissolve. But that is the place to ask the question.

The immediately preceding argument is necessarily sketchy. In its competent form it is necessarily quite lengthy. A very competent variant of that form, couched in the context of language as a problem for behavioral analysis, is given by Segal (1977); students of behavioral structure as an analytic point on a continuum between structure and function are commended to its 25 pages.

Negative co-occurrence. Few complex organisms have only one response with which to fulfill an environmental function: alternative ways to the same goal abound in most repertoires. These alternatives often appear as cases of negative co-occurrence: when one response is extinguished, punished, or otherwise prevented, another emerges systematically to fill the same function—or at least

---

than *why* there should be such phenomena at all. (But see Teitelbaum 1977 for an example of the occasional scientist attempting to connect two presumably contiguous realms to make a larger definitional domain.) Whereas reinforcement is behaviorally primitive, conditioned reinforcement is not. It is amenable to explanation by appeal to the discrimination phenomenon and its scheduling with other reinforcers (sometimes: cf. Kelleher & Gollub, 1962; Kelleher, 1966; Gollub, 1977) that are primitive or near-primitive terms in behavioral theory. But the developing behavioral explanation of conditioned reinforcement does not seem likely to accomplish a similarly behavioral explanation of all reinforcement, because conditioned reinforcement seems to require an already-effective reinforcer as a basic part of its process; thus not all reinforcers can be conditioned reinforcers, and so the explanation of why the primal reinforcer reinforces is left untouched. Response classes also can be described in procedural terms, much as conditioned reinforcement can be; but whereas the effects produced by the procedures that generate conditioned reinforcement do not fly in the face of other behavioral principles, those produced by the procedures that generate response classes do: more behavior is generated than was reinforced, and this surplus behavior continues to be maintained in the face of long-term cleanly differential reinforcement that, in virtually all other contexts, would long since have produced its extinction. Furthermore, this surplus behavior continues to respond to the behavior-changing operations applied not to it but to the other members of its class. Even though the procedures for establishing such phenomena are clear enough (but certainly not yet completely investigated), some of their effects strike at least some behavioral scientists as sufficiently paradoxical to require explanation.

to fill the same time in the organism's day. Thus one response is apparently a substitute for the other. Such responses may come in pairs, but more likely they will be found in larger numbers than two and will be arranged in a hierarchy of substitution: response A will be displayed until prevented, whereupon B will be displayed until it too is prevented, whereupon C will be seen until it also cannot occur anymore, whereupon. . . . This hierarchical substitutability is certainly a structure of these responses. Is it a necessary structure?

A common example of such structure is seen in the attention-seeking of many children. In some children attention-seeking has been shaped into an undesirable set of skills; when their undesirability becomes too extreme, behavior modification is sometimes applied. In those cases a likely procedure is extinction: the suspected attention-seeking response is no longer attended to. Usually that succeeds in reducing the undesired behavior. Sometimes, however, another behavior then emerges, which also seems to command attention and often is also undesirable to those whose attention is commanded. Dynamic psychologists on these occasions refer knowingly to "symptom substitution" as prima facie evidence that the entire approach is misguided and dysfunctional. However, the fairly common experience of applied behavior analysts is that the second undesirable response can be dealt with just as was the first; it too is ignored, and it too extinguishes. Often this is the end of the problem; occasionally it is not, in that a third behavior now emerges, which again seems to be attention-seeking in its function and again is undesirable. Indeed, it is not uncommon to note that the third response is more undesirable than was the second, and the second more undesirable than the first. If those dealing with the problem do not lose courage at this point, but extinguish the third response just as they did its two predecessors, they may well find that *this* is indeed the end of the problem—or sometimes they will discover that a fourth response, attention-demanding and even more undesirable than all its predecessors, has now emerged. However, it is significant that these successive emergences do not go on indefinitely; if each is dealt with in its turn, eventually no more will appear. (In my experience with normal and retarded children, the length of these sequences ranges between two and six.) Furthermore, the reduction of each successive behavior typically will go faster.

Research experience in the field deals almost entirely with the demolition of such structures, rather than with their construction. However, from that experience and from the well-known principles of behavior, it is easy to see how such structures could be made, and made arbitrarily.

Most children are reared under contingencies that establish attention as a conditioned reinforcer (cf. Bijou & Baer, 1965, chap. 8). Some of the behaviors they emit systematically produce attention; of these, those that annoy the children's caretakers and others in their audience are likely to produce the richest schedules of attention. They also are likely to produce schedules of disapproval, but children can differ much more in their responsiveness to the effectiveness of disapproval as a punisher than in their responsiveness to the effectiveness of attention as a reinforcer, and so at least some children are likely to have annoying, attention-commanding responses strongly reinforced in their repertoires. Of these, some inevitably will be better taught than others. They will differ by happenstance, and also systematically, in that some will command adult attention better than others (depending on the characteristics of the adults, of course), some will also generate punishment occasionally, and some will prove more effortful or time-consuming than others. Thus a hierarchy of these responses is established as the responses are learned. First in that hierarchy should be the response with the best combination of attention-commanding schedules, least effort, and lowest probability of punishment; the others will be arranged in a rank order according to the same kind of criteria. Thus, on any occasion when attention is available, the response first in this hierarchy will be seen, unless it is prevented (e.g., by extinction, punishment, or physical impossibility); then the next will be seen, and so forth. It is reasonable that successive responses in the hierarchy will be considered successively worse by their adult audience, in that those responses considered worst when they were learned probably were also punished occasionally, to the degree of their badness; thus, the worse they are the more mixed their establishing contingencies and the lower their position in the hierarchy. (Small wonder that as the problem is dealt with it seems to grow worse, in that its successive instances are more and more undesirable.) In a hierarchy like this, it will be difficult or impossible to appreciate the range of the hierarchy or its internal rank-ordering merely by observation. The first response in the hierarchy is first because it best serves the environment, and so the others are rarely if ever seen and thus are difficult to evaluate. It is when the environment changes to make the first response unlikely or impossible that an observer can see that there is a second response; and it is only when the environment changes again to make the second response unlikely or impossible that an observer can see that there is a third response (if there is). Thus, what will look to a romantic observer like some internal structure of behavior insisting ever more forcefully on expression, despite environmental obstacles or interference, could easily be the result of an arbitrary set of earlier conditionings, any or all of which could have been done differently or not at all, and which can be demolished now and either left demolished or replaced with a different hierarchy (preferably, for clinical purposes, a desirable hierarchy, which may require the development of approval as a more powerful reinforcer for the client than attention, given the nature of the society).

When the example is attention-seeking, experience suggests that most hierarchies are relatively small in number—attention is easily commanded. When the example is aggression, more complex effects often are seen, which nevertheless follow the same principles. Aggressive behaviors by children are reinforced less dependably, and they often generate counteraggression, which can punish them. Furthermore, the targets of aggression differ more widely in what kind of response must be applied to them to gain their reinforcers; in that they range widely from coercible to not so coercible, the repertoire of aggressive behavior to be applied to them also will range widely and will be subject to a corresponding range of stimulus controls. Thus aggressive hierarchies tend to be longer and more diverse, and to be seen not as merely one response at a time, but a number of responses at a time, depending on local circumstances (apart from any systematic attempt to suppress any one of them). But they too can be unmade (Pinkston, Reese, Le-Blanc, & Baer, 1973).

In institutionalized children, a comparable response class often is that set of behaviors called *self-stimulatory*. Sometimes these behaviors function to gain attention; sometimes it is not clear how they function, other than to fill time. But very often they represent a small class of negatively co-occurring responses: a favorite is seen until it is made unlikely or impossible, whereupon a systematic second choice is seen, and so on. Thus some children frequently display stereotyped, bizarre hand-waving close to their faces; if their hands are held or muffed, they turn systematically to foot-drumming, head-banging, echoic behaviors, rocking, and such. These behaviors can be dealt with by suppressing them, one at a time, until the class disappears, just like the previous examples.

Why call negatively co-occurring behaviors a response class? The hallmark of a response class is that behavior-changing procedures applied to a subset of the class produce similar results on all members of the class; in the case of negatively co-occurring behaviors, that seems almost the opposite of what is observed—as one is suppressed, another emerges.

It is possible, but not yet convincingly demonstrated, that negatively co-occurring behaviors often represent a response class within which a hierarchy also operates. In that case the hierarchy will be the more prominent phenomenon. To see the response-class structure as well, it will be necessary to know the membership of the class and the rank order of the behaviors that constitutes their hierarchy. Then it will be possible to apply behavior-changing procedures to a subset of them to see if, after a sufficient subset has been changed, the rest change similarly without the behavior-changing procedures having been applied directly to them. The nature of a simple hierarchy makes such knowledge difficult to obtain, short of doing the behavior change, because not until the first member of the hierarchy is suppressed will the second member appear, to be cataloged by the researcher. If this tactic is used, then at some point new members no longer emerge, but the researcher cannot tell if this is because a sufficient subset of the supposedly larger response class has been suppressed so that all members become suppressed with their class, or if there are no other members and thus no evidence for class structure at all.

In the case of complex hierarchies, such as many cases of aggression represent, a large part of the response class is seen during preliminary observation, because, as circumstances change, different hierarchies within the class are evoked; thus some of the membership in some of its hierarchies becomes apparent. Applied behavior analysts reducing large aggressive repertoires often see that a larger repertoire disappears (or is reduced) than was dealt with directly by the behavior-changing operations applied; thus they can see the response-class structure of what also seems to be a complex set of hierarchies of negatively co-occurring behaviors. Unfortunately, they rarely if ever document these details of their cases.

The strongest kind of demonstration, of course, would be the experimental construction of a response class, within which is constructed a hierarchy of its members. Given knowledge of the construction of such a class, it would then be possible to demonstrate its actual structure as a response class despite its internal hierarchical structure. This would establish it as an instance of behavioral structure; at the same time, it would establish it as a case of nonnecessary structure, in that it would be obvious that the structure was made experimentally, could have been made differently, can now be unmade, and can be remade differently. No such demonstration seems available at present; yet the probability of accomplishing just that kind of demonstration seems high, given the other kinds of knowledge available to us and sketched above.

Within this argument there lies at least one theoretical trap that ought to be avoided. It is constituted by the word *some* within the usual definition of a response class—a set of responses so organized that behavior-changing procedures applied to only some of them produce similar changes in all of them. Obviously the operative term in that definition is *some*, and a better rendition of it would be *sufficient*, because the number it represents has the character of a threshold. The problem is that *sufficient* has no independent definition. You know that you have dealt with a sufficient number of the members of a response class only when the rest of the class changes as the dealt-with members have changed; until then you do not know whether you have dealt with an insufficient number of class members or whether you are not dealing with a class at all, real or potential. Enough examples have been encountered in which there *was* a sufficient number to establish inductively that there often is a sufficient number, and that its value can vary widely from case to case. But an inductive case of that sort does not establish that there always is a response class in operation or capable of being constructed; it indicates only the possibility of them. The trap, then, is to proceed in any given example as if there were of course a response class operating or capable of operating there, and interpreting current failure to demonstrate the characteristics of a response class as merely the result of not yet having dealt with a "sufficient" number of members. Sometimes that will be exactly the truth; sometimes it will be an excuse for insisting on a behavioral structure where in fact there is none operating or none possible. Perhaps the best tactic is to proceed through a reasonable number of potential members, alert to possible response-class structure but silent about its reality, and remembering that, in a case like attention-seeking or self-stimulatory behaviors, a reasonable number is probably on the order of 10, and that, in a case such as establishing a class of generalized imitation, a reasonable number can vary between 10 and several hundred.

In summary, this argument has asserted that negatively co-occurring behaviors can represent response classes similar in essence to the response classes that contain positively co-occurring behaviors. There are differences, of course. One is obvious. The positively co-occurring cases represent responses serving the same function but responsive to individual stimulus controls within a common discriminative context (in imitation, each member is responsive to its model, not to the models of other members; in compliance, each member is responsive to its instruction, not to the instructions for other members, and so forth). The negatively co-occurring cases represent responses serving the same function but responsive to one or a small number of common stimulus controls (in attention-seeking, the availability of attention controls any member of the class of attention-seeking behaviors; in aggression, the role of another person as an obstacle to reinforcement controls any member of the person-coercing class, with subcontrols depending on the apparent coercibility of that person, etc.). Another difference is subtle: the negatively co-occurring cases represent one or more hierarchies operating within a class; the positively co-occurring cases represent a relative absence of hierarchy. But these differences are not of the essence of response classes as a structure of behavior. That essence lies in the observation that behavior-changing procedures applied to only some members of a class (a "sufficient" number) affect all other members of the class in the same way. In some cases it is experimentally clear that structure of that sort can be arbitrary rather than necessary; in other cases it is reasonable that structure of that sort can be arbitrary rather than necessary. Future research may well show that in those cases where that thesis now is merely reasonable, it can actually be demonstrated experimentally; the nature of such research has been sketched. What research could show that such structure is sometimes necessary rather than arbitrary?

PROGRAMMED INSTRUCTION

Many examples of concept learning, especially in young and variously handicapped students, show that a given concept may not be learned by a particular student despite long, intensive differential reinforcement with stimuli demonstrated to be effective reinforcers for controlling other, seemingly comparable behaviors of that very student in the same setting. Yet, when a sequence of carefully constructed, tightly interrelated instances of that concept is offered, each member of this sequence may be learned without error, and the sequence may lead inexorably to a final skill identical to the concept that originally resisted acquisition through differential reinforcement. The construction of such sequences is *programmed instruction*, sometimes called *errorless programming, task analysis,* and *response analysis.*

Programmed instruction is characterized by a low rate of errors in learning each of its sequenced instances; a high rate of errors on any instance is usually taken as evidence of poor programming at that point, and a new portion of the program is developed to accomplish the learning of that instance with fewer errors. Sometimes this logic is carried to its ultimate, and programs are designed (or at least sought) that accomplish concept acquisition without any error at all. The ability to do this at least sometimes is now clear (cf. Etzel, LeBlanc, Schilmoeller, & Stella, 1981; Schilmoeller & Etzel, 1977; Terrace, 1963).

The significance of errorless concept acquisition through such a carefully designed sequence of instruction is considerable. It can have practical advantages, in that it offers students very consistent experiences with successful acquisition of new concepts. Some students' previous experiences have been consistently full of failure, which can produce a very undesirable set of side effects that can cumulate to make the students almost unteachable.

It also has a theoretical significance relevant to the present argument.[6] When a student moves from incompetence in a concept to mastery of it, through a sequence of steps entirely free of error, that suggests very strongly that the structure of the sequence—the succession of stimuli controlling a succession of responses to them—is the structure of the concept that the student has just attained. In other words, concepts have structures—the sequences of instances that must be acquired in order to acquire the concept or to constitute the concept. These structures are manifest as the structure of the program that teaches these concepts to students previously deficient in them. But these structures are manifest in their teaching programs *only* if no errors are made by students progressing through the program. For errors can mean that a necessary element of structure is missing at that point in the program. A flurry of errors at a given point that eventually disappears as mastery of that point emerges probably represents the student's solving the problem left unstructured there, and solving it by private means. These private means are very valuable to the student, of course; unfortunately, they also represent a process that is part of the learning at that point

6. It has other theoretical significance, not related strongly to the present argument, but nonetheless profound. An excellent review has been made by Rilling (1977; cf. especially pp. 464–475).

but is hidden from direct study by the teacher-analyst of the concept being programmed. That process—or *a* process adequate to the same function—can be made manifest rather than hidden by reconstructing the program at that point so that its new instances take the student through that point without error. The structure of its new instances is either the structure of the process that the student went through privately to solve that problem or is the structure of a process that the student *could have* gone through in solving that problem. A totally error-free performance by a previously incompetent student in acquiring a new concept indicates a correspondingly complete statement of the structure—or at least *a* structure—of that concept.

If some concepts cannot be acquired through differential reinforcement of trial-and-error responding to them but can be acquired errorlessly through a properly programmed sequence of instruction, then it can be argued that such behavior (the concept) has a structure, in the sense that it has prerequisites, and that the structure is necessary to the behavior, in that the behavior cannot be attained otherwise. The essential question in the evaluation of whether this structure is a necessary structure is exactly that "otherwise." An errorless teaching program for a concept represents its structure clearly enough; and if we grant that the concept was not teachable simply by intensively conducted differential reinforcement, then we may well agree that there is some structure to this behavior, at least for this student, and that the structure will have to be built, at least for this student.

Whether this successful program represents the necessary structure of this behavior for this student depends on whether there are any other programs that could have taught the same concept to the same student but through a significantly different sequence of instances. If there is one such program and only one, then the structure of that program is the necessary structure of that behavior for that student. But if there are many such programs, then no one of them is the necessary structure of this behavior. Each is a sufficient structure, and in their numerousness they greatly diminish the whole idea of structure: a concept that can have a great many structures need hardly be considered in terms of structure, just as an infinite number of paths to a goal cancels the meaning of *path*. To put the same argument in another way, if we cannot teach a concept other than by programming it, a notion of structure emerges necessarily. As we discover a successful errorless program for this concept, the notion of concept structure becomes equated with the structure of the program. If we discover more than one errorless program for this concept, and if they are appreciably different from each other, the notion of a necessary structure to this concept begins to dissolve. If we discover more and more significantly different errorless programs for this concept, the notion of necessary structure approaches invisibility, and the whole notion of structure, necessary or arbitrary, becomes increasingly trivial. Its last residue of meaning is simply that the behavior could not have been taught without some program.

To say that the behavior could not have been taught without some program is to say more than a researcher could possibly know. The usual case is one in which very good unprogrammed differential-reinforcement techniques have been applied intensively and for a long time by sophisticated researcher-teachers and have failed to produce the behavior. Thereupon a program succeeds. It is always possible that an even more intensive unprogrammed effort would have succeeded; it simply seems unlikely. But the argument outlined above has much the same force, even if this were true. A behavior that is difficult to acquire through unprogrammed differential reinforcement, but easy to acquire without errors through a properly designed program, still testifies that it has, if not prerequisites, at least predispositions important to its acquisition. Then the predispositions are the statement of its structure, and conceivably of its necessary structure, because, for all we know, the student who learns the behavior with difficulty under unprogrammed differential reinforcement does so only by privately constructing just that program of predispositions. Perhaps it is the time necessary for the private construction, which we of course do not see happen, that makes the acquisition "difficult."

What is the current demography of errorless programming of otherwise impossible or difficult-to-acquire behaviors? Specifically, do we typically find one successful errorless program per concept, or very many of them per concept? Unfortunately, those facts are not in hand. Very few concepts have been programmed errorlessly. No doubt that is because the idea is relatively new and because the construction of such programs is very difficult and time-consuming; indeed, it requires exceptionally sophisticated effort, in that it is *not* the kind of task analysis that can be done simply by looking at the concept to see what its components are. Thus, few exist, and their rarity means that it is not yet possible to say whether concepts typically have one errorless structure or more than one, let alone how many. If errorless programming is pursued energetically in the future, then it may become evident that there are many significantly different programs serving the same concept. However, it is not highly likely, because many of those programs are constructed by researchers striving to solve some practical problem of conceptual deficit; once they have constructed an errorless program remedying that deficit, they are not likely to invest several more years of their lives in developing others, just to see if they exist (cf. Baer, 1981b).

Even if the crucial research is highly unlikely, it is at least possible. What it could show is that there are many alternative structures to a concept. What it could not show is that there are not many alternative structures to a concept. The only conclusion that failure to produce alternative programs would allow is that hard, intelligent, and sophisticated work aimed at producing them has failed so far. But it will never be logically possible to say that there are no more of them, and that the extant program is the only possible structure of the concept. Thus, once again, nonnecessity of structure could be proved, necessity could not. Even so, the area of programmed instruction seems to be one of the most useful for suspicions that behavior has structure, in that errorless programs (even in their small numbers) are remarkably impressive for the new concepts that they can build in students whose prior resistance to the unprogrammed differential reinforcement of those same concepts seemed so unrelenting. The structure revealed by these programs may never be amenable to proof as necessarily prerequisite, but it is readily amenable to documentation as importantly predisposing. Here is a case where nonnecessity of structure may be less interesting than the frequency with which these predispositions function as structure, whether necessary or not, and less interesting than the importance of having these predispositions function as structure, whether necessary or not.

THE LIMITED AMOUNT OF TIME WITHIN WHICH TO PERFORM BEHAVIORS

If all responses were instantaneous, or as nearly so as the key peck, then an almost infinite number of them could be fitted into a finite amount of time. Alternatively, if organisms lived forever, then even noninstantaneous, long-duration responses could be performed without restraint in an infinity of time. Neither is the case. Consider me as an example. Some of my high-rate behaviors are reading, playing my flute, and playing chess against my computer. I choose these as examples for this discussion because it is easy to see that behaviors like these have no function for me, or for most people, unless they can be performed for at least a few minutes at a time. Reading has no function unless I have time to scan at least enough sentences to collect a meaning from the text—at least, a small meaning. I have no use for a word or two; I probably will not remember them by the time when I can read the next word or two, and so trying to cumulate them over separated episodes until they mean something is not reinforcing enough to maintain that behavior. Similarly, flute-playing requires at least enough time to make a phrase, if it is to have function; and chess-playing requires at least enough time to choose a move from the alternatives I can see and evaluate. Indeed, the more continuous time I can give to activities like these, the stronger their reinforcing function (within very definite limits, of course—after sufficient time, each of these activities would become boring, and if I were somehow forced to continue them beyond that, aversive). Because I will not live forever, and have already left only a small part of every day for these behaviors, they have necessary interdependencies: time devoted to any one of them must be made up by time taken away from another. In other words, I trade these behaviors for one another. Thus they have a necessary mutual structure for me. The necessity is not that I engage in them, or engage in them in any order; the necessity is that to engage more in any of them means engaging less in at least one other. I trade these behaviors for one another because I *must* trade these behaviors for one another.

Here then is an instance in which the null hypothesis that behavior has no necessary structure apparently can be rejected immediately, with no more research required than the recognition by each of us that we do indeed trade off behaviors among themselves, and that we have no choice in this. However, recall that the null hypothesis was that behavior has no necessary structure other than trivial. Is there any more structure imposed on behavior by the fact that, to have function, it often requires time? The question is how organisms go about trading one behavior for another within themselves, or how the environment teaches them or constrains them to trade one behavior for another.

The first pattern to this structure that is likely to appear is a set of rank-orderings, or currency, for an individual, within which it will be true that this much time for one behavior is worth that much time for another behavior. A reinforcer currency is of course an old and familiar concept, especially to applied behavior analysts managing token-reinforcement economies; thus the corresponding notion of a response currency should be equally acceptable and useful. One quirk of terminology must be recognized and dealt with, however: this concept of a response currency to describe their trade-off relationships is implicitly an equation of responses to reinforcers. But responses cannot be equated to reinforcers. A reinforcer, by definition, is an event that can be programmed contingent on a response and thereby will alter the probability of that response. Responses of an organism *cannot* be programmed contingent on other responses of the same organism. You simply cannot deliver to an organism one of its own responses, let alone do so contingent on another of its own responses. What you can deliver to an organism, in a contingency with another of its behaviors if you wish, is the *opportunity* to engage in one of its own behaviors, or the coercive *demand* to engage in one of its own behaviors (accompanied by the opportunity to do so, of course). The opportunity to respond and the demand to respond are not behaviors but stimuli. Opportunities are places, apparatus, tools, gates, permissions, and such—all eminently stimuli. Demands are instructions, threats, put-throughs, descriptions or signals of contingencies, and such—all eminently stimuli.

True, organisms may seem to deliver one of their behaviors to themselves, as when I put down my flute and turn to my chessboard and computer, apparently without cue, permission, signal, instruction, request, invitation, or suddenly changed availability. But to establish that one of these activities has reinforcing function for me (for another of my behaviors), it will be necessary to intercede experimentally rather than leaving the trade-off of one behavior for another in my hands. An experimenter will perforce take control of the opportunity to engage in these behaviors and will have to deliver that opportunity to me contingent on some response, to see what reinforcing function that opportunity (to engage in that behavior) may have. Catania (1975) has made exactly this point in the context of self-control; it applies equally here.

Then studies that purport to show that behavior has a structure, which is the relative rank-ordering of one behavior's value relative to another's, are, when they are competent to show that, functionally studies of the structure of reinforcers—specifically those reinforcers that function as reinforcers because they constitute the opportunity to perform some response. Upon examination, most reinforcers turn out to be just that—the opportunity to do something else. Food is the opportunity to eat, water is the opportunity to drink, approval is the opportunity to thank the approving person and to ask for a favor (a reinforcer), on some schedule. Similarly, aversive stimuli are the opportunities to escape them or reduce them—to flee or fight, quite often.[7]

Nevertheless these studies, reinforcement studies though they be, still are studies of behaviors that require time to have function, and thus they have some necessary structure among themselves, as trade-offs. If the nature of those trade-offs is simple and obvious, the importance of the necessity of this structure may pale beside its banality. On the other hand, if the relationships are not utterly predictable—if, for example, making the opportunity to perform behavior A for a certain amount of time contingent on the necessity of performing behavior B for a certain amount of time, not only controls B but also detracts from the time previously available to behaviors C, D, and E, which thereupon rearrange themselves from their prior rank-ordering into a new one—then the structure necessary to those interrelationships may prove not only necessary but interesting. Like the case for programmed instruction, necessity of structure is not much at issue in the research that the immediate future probably holds, but importance of structure, necessary or arbitrary, probably is. We must wait and see—and perhaps do some of the research ourselves.

Summary

Behavioral structures abound, and they are easy to make. Still, it is possible that some structures are necessary rather than arbitrary and existential rather than constructed. However, traditional scientific conservatism combines with the observation that making behavioral structures is relatively easy to generate a null hypothesis, namely, that behavior has no necessary structure other than trivial. Six sources of behavioral structure that might support rejection of this null hypothesis were considered. The operant-respondent distinction, species-specific stereotyped instinctive chains, stimulus- and response-generalization gradients, and response classes all seemed to be more validly viewed as plausible cases of unnecessary, constructed structures than of necessary ones;

7. Punishing stimuli are more difficult to place in this context. What opportunity does response-contingent electric shock afford an organism? To hurt? To nonperform the punished response? Does it strain the semantics of this formulation to assert that punishment allows an organism the opportunity to nonperform the punished response?

programmed instruction seemed difficult to establish as a case of necessary structure, yet it is very compelling as a case of important structure that might also be necessary but was worth intensive research, whether necessary or not. And that some behaviors require time to have function, and thus enter into necessary trade-off structures with one another, constitutes a prima facie case of necessary structure, the importance of which remains to be seen.

It is important to remember that in behavioral structures importance is as significant a question as necessity. Some structures of behavior may be quite arbitrary, in terms of the structure of the universe and the laws of behavior, but may be extremely common and urgently important, in terms of the organization of our society and its effects on our behavior. The papers by Reid and Wahler in this volume should be considered in that light, rather than in terms of the null hypothesis of this chapter. But the rest of this symposium might well be considered exactly in reaction to the null hypothesis of this paper.

REFERENCES

Baer, D. M. A hung jury and a Scottish verdict: "Not proven." *Analysis and Intervention in Developmental Disabilities*, 1981, **1**, 91–97. (a)

Baer, D. M. The nature of intervention research. In R. L. Schiefelbusch and S. D. Bricker (Eds.), *Early language: Acquisition and intervention* (Chap. 17). Baltimore: University Park Press, 1981. (b)

Baer, D. M., Peterson, R. F., & Sherman, J. A. The development of imitation by reinforcing behavioral similarity to a model. *Journal of the Experimental Analysis of Behavior*, 1967, **10**, 405–416.

Baer, D. M., & Sherman, J. A. Reinforcement control of generalized imitation in young children. *Journal of Experimental Child Psychology*, 1964, **1**, 37–49.

Bandura, A., & Barab, P. G. Conditions governing nonreinforced imitation. *Developmental Psychology*, 1971, **5**, 244–255.

Beach, F. A. The descent of instinct. *Psychological Review*, 1955, **62**, 401–410.

Bijou, S. W., & Baer, D. M. *Child development*. Vol. 2. *Universal stage of infancy*. New York: Appleton-Century-Crofts, 1965.

Bucher, B. Some variables affecting children's compliance with instructions. *Journal of Experimental Child Psychology*, 1973, **15**, 10–21.

Catania, A. C. The concept of the operant in the analysis of behavior. *Behaviorism*, 1973, **1**, 103–116.

Catania, A. C. The myth of self-reinforcement. *Behaviorism*, 1975, **3**, 192–199.

Catania, A. C. *Learning*. Englewood Cliffs, N.J.: Prentice-Hall, 1979.

Doleys, D. M., Wells, K. C., Hobbs, S. A., Roberts, M. W., & Cartelli, L. The effects of social punishment on noncompliance: A comparison with time out and positive practice. *Journal of Applied Behavior Analysis*, 1976, **9**, 471–482.

Etzel, B. C., LeBlanc, J. M., Schilmoeller, K. J. & Stella, M. E. Stimulus control procedures in the education of young children. In S. W. Bijou & R. Ruiz (Eds.), *Contributions of behavior modification to education* (Chap. 1). Hillsdale, N.J.: Lawrence Erlbaum Associates, 1981. (Also Mexico City: Editorial Trillas, 1981.)

Ferster, C. B., & Skinner, B. F. *Schedules of reinforcement*. New York: Appleton-Century-Crofts, 1957.

Garcia, E., Baer, D. M., & Firestone, I. The development of generalized imitation within topographically determined boundaries. *Journal of Applied Behavior Analysis*, 1971, **4**, 101–112.

Garcia, E., Guess, D., & Byrnes, J. Development of syntax in a retarded girl using procedures of imitation, reinforcement, and modelling. *Journal of Applied Behavior Analysis*, 1973, **6**, 299–310.

Gewirtz, J. L. The roles of overt responding and extrinsic reinforcement in "self-" and "vicarious reinforcement" and in "observational learning and imitation." In R. Glaser (Ed.), *The nature of reinforcement*. New York: Academic Press, 1971.

Gollub, L. Conditioned reinforcement: Schedule effects. In W. K. Honig & J. E. R. Staddon (Eds.), *Handbook of operant behavior* (Chap. 10). Englewood Cliffs, N.J.: Prentice-Hall, 1977.

Guess, D., & Baer, D. M. An analysis of individual differences in generalization between receptive and productive language in retarded children. *Journal of Applied Behavior Analysis*, 1973, **6**, 311–329.

Guess, D., Sailor, W., Rutherford, G., & Baer, D. M. An experimental analysis of linguistic development: The productive use of the plural morpheme. *Journal of Applied Behavior Analysis*, 1968, **1**, 297–306.

Honig, W. K. Discrimination, generalization, and transfer on the basis of stimulus differences. In D. I. Mostofsky (Ed.), *Stimulus generalization*. Stanford, Calif.: Stanford University Press, 1965.

Honig, W. K. (Ed.). *Operant behavior: Areas of research and application*. Englewood Cliffs, N.J.: Prentice-Hall, 1966.

Honig, W. K., & Staddon, J. E. R. (Eds.). *Handbook of operant behavior*. Englewood Cliffs, N.J.: Prentice-Hall, 1977.

Kazdin, A. E. *History of behavior modification: Experimental foundations of contemporary research*. Baltimore: University Park Press, 1978.

Kelleher, R. T. Chaining and conditioned reinforcement. In W. K. Honig (Ed.), *Operant behavior: Areas of research and application*. Englewood Cliffs, N.J.: Prentice-Hall, 1966.

Kelleher, R. T., & Gollub, L. R. A review of conditioned reinforcement. *Journal of the Experimental Analysis of Behavior*, 1962, **5**, 543–597.

Keller, F. S., & Schoenfeld, W. N. *Principles of psychology*. New York: Appleton-Century-Crofts, 1950.

Leitenberg, H. (Ed.). *Handbook of behavior modification and behavior therapy.* Englewood Cliffs, N.J.: Prentice-Hall, 1976.

Lutzker, J. R., & Sherman, J. A. Producing generative sentence usage by imitation and reinforcement procedures. *Journal of Applied Behavior Analysis,* 1974, **7,** 447–460.

Malott, R. W., & Malott, M. K. Perception and stimulus generalization. In W. C. Stebbins (Ed.), *Animal psychophysics.* Englewood Cliffs, N.J.: Prentice-Hall, 1970.

Millenson, J. *Principles of behavioral analysis.* New York: Macmillan, 1967.

Munn, N. L. *The evolution and growth of human behavior.* Boston: Houghton Mifflin, 1955.

Peterson, R. F. Some experiments on the organization of a class of imitative behaviors. *Journal of Applied Behavior Analysis,* 1968, **1,** 225–235.

Peterson, R. F., Merwin, M. R., Moyer, T. J., & Whitehurst, G. J. Generalized imitation: The effects of experimenter absence, differential reinforcement and stimulus complexity. *Journal of Experimental Child Psychology,* 1971, **12,** 114–128.

Peterson, R. F., & Whitehurst, G. J. A variable influencing the performance of nonreinforced imitative behavior. *Journal of Applied Behavior Analysis,* 1971, **4,** 1–10.

Pinkston, E. M., Reese, N. M., LeBlanc, J. M., & Baer, D. M. Independent control of a preschool child's aggression and peer interaction by contingent teacher attention. *Journal of Applied Behavior Analysis,* 1973, **6,** 115–124.

Rilling, M. Stimulus control and inhibitory processes. In W. K. Honig and J. E. R. Staddon (Eds.), *Handbook of operant behavior* (Chap. 15). Englewood Cliffs, N.J.: Prentice-Hall, 1977.

Schilmoeller, K. J., & Etzel, B. C. An experimental analysis of criterion-related and noncriterion-related cues in "errorless" stimulus control procedures. In B. C. Etzel, J. M. LeBlanc, & D. M. Baer (Eds.), *New developments in behavior research: Theory, method, and application* (Chap. 19). Hillsdale, N.J.: Lawrence Erlbaum Associates, 1977.

Schumaker, J., & Sherman, J. A. Training generative verb usage by imitation and reinforcement procedures. *Journal of Applied Behavior Analysis,* 1970, **3,** 273–287.

Segal, E. Toward a coherent psychology of language. In W. K. Honig & J. E. R. Staddon (Eds.), *Handbook of operant behavior* (Chap. 22). Englewood Cliffs, N.J.: Prentice-Hall, 1977.

Skinner, B. F. *The behavior of organisms: An experimental analysis.* New York: Appleton-Century-Crofts, 1938.

Skinner, B. F. *Science and human behavior.* New York: Macmillan, 1953.

Staddon, J. E. R. Schedule-induced behavior. In W. K. Honig & J. E. R. Staddon (Eds.), *Handbook of operant behavior* (Chap. 3). Englewood Cliffs, N.J.: Prentice-Hall, 1977.

Steinman, W. M. Generalized imitation and the discrimination hypothesis. *Journal of Experimental Child Psychology,* 1970, **10,** 79–99.

Steinman, W. M., & Boyce, K. D. Generalized imitation as a function of discrimination difficulty and choice. *Journal of Experimental Child Psychology*, 1971, **11**, 251–265.

Teitelbaum, P. Levels of integration of the operant. In W. K. Honig & J. E. R. Staddon (Eds.), *Handbook of operant behavior* (Chap. 1). Englewood Cliffs, N.J.: Prentice-Hall, 1977.

Terrace, H. J. Discrimination learning with and without "errors." *Journal of the Experimental Analysis of Behavior*, 1963, **6**, 1–27.

Tinbergen, N. *The study of instinct*. London: Oxford University Press, 1951. (Reissued in 1969.)

Subject Index

activity factor, 3
adaptedness, 198
adaptive averaging, 192–195
aggression, 240, 243
animals
  carnivores, 82, 96
  closed economy, 85–87
  and environment, 116–122
  feeding studies on, 71–76, 105–114
  food-deprived, 76–79, 91–94, 132, 135–139, 171–172
  herbivores, 80–82, 96
  learning theory, 121–122
  memory research on, 70
  omnivores, 82, 96
  open economy, 87–90
  stimulus control studies on, 27–28
  test environments, 79–80
arm-swinging, 20
arousal, 169–173
  constraints on, 202
  decay in, 190, 205–206
  level of, 177
  theory of, 175
asymptotic rates, 170, 173, 179–180
attention/time-out contingency, 14
autism, 2, 3, 17, 19, 21, 22, 28
averaging theory, 173–177, 187

babbling, 18
Beck Depression Inventory, 24, 26

behavior
  across-setting, 4–5
  acquired, 236–237
  adaptive, 75
  aggressive, 2, 240
  analytic study of, 218–219
  animal, 150
  assumptions about, ix, 4
  asymptotic, 193
  covariation between, 8–9
  choice, 70, 82, 170, 189, 190
  compliance, 232–234, 243
  constraints on, 146
  descriptive study of, 217–218
  disruptive, 29
  dynamics of, 169, 170
  economic, 198–199, 201, 206
  and environment, 5–6, 220–221
  feeding, 71–76, 77–78, 80–83, 101–105, 117–121, 122
  genetically controlled, 227
  "homing," 121
  hyperactive, 19
  imitative, 9–10, 19, 28, 231–234
  incentive effect on, 170
  learned, 228–229
  measures of, 186
  methodological approach to, x
  modification, 4, 238–241
  on-going, 169
  operant, 220
  oppositional, 13–17, 21
  patterns of, x, 5

Author Index